Move over, Strunk & White . . . Dianna Booher has created the ultimate writer's desk reference for a whole new age.

E-WRITING

21st-Century Tools for Effective Communication

DIANNA BOOHER'S CLIENTS PRAISE *E-WRITING*

"Dianna Booher clearly understands the challenges of e-mail communication and has, once again, given valuable advice that is useful to everyone in corporate America! I'll begin using her tips right away."
—*Gay L. Knight, consulting education specialist, IBM Global Services*

"This step-by-step approach could easily form the syllabus for a college course on the subject. It's about time someone tackled this timely subject and I'm not surprised to see Dianna Booher do it first."
—*Timothy C. Violette, director, human resources, The Boeing Company*

"The impact of my team has been greatly enhanced by Dianna's previous work. This new book is right on target for the next step."
—*Jennifer Raymond, research manager, Frito-Lay*

"Splendid insights on how to improve the critical communication skill sets necessary for the ever-changing individual and business challenges we face. A must-read for anyone 'learning a living.'"
—*Leon Abbott, Ph.D., program director, University Partnerships/Relations, Lockheed Martin Aeronautics Company*

ALSO BY DIANNA BOOHER

BOOKS (SELECTED TITLES)

Communicate with Confidence: How to Say it Right the First Time and Every Time

Good Grief, Good Grammar

To the Letter: A Handbook of Model Letters for the Busy Executive

Great Personal Letters for Busy People

The Complete Letterwriter's Almanac

Clean Up Your Act: Effective Ways to Organize Paperwork and Get It Out of Your Life

Cutting Paperwork in the Corporate Culture

Executive's Portfolio of Model Speeches for All Occasions

The New Secretary: How to Handle People as Well as You Handle Paper

Send Me a Memo: A Handbook of Model Memos

Writing for Technical Professionals

Winning Sales Letters

67 Presentation Secrets to Wow Any Audience

Get a Life Without Sacrificing Your Career

Ten Smart Moves for Women

Get Ahead, Stay Ahead

The Worth of a Woman's Words

Well Connected: Power Your Own Soul by Plugging into Others

Mother's Gifts to Me

Little Book of Big Questions: Answers to Life's Perplexing Questions

Love Notes: From My Heart to Yours

Fresh-cut Flowers for a Friend

First Thing Monday Morning

VIDEOS

Writing for Results
Writing in Sensitive Situations
Building Rapport with Your Customers
Giving and Receiving Feedback Without Punching Someone Out!
Thinking on Your Feet: What to Say During Q & A
Basic Steps for Better Business Writing (series)
Business Writing: Quick, Clear, Concise
Closing the Gap: Gender Communication Skills
Cutting Paperwork: Management Strategies
Cutting Paperwork: Support Staff Strategies

AUDIOS

Get Your Book Published
People Power
Writing to the Point: Business Communications from Memos to Meetings

SOFTWARE

Effective Writing
Effective Editing
Good Grief, Good Grammar
More Good Grief, Good Grammar
Ready, Set, NeGOtiate
2001 Model Business Letters
2001 Sales and Marketing Letters
8005 Model Quotes, Speeches, & Toasts
Model Personal Letters That Work

E-WRITING

21st-Century Tools for Effective Communication

DIANNA BOOHER

POCKET BOOKS
New York   London   Toronto   Sydney

An *Original* Publication of POCKET BOOKS

POCKET BOOKS, a division of Simon & Schuster, Inc.
1230 Avenue of the Americas, New York, NY 10020

Library of Congress Cataloging-in-Publication Data

Booher, Dianna Daniels.
    E-Writing : 21st-century tools for effective communication / Dianna Booher.
        p. cm.
    Includes bibliographical references and index.
    ISBN-13: 978-0-7434-1258-2
    ISBN-10:   0-7434-1258-3
        1. Electronic mail messages—Handbooks, manuals, etc. 2. Electronic mail
systems—Handbooks, manuals, etc. 3. Business writing—Handbooks, manuals,
etc. 4. Business communication—Handbooks, manuals, etc. I. Title.

HE7551.B66 2001
651.7'9—dc21   00-051658

First Pocket Books trade paperback printing February 2001

10 9 8 7

Cover design by Anna Dorfman
Interior design by Nancy Singer Olaguera

Printed in the U.S.A.

CONTENTS

INTRODUCTION

WRITING ELECTRONICALLY

Put it before them briefly so they will read it,
clearly so they will appreciate it,
picturesquely so they will remember it
and, above all, accurately so they will be guided by its light.
—*Joseph Pulitzer*

We do most of our business by e-mail. Our marketing information is on the web, and our staff is putting our internal information—policies and procedures—on the intranet. Our people just don't write much anymore." A rather odd, but common, comment. What else do people read on the web and in their e-mail? Words.

More, not fewer, people write. And more people write more. We used to pick up the phone for day-to-day tasks. But so many people now screen their calls with voice mail that we've found it easier to reach them by e-mail.

Just two years ago, the most "important" writing tasks were still done primarily by professionals at the top: engineers, lawyers, auditors, analysts, controllers, sales and marketing executives, and middle managers. But with the advent of e-mail, even entry-level workers write—to inform customers when they can expect to receive their razor or robe; to apologize for a billing error; to let their team know that the Friday meeting has been postponed; to ask a vendor for a faster delivery; or to tell their coworkers about new procedures.

Screen or paper matters not.

How do we write thee? Let us count the ways: e-mail, websites, bulletin boards and chat rooms, online information centers for employees, form letters to customers, boilerplate fill-in-the-blank proposals loaded on account

1

executives' laptops, team reports edited simultaneously online, job postings on the Internet that generate electronic résumés.

In today's e-commerce, written communication makes the competitive difference in overall organizational success. Customers, clients, and prospective business partners often check out your website before they even phone or fax you. If your words on the website don't communicate what they need to know or help to build your credibility, you'll never get a chance to connect with prospects by phone or face to face. Ask any salesperson how many real-time conversations they have with prospects or customers.

Today, more than ever, poor writing tempts a customer to click away, doubting that your technology or service is any better than your written communication. An e-mail, a web headline, or a product proposal that contains disorganized ideas, convoluted wording, intimidating layout, or grammatically incorrect sentences, tells clients that you won't service their engines well, amortize their mortgage correctly, or interpret their insurance coverage fairly.

First impressions stay around a long time. But what's the payoff when people and organizations write things correctly? Increased profits and productivity.

Case in point: Thirty-something Angie recently landed a new job without ever having met her new boss in person. She works for a Fortune 50 telecommunications company, and for the past seventeen years there, she has enjoyed her share of all-expenses-paid trips to Hawaii as a reward for her contributions to the company. She has worldwide responsibilities and administers a budget of hundreds of millions of dollars. In short, she's obviously no slouch at what she does.

But after spending eight years in one job position, she developed an itch for a new challenge. After learning through the grapevine about a new position being created, she e-mailed a résumé to the vice-president in charge and expressed a willingness to fly in for an interview. The vice-president e-mailed a response with mild interest, stating that the job required relocating to Atlanta, and that the position demanded high-level thinking and interaction with senior executives at client firms. In her job overview, the hiring executive emphasized that 50 percent of the job would involve writing documents (letters, summary reports, proposals, and marketing materials) to demonstrate the value-added service the firm offered to client organizations worldwide.

Angie responded that for personal reasons she could not relocate to Atlanta, but she still wanted to set up at least an interview. She mentioned that she had another job offer in the wings, but while she was making a career move anyway, she wanted to be sure she had considered all her options.

Rather than decide yes or no about the interview, the vice-president asked her to e-mail a few samples of her writing so that she could compare them to those of other candidates under consideration. Within the hour, Angie responded with the samples. Within eight hours, the hiring vice-president picked up the phone and offered Angie the job—solely on the basis of her writing talents. And never mind the move to Atlanta.

Such is the power of high-impact writing.

This Fortune 50 company is not the first to hire or fire based on impressions created by writing skills. Consider the traffic on websites such as hotjobs.com, computerjobs.com, CareerMosaic.com, monster.com, and the e-mail exchanges these sites generate.

A few years ago, *USA Today* carried a front-page headline: "What Employers Look For." The accompanying story reported a nationwide survey among 3,000 hiring executives who were asked for their top criteria in hiring professionals. Number one was attitude. Number two was communication skills. Communication skills ranked ahead of both work experience and academic or technical training.

That ranking is no surprise. Peter Drucker, the most internationally respected name in modern management, has been saying the same thing for years. In *People and Performance*, he writes:

> The further away your job is from manual work, the larger the organization of which you are an employee, the more important it will be that you know how to convey your thoughts in writing or speaking. In the very large organization, whether it is the government, the large business corporation, or the Army, this ability to express yourself is perhaps the most important of all skills you can possess. . . . This one basic skill is the ability to organize and express ideas in writing and speaking.

Universities today, even the best ones, are suffering from arteriosclerosis, according to Warren Bennis, author of numerous books on leadership and professor at the University of Southern California. Why that glum conclusion? After interviewing business leaders and graduate students five years into their careers about ingredients missing from their formal education, Bennis has discovered a big hole in their skills set. The skills most frequently cited as missing? "More leadership and interpersonal communication skills, writing, oral communication, and presentation of self—that is what our graduates five years out are telling us they lack."

Does this lack hit us personally in the pocketbook? Stephen Reder, a linguist at Portland State University, working in conjunction with the U.S. Department of Education, has measured how American adults' verbal skills affect their earning power. He found that among people with a two- or four-year college degree, those with the best skills in writing ability earn, on average, more than three times what those with the worst skills earn.

The importance of writing stands to reason. Your boss, coworkers, or customers can't or don't follow you around on the job. They don't see how you handle people or projects day to day. They simply see the *results* of your work—documented in database notes, in your e-mail, or in your reports and proposals to them. Clear writing reflects clear thinking. Your writing becomes your face on the page or screen.

Giving information isn't enough. Information doesn't necessarily result in proper communication. We have intranet and Internet information sprawling around the globe, yet still we hear the ubiquitous employee complaint: "There's just no communication around here." With a computer on every desk, in-boxes overflowing with e-mail, paper printouts piled high, and faxes on every front, what do people mean by that statement?

People know how to use the medium, but they have difficulty shaping and sharing the message.

Readers Complain

- "I get six or seven copies of the same e-mail forwarded by different people. Although I delete a lot of it without reading it, I'm always worried that I'll miss something important."
- "I hate websites where you can read pages and pages of information and still don't know what the organization does."
- "I can't tell exactly what the writer wants me to do."
- "The writer doesn't get to the point soon enough. I don't have time to go to the second screen."
- "People ramble. I have to dig out the main idea."
- "What the writer assumes is obvious, is not."
- "People put in too much background detail."
- "They use too much technical jargon and too many acronyms for anybody outside their area of expertise."
- "There's too much hedging and avoiding the issue."

- "The writing is too formal. It sounds pompous and silly."
- "The writing is too informal. Vendors offend me when they're flippant or use colloquialisms or make personal comments as if we're good buddies when I've never laid eyes on them."
- "The tone causes an adverse gut reaction—particularly in directives from a peer who doesn't have the authority to tell me to do anything."
- "Some people sound wishy-washy. They try to be so careful to be tactful and not hurt your feelings that you can't even figure out the real message."
- "Subject lines are unhelpful. I can't tell what needs an immediate response and what can wait."
- "When I get copied on something, I often can't tell if I'm supposed to take some action or if things have already been handled. So I'm left thinking: Why did they tell me that?"
- "Our policy and procedure manuals—and even the online help and hyperlinks—look too intimidating. I have trouble just finding what I need to know."

Writers Complain

- "We do a lot of things by committee or team—even writing up formal reports and presentations. By the time everybody puts in their two cents' worth, we've gone through six or seven drafts. It's a waste of time for everybody."
- "We have lousy boilerplate proposals that we try to customize, but some manager somewhere thinks they're good, and so we're all forced to follow that dictated format."
- "My boss never tells me why a report or letter or proposal was revised before it got passed on. So how do I know how to do it any differently the next time?"
- "When my manager asks me to revise something, she never gives me suggestions. So it's a shot in the dark whether I'm going to get it right the second time. Or the third. Why can't managers tell you exactly what they want—rather than always what they *don't* want?"
- "I can't find good writing samples to follow, and setting up new formats takes time."
- "I'm fuzzy on grammatical points. And I don't even have a clue whether the grammar checker on my software is right when it highlights things for me to change."

- "I don't like to write, so it's difficult for me."
- "My supervisor is on an ego trip when he edits my work; everything has to be said *his* way."
- "I spend so much time staring at the screen, trying to decide how to start."
- "I never know who the reader will be—we typically write to a wide audience."
- "How do you know how detailed to get? I have trouble deciding what I can assume my reader understands and what I need to explain."
- "I get e-mail and letters on my desk that I'm supposed to respond to, yet I'm usually the one with the least information about the whole situation. How can I respond if I don't have all the information?"
- "Writing takes too much time. I'd rather just walk in and tell somebody what I want. But the trouble is, my competitors leave behind a proposal. And by the time my buyers go to their team with an overview of what we're offering, they've forgotten what I told them on the phone or in their office. I'm clearly at a disadvantage when I don't sum up meetings or phone calls in writing."
- "Liability is a big fear. When I'm writing to a customer about a problem, the lawyers have us half scared to death that we're going to cause a lawsuit."
- "Sometimes I see errors in my team's reports, but when I point them out without using the exact terminology or citing the specific rule, people think I don't know what I'm talking about. It's hard to keep quiet when you know something's unclear or grammatically incorrect. Worse, *my* reputation suffers because *my* name's on the document, too."
- "Why bother? My boss rewrites most everything I do anyway."

The burden for untangling these communication crosswires falls on you, the writer. If the reader has not understood your message, you have not written well.

Why is e-writing any different from the writing of twenty years ago? Volume, for one thing. In our surveys among 17 companies across ten different industries, 72 percent of respondents say they spend 1–2 hours daily handling e-mail. Ten percent of those e-mails received are unnecessary and unwanted. The biggest recent complaint about e-mail, cited by 30 percent of respondents, is disorganized, irrelevant, missing information. Another 26 percent complain that the e-mail they receive is too technical for their purpose.

Another difference: Not only must your writing be clear, correct, complete, and concise, but it also has to connect.

Years ago, if your letter or memo sounded too stiff or formal, you could overcome that weakness by being personable face-to-face. If your proposal confused your coworkers or clients, you could clear up the issue orally in a meeting. If your instructions muddled a coworker's mind, you could walk down the hall and demonstrate how to do the job.

Today, these clarifying measures often no longer apply. Your entire relationship with coworkers or customers may rest solely on your e-mail exchanges. You may complete a $50 million project without ever meeting your coworker or client face-to-face. You may report to a boss who's never walked into your cubicle. You may deliver a sales pitch by written proposal rather than by plane.

This book is for those who want to accept the challenge of making a significant cultural change and leap in personal productivity. We have to tame the tongue's technology to make it work for, rather than against, us.

The good news: There's a process and there's a format. The bad news: It'll take you a few hours or days of practice to learn them. But my guarantee is that if you'll use the five-step thinking process detailed in the following pages and embrace the e-mail protocol and productivity tips, you'll increase your credibility and strengthen your relationships.

Specifically, you'll learn to:

- Reduce your writing time.
- Improve clarity.
- Organize your ideas succinctly.
- Select appropriate details and data.
- Reduce document length, thereby saving reader time.
- Write authoritatively and persuasively.
- Respond efficiently and effectively by e-mail or letter.
- Eliminate irritants for recipients, caused by an inappropriate tone.
- Build rapport with your customers and coworkers by selecting an appropriate tone.
- Avoid liability issues caused by communications blunders.
- Protect your privacy and that of your organization.
- Project a professional image.

You can translate these outcomes any way you like in your organization.

Now that the gee-whiz has worn off our communication technology, what do you say we make life easier, rather than harder, for one another?

A very great part of the mischiefs that vex this world
arises from words.
—*Edmund Burke*

PART 1

E-MAIL EXCHANGE

Clear writing represents clear thinking—in whatever form: e-mails, reports, or yard signs. This book will detail a five-step thinking process for writing:

Step 1: Consider your audience—what they know, what they want, what they need, how they'll use it.

Step 2: Anticipate special reader reactions.

Step 3: Plan the message functionally in the MADE Format™.

Step 4: Draft quickly.

Step 5: Edit for content, layout, grammar, clarity, conciseness, and style.

This same process holds true even for e-mail messages. But with the day-to-day, two- to ten-liners so prevalent, most people start—and end—with only Step 4.

They log on. They draft. They send.

And that's acceptable for the most part. The efficiency of a fast reply, mass distribution, and paperless communications tempts us to put all kinds of messages in e-mail format. But with those benefits acknowledged, let's focus on the similarities in clear messages—whether they be e-mail, voice mail, or paper. In a nutshell: E-mail should be concise, complete, clear, correct, and quick. As a result, you, as well as your organization, will be thought of as competent.

1

SELECT THE RIGHT MEDIUM
TO COMMUNICATE

We began the last millennium in unity and ended it in isolation. At the turn of the twentieth century, people gathered in town halls to talk politics, went to the theater to watch silent movies, heard news from the same few radio broadcasts, bought gifts and tools at the general store, read about new trends from the same monthly magazines, and studied all subjects in the same classroom.

At the dawn of the twenty-first century, we talk politics in virtual chat rooms, select our movies for home viewing from any of 500 television stations or the corner video-rental shop, buy our gifts and tools from the paper or online catalog, hear our news on television while in the bathroom, read about new trends while in Latvia with our laptop connection to the Internet, and study our online courses at home alone at midnight.

In such a world of emotional disconnection, there's a growing sense of discontent. Customers and coworkers long to be treated as special, important individuals. An automated tracking system that responds to our log-on with "Hi, Bob. Welcome back. The last time you visited, you ordered X" does not exactly leave us with a warm, fuzzy feeling. It has been a long time since having our name inserted in the middle of a direct-marketing letter impressed us.

In an age of impersonal "customization," customers and clients want personal communication. They want a live person to send them an individual e-mail with an answer to their specific question or a suggestion for their specific problem. To confirm the phenomenon, you have only to take a look at your mailbox to see how many chain letters, jokes, and inspirational stories and poems get forwarded to you by friends, coworkers, and customers.

These are attempts to say "Let's connect. Let's share a laugh or a tear. Is anybody out there? Do you remember me?"

The e-mail, letter, or proposal writers who can make a positive emotional connection with their writing will win coworkers' and customers' attention, business, goodwill, and loyalty.

Know When to Send an E-Mail, Fax, or Formal Letter or Report

Impact, reference, speed, and distribution are the key criteria. Let's take them one at a time:

Impact: It's an image decision: tux or blue jeans. *Protocol* may demand a formal report or letter. When introducing yourself, your product, or your service to a new organization or to a new individual within the organization, most people still expect a formal letter, proposal, or other literature to arrive in hard copy, to be read at their leisure. In other words, if you're writing to the CEO, he or she will generally consider an e-mail a breach of etiquette as a first-time communication from an outsider.

Protocol aside, consider *the look.* Prefer to prepare a formal report or letter if the content requires editing and formatting capabilities not available on your e-mail software or that of the reader's.

Finally, consider the *formality or informality:* Because e-mail is commonly used for routine day-to-day business, the recipient doesn't attach as much importance to an e-mail message as to a formal report, letter, or proposal.

Reference: Will the recipient need to find your information three years from now? With most software programs, you can easily delete all e-mail older than a preset date with a few keystrokes—or routinely during the archiving process. Although e-mails *can* be kept indefinitely, most users don't bother to make an exception with their file command on a document-by-document basis.

Speed: Yes, you can send a report across town or cross-country by courier in a few hours. But e-mail takes mere seconds. (Of course, when the e-mail may get read is an altogether different matter.)

Distribution: Yes, you can make 50 copies of a 20-page report and distribute it around the building or fax it cross-country. But that's definitely more expensive and more trouble than hitting a few keys. Second, consider the ease of a recipient forwarding your information to others.

That's easier done (with you controlling the quality of the "reprint") by e-mail.

Impact, reference, speed, distribution. Consider each in making your decision about which medium to use e-mail for a specific message.

Know When to Phone Instead of Writing E-Mail or Letters

Prefer to phone when:

- You need an immediate response. (You can't guarantee when someone will answer e-mail, but if you catch him or her answering the phone, you may get an immediate response.)
- You want to hear someone's voice tone to "read between the lines" about the message, information, personal commitment, and so forth. People are typically less on guard when speaking than when writing.
- You need to ask questions and negotiate issues, and the answers to the questions determine your immediate direction in the negotiations.
- You are concerned about the privacy of your comments.

Prefer e-mail to the phone when:

- The information is complex and will warrant repeating (rereading).
- A written copy will be more convenient for later reference.

Nothing makes another person as angry about the wrong choice of media as the following situations: 1) when someone leaves a voice mail with detailed information that needs to be transcribed almost in its entirety; or 2) when someone e-mails about a situation that has too many discussion points, requiring either an ongoing saga or an extended, time-consuming response.

Understand the Dangers of E-Mail Misunderstandings and Major Faux Pas

For all its convenience, e-mail has a few drawbacks. Consider them carefully. First, humor doesn't travel well in typical e-mails—unless authored by skilled comedy writers. In the absence of tone of voice, facial expression, and body language, readers may interpret your flippant or witty remark as literal and stupid.

Second, you risk losing control of what you've written. Yes, others should not forward your sensitive messages without your permission. But they often do. Forwarding other people's e-mail tempts people of even the highest integrity.

Two good questions to ask yourself before putting anything in e-mail: 1) What might happen if this e-mail were forwarded to everyone in the company? 2) What might happen if a client or supplier sued us, and all our e-mail records were subpoenaed for court?

Commit your information and opinions to e-mail accordingly.

2

FOLLOW THE RULES OF E-MAIL ETIQUETTE TO CREATE THE PROPER IMAGE

Even though technology changes rapidly, the rules of business and social etiquette do not. It has always been considered rude to interrupt private conversations, to conduct private conversations in front of other people, to monopolize a conversation, and to push your business wares in a social setting. These same rules apply to e-mail, Internet, and intranet settings.

Additionally, etiquette in any situation—e-mail included—involves standard common-sense considerations. Avoid remarks that are vulgar, repetitive, and verbose.

Check Multiple E-Mail Accounts Promptly

When you are in a job transition, when you want to separate your social correspondence from that of your business, or when you're on the road, you may make use of multiple e-mail boxes. That's understandable and inexpensive.

But if you have multiple e-mail accounts for whatever reason, check your mail on all accounts promptly. *You* may know that one address is your primary mailbox, but others may not. And because the medium is e-mail, senders expect a much faster response than a look-see once a week.

Avoid Using All Uppercase or All Lowercase

Writers use either all uppercase or lowercase because they think it's faster to keyboard without hitting the Shift key. They're correct—it is faster for the *sender* . . . but not for the reader.

Which of the following two e-mails do you prefer to read?

DO NOT STOP BY. FYI I'M LEAVING FOR THE NEA ASAP VIA LA. I'M HOPING TO CONNECT WITH JOHN IN INTERNATIONAL COFFEE SHOP. SO IF HE CALLS HAVE SUE TELL HIM WHERE OFF AIRPORT ROUTE. ETA STILL NOT CLEAR. SEMINAR ROOM TBD. TELL HIM TO BRING THE MDG MODEL WITH HIM. MAY NEED TO DEMO.

do not stop by. fyi i'm leaving for the nea asap via la. i'm hoping to connect with john in international coffee shop. so if he calls have sue tell him where off airport route. eta still not clear. seminar room tbd. tell him to bring the mdg model with him. may need to demo.

Neither would be immediately clear. Uppercase and lowercase letters are reading aids that signal a reader about sentence beginnings (new thoughts), proper nouns, and acronyms. Besides making your e-mail more difficult to read, all uppercase is interpreted as shouting, and all lowercase, as lazy.

Never Double-Space Your Entire Message

Readers need to grasp sentences, paragraphs, and lists as single units; double-spacing on the screen makes that more difficult to do.

Double-spacing *between* paragraphs, however, aids readability—for the same reason just mentioned.

Highlight Responses in Color to Aid Reading

Rather than simply hitting the Reply key and keyboarding your answers after each specific question or keyboarding all your answers either above or below the original message, use your color pen to highlight your responses (provided, of course, you know your other internal readers' e-mail programs support color). Your answers will stand out dramatically.

Cut and Paste Rather Than Hit "Reply" on Long, Continuing E-Mails

Don't make recipients read through long lines of their previous e-mail to find your two-sentence reply. Delete all the other background or explanatory information originally sent and leave only the pertinent questions, along with your responses. Or cut the pertinent questions and paste them into a new e-mail, accompanied by your responses.

Although this point is not so critical when you're responding only to the original writer of the e-mail (because he or she can more easily distinguish between the original message and your responses), others who may be copied on your reply will have difficulty separating the original comments from the responses.

Be Wary of Humor or Sarcasm

Humor is extremely difficult to convey in writing because you do not have the same body language "softeners" (a twinkle in the eye, a smile, a shrug of the shoulders) that provide interpretation clues in face-to-face conversations. That's why comedy writers earn big bucks. Either be sure your humor works, use the typical sideways smiley face as a label, or don't try your wit at all.

Neither is sarcasm any more acceptable in e-mail than in face-to-face communication. Sending off a scathing attack with some disclaimer about how "the humor-impaired should skip this message" does not rule out offense and mitigate the criticism. In short, don't write anything in e-mail that you wouldn't want forwarded to your CEO, your customers, your family, or your friends.

Allow Cool-Off Time Before Sending a Flame or Any Emotional Message

Sending a negative message that contains insensitive, insulting, negative, and critical comments is called a flame. Before you flame, cool off. Once you hit the Send button, you're committed.

As a safety valve, leave an emotionally charged message in your outbox or drafts folder for at least an hour or, better, a day. Ask yourself: Would I say this face-to-face? Remember, there really is a live person on the receiving end of your communication.

Particularly, avoid flaming in public. If you must send a negative message to someone who originated a message, do not post your flame or send it to an entire distribution list. Even in the old TV westerns, the cowboys always "stepped outside" to have a showdown. Others really do not appreciate being involved in a personal debate or insulting e-mail duel.

Use Receipts Sparingly

In urgent matters, when you must be assured that someone has read your e-mail, use of a receipt is appropriate. However, generally, readers interpret a receipt to mean "I got you. Now I have proof that you received this message, so don't give me any excuses for not responding or doing what I asked."

A good rule of thumb is to use receipts only for emergencies.

Don't Forward Sensitive Messages or Copyrighted Articles Without Permission

Copyright on e-mail belongs to the writer of the message, not the recipient. If there's any doubt in your mind about forwarding another person's e-mail, don't.

Granted, in our routine business e-mail, it's standard practice to forward e-mail to someone else who can or should handle a situation (or know about it). But standard practice is not legal practice.

Ask yourself these filter questions about e-mails you plan to forward: 1) Will the author be upset that I forwarded the message? 2) Does this information contain a copyright note? It's *not* necessary for the author to place a copyright note on a document for it to have legal protection. But you can be sure that when there's a formal copyright note, the author is dead serious about copyright infringement.

If there's a question about forwarding someone's e-mail, reconsider before you risk ire and the law.

If You Don't Have Something to Say, Don't Say It— Not All E-Mails Deserve Responses

On the street, when someone you know speaks to you, etiquette dictates that you return the greeting. And if you're from some particularly friendly parts of the country, people greet and return greetings—and even engage in small talk over an extended period—from total strangers.

Not so with e-mail. Don't reply to a message unless you have something to add. If you're "tagged," don't feel as though you're obligated or expected to reply.

Some of the biggest time-wasters are silly responses, such as in the following situation with an e-mail from Bryan to his coworkers:

I'm considering switching software for handling our geological maps. I'm investigating Brand XYZ from ABC Company. If you have any experience with this software, I'd appreciate an opinion about it. Thanks.

More than 60 responses flooded Bryan's box, and they all basically said "Never heard of it."

If you don't have anything to say, don't say it.

Use a Signature Block or Line

The signature line identifies who you are and includes alternative ways to contact you (usually phone and fax numbers). When your return address is the only item identifying the message source, your signature block may be all that people find to identify you.

You may need to use different signature blocks for internal and external correspondence. If you're sending e-mail outside your organization, identify yourself completely, stating your position and the name of your organization. For internal use, you may mention only your department and sometimes include a descriptive line about the key project you're leading if most of your e-mail relates to your role in that capacity.

And, in fact, the signature block containing a full name may be the only way the recipient can decipher the name. With an e-mail address like pconeil@aol.com (Is it Paul Coneil or P.C. O'Neil?), tray@hotmail.net (Is it T. Ray or someone with the first name Tray?), or johnspeaks4U2@compuserve.com, readers may have difficulty recognizing even a friend's name.

To avoid this difficulty, be sure to enter your full name, as well as your e-mail address. Both should appear in the sender line.

To go one step further, use the "v-card" (virtual card—this contains items such as your full name, title, organization, phone, or fax). Keep looking through your e-mail program options until you find this great little feature. This small file, automatically attached to your outgoing e-mail, can populate a contact record with all your contact information for the benefit of the person receiving your message.

In other words, as a customer, if I e-mail a company about a product, this v-card information would automatically go into the company's customer database in the correct fields so that I'd be on the mailing list for the next catalog. A nice feature for both parties.

Limit Your Signature Block

Keep your block short, generally no more than four lines, with possibly an additional two to three lines for alternative methods of contact (your fax or phone number). But don't include another screen full of hype, thinly disguised as a signature block.

Limit Emoticons or Smileys

Emoticons composed of various keyboard characters to create faces of emotion equate to e-mail slang.

:)   Smile

: (Sad, anger, disappointment

;)   Winking, just joking

:-D Shock or surprise

;-} Leer

:-Q Smoker

:-@ Scream

For trivial e-mail, emoticons may be appropriate. But when communicating about serious topics to important people, they detract from your authority and distract the reader.

And as a second filter, if you find that you need to underscore the emotion with a smiley, make sure that a smiley will do the trick. A smiley won't disguise an offensive remark as a joke. And there is a bigger danger: After almost a decade of e-mail, emoticons are proliferating, and their meanings are by no means universal.

Use Internationally Recognizable Dates, Times, and Measurements When Appropriate

If you're communicating around the globe, use both metric measurements and their English-system equivalents (examples: gallons and liters; miles and kilometers).

Also, be clear about whether you're using the international or United States format for dates and times. Placement of digits varies: Is 3/9 meant to be read as March 9 or September 3? If you're communicating with your team leader in Rome, prefer 1430 hours for a conference call rather than 2:30 P.M.

Act on E-Mail Promptly, or Notify Others That You're Unavailable

With the speed of transmission, users assume speedy replies. Whether a good or bad assumption, people appreciate knowing when you will be offline for extended periods.

Some e-mail programs have built-in out-of-the-office features. Others do not.

You have two choices: 1) Use the auto-responder that tells people you're offline. (In preparing your automatic response to incoming e-mail, you can be as specific or vague as you want about if and when you'll respond.) 2) Have someone else check your e-mail and respond in your absence.

Although there are exceptions in every culture, generally, if you'll not be responding to your e-mail for more than 48 hours, use the auto-responder to let others know you have not read their incoming messages.

Don't Post "Action or Else" Messages If Action Is Irreversible

For years, businesspeople have used the "If I don't hear from you, I'll assume that X, and I will go ahead and do Y." They come to that decision when dealing routinely with someone who often stalls on decisions and actions. If you can't reverse the action, and if you care that the other person may not like the action you're proposing, ask for confirmation of your message. Otherwise, you may mistake that person's silence during a three-week vacation as agreement.

Judge Reading Time to Determine Length, Not Screen Space or Page Count

Screen space and paper are cheap; reading time is expensive. For years, you've probably heard people say, "Put it on one page. My boss won't read more than one page." The concept is correct; the attempt, admirable. To be concise is good.

But to be read is better.

In a false attempt to be brief, writers have frequently crowded their words, omitting paragraph breaks, headings, or bulleted lists to save a line or two. They often accomplish the task of getting everything to a single screen or page—and lose the ability to win over the reader.

Short paragraphs, lists, and informative headings all aid readers in skimming your document quickly, tempting them to keep reading until the end.

In determining the length of your document, make reading time the criterion for brevity, not word count, screens, or pages used.

Use "For Your Information Only" Tags to Help Others Manage Their E-Mail Volume

Some FYI documents with an informative subject line will be self-explanatory. For example, with an e-zine or e-newsletter, you automatically know no action is required. The same is true with subject lines such as "XYZ Project Update" or "Monthly Sales Report."

On the other hand, those e-mails addressing current situations or projects may routinely fit in either category—"know something" or "do something." If you can add an "FYI only" or "immediate action" phrase in your subject lines, that tag will help readers prioritize their e-mail reading.

When Traveling, Take Care to Verify Your "Reply to" Address on Forwarded Responses

It's not uncommon for e-mail users to have multiple addresses: one at the office, one for personal use, and one for a hobby or special-interest project. Because users often have remote access to their office mail, they can receive Internet e-mail almost anywhere. It's easy to get in the habit of hitting Reply to a business e-mail forwarded to you while logged on to your office system from home. The problem is failing to have your remote computer set up with the appropriate business "reply to" e-mail address.

That means your business colleague gets an e-mail from Jerry&Toots@hotmail.com and doesn't recognize the sender. Worse, the recipient in turn hits his or her Reply button and sends an answer back to your Jerry&Toots@hotmail.com address, which you don't access for the next week.

Either change the address manually when replying to specific e-mails, or set up another e-mail log-on with the different "reply to" address.

3

COMPOSE CLEAR,
TO-THE-POINT MESSAGES

Avoid Knee-Jerk Responses

E-Mail is quick. That's why we use it. But its greatest benefit can also be its greatest drawback. When we sit down at the keyboard "to do e-mail," our mind-set is typically to get through it all—to empty our e-mail box and go on to other business.

That mind-set generates knee-jerk reactions to others' questions, solicitations of opinions, requests, and recommendations. We open. We read. We reply. Then we think—or don't—as the case may be.

We nix a promising idea because it has a few glitches that we don't take the time to consider seriously. We turn down a request to provide information because our day is already overscheduled. We offer a make-do explanation or assessment rather than a reasoned one because speed, rather than thoroughness, is the goal.

Be mindful of speed as a potentially negative habit.

Give Messages a Context When Replying

Include enough of the original message to provide a context for your response. You need not include the entire message, but do include the relevant part to remind your reader of the pertinent issues or questions.

Also, be sure to use a visual marker to help the reader distinguish between your comments and the original message you're forwarding or replying to with your current e-mail.

Understand the Difference Between Being Informal and Seeming Careless and Ignorant

Yes, e-mail is an informal method of communicating. To be informal means using a conversational tone, a breezy style, colloquial words and phrases, intentional sentence fragments, abbreviations, and acronyms. All of these are conventions you may use in speaking face-to-face with someone, and they are certainly appropriate in specific types of e-mail.

On the other hand, being informal does *not* mean using unclear and incomplete thoughts, ambiguous references, irrelevant details, repetitive information, disorganized ideas, misspelled words, and grammatical errors.

Such e-mail demonstrates your thinking process to coworkers. Never forget that your reputation sometimes rests on your ability to communicate internally with your coworkers as much as it does on your external communication with clients and customers.

Yes, software programs have spelling and grammar checks that can be automatically set to prompt users. The problem is that many people don't use them. In their attempt to save the 10 to 20 seconds that the checks might require to review the document, users can lose the career opportunity of a lifetime.

The bigger issue is that grammatical mistakes often affect clarity. They cost time in rereading to decipher messages and often create misunderstandings. If your e-mail is worth composing and sending, it's worth being written well enough to be understood.

Your communication reflects your competence. Compose e-mail with your reputation in mind.

Avoid Composing and Then Asking, "Who Should Get a Copy?"

A typical writing habit is to keyboard a message (such as a project update, a new policy statement, or a change in procedure), and then ask, "Now, who should get a copy of this?"

Wrong approach. When you copy people on your e-mail, it should be because they have a need to know. And if they have a need to know, they should be able to understand the jargon and acronyms, get the answers to their questions, and understand how the message specifically affects them.

This means the e-mail should be written with all these issues in mind: a focus on the readers' interest, the necessary details, and the language.

Best approach: Consider first who needs to know what you're writing. Then tailor your message to their interests, their questions, their details. Not the reverse.

Highlight the Readers' Action

You have two ways to alert your readers to the action you want: subject lines and action statements up front in the e-mail.

If your e-mail requests action that will be a low priority or difficult, don't force readers to hunt for the necessary details or to assume the action by "reading between the lines." You'll most likely not get a quick, complete, or appropriate response.

Don't Be Cryptic and Remove the Actors

Because e-mail is fast and informal, many people tend to use a cryptic style, dropping the "actors" and using fragments instead of sentences. The resulting comments become unclear. Who does what is often the most important part of the message. Consider this example:

> Carol Frazier of Global United is trying to help us get into her company to do business. Called about the possibility of arranging a meeting with the sales development managers about their needs for fully automating their field offices. Told them such automation was essential to compete in today's environment and that laptops for everybody were essential to do business. Negotiations began last week. Will call at the end of next month with firm date when everyone can get together.

Who initiated the call—Carol or the writer? Whose needs does the writer refer to—the company's, or sales development managers only? Who told whom that the automation was essential? (Is Carol trying to sell her own people, or is the writer of the e-mail trying to persuade Carol?) Who began negotiations? (Carol, to "sell" her own managers on spending the money, or the writer representative negotiating with Carol to get Global United's business?) Who will call at the end of next month? (Will Carol call the writer, or the writer will call Carol?) Who is "everyone"?

The reader doesn't always make the same assumptions that the writer intends. Name the specific actors to eliminate any guesswork.

Distinguish Between Fact and Opinion When the Difference Is Not Obvious to Casual Readers

"Universal Corporation uses deceptive advertising in all its campaigns" stated in an e-mail as fact and distributed to a list of hundreds can result in a lawsuit. If you're making a personal judgment, say so, lest your words come back to haunt you later. And even then, be sure you really want to state your personal opinion in potentially libelous situations.

Avoid Offbeat Acronyms

Acronyms such as *bcnu* (be seeing you), *imho* (in my humble opinion), *fwiw* (for what it's worth), *obo* (or best offer), *rtfm* (read the funny manual), and *tnstaafl* (there's no such thing as a free lunch) annoy people rather than amuse them. If you're using these as shortcuts, remember that artificial acronyms may be a shortcut for the writer, but they will not be easily interpreted by those unfamiliar with them.

Avoid Stream-of-Consciousness Rambling

Be careful about stream-of-consciousness rambling in e-mails. Just as the penny is the basis for our monetary system, the sentence is our basic unit of thought. For the most part, one sentence should convey one thought. To be readable, sentences in a passage should not average more than 15 to 20 words. Time yourself in reading the following two passages. Notice also that in addition to the time consideration, shorter sentences are generally clearer.

Stream-of-Consciousness Writing

I maintain that we already have "implemented procedures" to determine that we do not issue title policies over $5 million without being reinsured, but I don't see why these procedures need to be converted to the hypertext procedures online because the mere fact that we have instructed people not to write policies without reinsurance over that amount should be adequate procedure, as with all the other instructions we send out routinely. (1 sentence)

Short, Clear Sentences

I maintain that we already have "implemented procedures" to determine that we do not issue title policies over $5 million without being reinsured. But I don't see why these procedures need to be converted to the hypertext procedures online. The mere fact that we have instructed people not to write policies over $5 million without reinsurance should be adequate. We send out other oral instructions routinely without writing them into formal procedures. (4 sentences)

Which version would you rather wade through? If the e-mail wasn't that interesting to read the first time, imagine forcing people to reread it.

Keep to One Subject in Each E-Mail

E-mails covering multiple topics are difficult to file. No, I take that back. They're not difficult to file; they're just difficult to retrieve when you need them for reference.

Multiple-topic messages also cause a problem when you need to forward only part of the information. The reader either has to cut and paste to create a new e-mail, or he or she has to send along your e-mail in its entirety—and leave it to the next reader to sort through the irrelevant material.

For ease of filing and forwarding, as a general rule, address only one topic in each e-mail.

Watch the Tone in Directives

Brevity breeds brusqueness. Notice the difference in these two versions:

Version 1:   Please return the shipment by June 1. Do not sign the form.

Version 2:   We're working against a short deadline on this project, so please return the shipment by June 1. Also, please leave the form unsigned.

Let's say you've just asked your boss if she thinks you should consider working toward an advanced degree in night school at a local university to pursue credentials that might position you for a promotion. Consider the difference in these two responses:

Response 1:   No.
Response 2:   No, Terry, I don't think an advanced degree would have any effect on the opportunity for promotion here.

A neutral question posed to a peer might generate the same uneasiness about a brief answer. Let's say you've asked a colleague if it's appropriate to dress casually for the office Christmas party.

Response 1:   No.
Response 2:   No, I think the proper attire is business dress.

Brief is good. Blunt is not. Sometimes an explanation adds a buffer to an otherwise cold, foreboding, or intimidating tone.

Distinguish Between Confirming Receipt and Confirming Action or Details

The point of a confirmation e-mail is just that—confirming action or details. Generally, it's not enough to confirm that you received a message. For example, knowing about a meeting is definitely not a commitment to attend.

If confirming an action, be specific about the details you're confirming: "Yes, I will be at the meeting on Friday, August 6, at 3:00 in the Loma Linda Conference Room."

Tell Others Why You're Sending an Attachment, and State What It Is

Avoid sending an e-mail that says only, "I'm sending you something. Look at it." The recipient understands that much from the subject line and attachment bar. Instead, summarize the salient point or issue from the attachment. Then state the action(s) you want: What do you want the reader to notice, believe, consider, approve, question, confirm, or review?

4

AIM TO GET ATTENTION FOR YOUR OWN E-MAIL

Create Informative Subject Lines That Get Quick Responses and Help Readers Prioritize

Prefer a specific subject line that informs to one that merely suggests a topic. And if you need action from your readers, state that in your subject line, too:

> *Not:* Staff Meeting
> *But:* Staff Meeting Rescheduled to June 6

> *Not:* Insurance Problems
> *But:* $2,000 Insurance Premium Uncollectable

> *Not:* Training Schedule
> *But:* Confirmation Requested: EWW Class May 4

> *Not:* Field Trip to Leichton
> *But:* Approval Requested for Leichton Field Trip

Informative subject lines allow people to determine priorities from their in-box list.

Update Subject Lines on Replies in Ongoing Sagas

When you hit the Reply button or the Forward button, the same subject line appears on the reply or forwarded document. That subject-line "thread" becomes a convenience in the first three or four responses—and then it becomes downright confusing.

When that same subject line keeps popping up in your mailbox five and six times, it begins to create questions: Is that the e-mail I just read and forgot to file, or is it a new one? If so, is the issue still a high priority?

Another drawback to retaining the thread in the subject line is an automatic list of uninformative subject lines captured in your contact manager database. If you later need to refer to a past e-mail, you'll need to open eight or ten of them to find the e-mail with the exact detail you need.

Worst still, after an issue has been volleyed back and forth several more times, chances are that the e-mail no longer matches the subject line. Or the subject line reads: *Subject: RE: RE: RE: RE: RE: RE:*, until the real subject is truncated and no longer appears at all.

Typically, after a few volleys, it's better to change the subject line to keep it focused and informative for the specific topic of the latest message.

Avoid Crying Wolf with "Urgent" Subject Lines

People, of course, skim their subject lines to prioritize reading. With people now often receiving from 20 to 200 e-mails a day, those subject lines become valuable ways to determine what must be read within the hour and what can wait until the end of the day.

Once you abuse the "urgent" label, your readers will learn to ignore other such e-mail in the future. Then what do you do for an encore?

Limit Distribution to Others' Need to Know: Understand That Less Equals More

In our writing workshops, the most frequent complaint about e-mail is this lament: "I get so much stuff that I just delete a lot without reading them. And in doing that, I probably miss things I should have read." Then these attendees go on to call names of people and departments that send e-mails to them for which they have no interest and often do not understand.

Sending e-mail to mass-distribution lists within your own organization is fast becoming a way to make yourself a nuisance. Do not e-mail to a prepared list simply because it's easier for you than customizing the distribution list for a specific communication. Instead of using mass distribution, post general information to an internal bulletin board or online discussion forum. Of course, if a message *needs* to be read by everyone, don't simply post it, because some people never check bulletin boards.

In short, be discerning about wide distribution, and use internal bulletin boards when they are more appropriate.

Don't Forward Messages Without Adding Your Own Note to Tell the Recipient Why

It may be perfectly clear to you why you're forwarding an attachment, but often recipients are left scratching their heads. Either add your explanation in a new subject line, or add a note to explain why you are forwarding the e-mail.

Generally, it's safer to put the explanation in the subject line. Otherwise, with only the original subject, when the reader sees a duplicate subject line, he or she may simply delete your copy, thinking one copy is as good as another. If your "cover" note contains specific instructions or explanations about the forwarded document, the recipient may miss those.

So prefer to change the subject line on forwarded documents if you have added a note.

Know the Implications (Uses and Misuses) of Using Receipts

Receipt-requested e-mail conveys one of three messages to your reader: 1) I'll sleep better tonight if I know you received this message; 2) I want to know exactly what time you read this message; or 3) In case you try to weasel out of something, I want proof that you received this message so you can't claim you didn't know about it.

When you request a receipt, understand that readers will give your gesture one of these interpretations. And you can't control which one.

Don't Diminish Your Authority with an Inappropriate Tone and Style

Twenty years ago, writers had difficulty distinguishing between a pompous and a formal writing style. Today, the bigger difficulty has become knowing the difference between a formal and an informal style.

For example, consider the following word choices:

INFORMAL	FORMAL
Look over the stuff and kick it back with your input.	Review the materials and give me your opinion.
Please have the contract okayed before forwarding the forms.	Please have the contract approved before forwarding the forms.
FYI, I'm outta here for the rest of the week.	For your information, I'll be traveling for the rest of the week.
The client has to come to grips with the deal. That's how we do business.	The client needs to understand this is our standard procedure.

To determine the appropriate style and tone, consider three things: 1) your relationship to the reader; 2) the subject of the e-mail; and 3) the purpose of the e-mail.

First: Who are you writing to, and how well do you know them? How would you talk to them on the phone or face-to-face?

Second: Is the subject casual and trivial, or is it a serious business issue?

Third: Will your readers review the message and delete it? Will the e-mail be filed? Will it possibly be printed out for distribution at a client meeting? Will it serve as evidence in a legal proceeding?

These three criteria will dictate the appropriate tone for specific situations: Know your audience; know your intentions; know the dangers of drivel.

5

MANAGE HIGH-VOLUME E-MAIL EFFECTIVELY

Use LIFO (Last In, First Out) as a Rule of Thumb

The last-in, first-out reading rule applies in two situations: multiple e-mails from the same person and all e-mails collectively.

First, let's talk about several e-mails from one person. If you read and respond to the e-mails in chronological order, you'll often find yourself responding to questions or issues that have been overcome by events. Read the last e-mail first and you may discover that the last e-mail summarizes all the issues or questions from the previous e-mails and the whole situation has been overcome by events—events in which you don't have any interest. When that's the case, you've saved yourself having to read several interim e-mails.

On the other hand, if you read the latest e-mail and find the situation of interest (even though resolved), then you will probably want to go back and review all the interim e-mails to get the full picture about issues and decisions along the way. It makes sense at that point to go back and read them chronologically.

Just don't *respond* to all those e-mails along the way, because you may be responding to the unnecessary on issues that have already changed or sorted themselves out. Read them from first to last, and *then* respond.

Now, to the second category of e-mail—e-mail accumulated over several days from multiple senders. Let's say that upon returning to the office from a business trip or vacation, you have 300 e-mails. If you start to read them in chronological order, by the time you get to the last half of the heavy volume, your responses will be late on those as well. As a result, you'll risk being tardy in responding to all 300 senders. If, on the other hand, you respond to the last day's e-mails first, those responses will not be late. And for the senders who have had e-mails in your box for the longest time, it probably won't make much difference to them whether your response was delayed three days or six days. It's simply late.

So after you prioritize by subject line or sender, adopt a last-in, first-out order.

Prioritize Your Reading According to Urgency

Yes, your e-mail software typically displays e-mails by date. But just because it's an easy pattern to open and close documents, don't let that automatically dictate your reading order.

Even if you intend to go through all the waiting e-mail in one sitting beginning at midnight, if you have a full box, you'll likely be tired by the time you get to the last few. If they happen to be the most important ones, you might be less likely to give them your fullest attention for a thoughtful response.

Don't lapse into a "whatever comes up" reading order.

Don't Be Teased into Reading What You Don't Need to See

Some people read their e-mail the way they read road signs. They read whatever meets the eye. But spending unnecessary reading time at your computer costs you much more than if you are reading signs in a subway, bus, train, or car.

Ignore e-mails from names you don't recognize and with subject lines that don't interest you. Or, if you're afraid to ignore them, sample them by reading the opening line or two. If the topic is only of minimal interest, force yourself to delete that e-mail.

Read with purpose, not by default. Curiosity killed the cat, and it can crowd your day.

Identify and Record the Essentials of Coworker or Customer Interactions: Integrate with Other Functions and Software to Avoid Duplication of Effort

Most of us work in a job in which we need to document our interactions with others so that coworkers can handle situations in our absence. That documentation is most often kept on a database contact manager. Rather than force coworker to wade through screens of disorganized comments, use the following structure to document your interaction:

Summary: Summarize the situation or interaction in a sentence or two.

Action Taken: State the last action taken.

Action Pending: State the next action required of you or the other person.

Details: Elaborate on any necessary details to make the summary or action clearer (usually the *how* and *why*).

Study the following example:

Summary: Ellen Pitts called to say that she left her cellular phone in the glove compartment of a green Taurus she rented from our St. Louis airport location June 28. She had an accident while driving, and the car was towed to a body shop for repairs. She needed the name and phone number of the body shop repairing the car.

Action Taken: I referred her to Don's Body Shop on Main Street.

Action Pending: If the body shop doesn't locate her phone, she'll call us again to get necessary paperwork to file a claim with her insurance company.

Details: She has informed the police about the accident. Her insurance will cover damages to our car.

Overview first, then elaborate. That structure holds true in most communication in general, and in database records in particular.

If you begrudge the time required to keep complete records, consider the time lost in trying to dig to the bottom of a situation before you can take further action.

Maintain Your Files Responsibly

Check your e-mail daily. Delete messages as soon as possible so they don't take up unnecessary storage space. Transfer your e-mail to your hard drive or download it onto a floppy disk for future reference. Use file folders to sort e-mail, and organize the folders.

Routinely scan your system for viruses, especially when receiving or downloading files from other systems. Keep up to date on any copyright or licensing arrangements.

Sort Mail into File Folders That Make Sense to *You*

Don't be unduly influenced by traditional filing systems that typically organize things by accounts (company or individual names), projects, or dates. Nor is the default, chronological setting the most efficient way to organize (and retrieve) files.

For e-mail purposes, it may be more logical to keep documents filed by sender (your boss, your three key clients, your assistant) or by category (marketing updates, nifty newsletters, training schedules).

Traditional files should be organized so that *anyone* can locate things. Your e-mail files should be organized so that *you* can find things.

File Thin Rather Than Fat

File folders that cover broad categories and dates fill faster than smaller files. Then when those files get fat and full, it takes you longer to browse through subject lines to find what you want. Therefore, when you're setting up your file folders, think thin. Name your file folders to collect fewer documents; you'll be able to browse them quickly to locate a single document.

Group "Read Later" E-Mails into a File and Out of Sight

It takes you longer to skim a long list of e-mails than a short list. And every time you leave unread mail in the box, you have to review the complete list again to find the new e-mail. (Of course, you can flag files, but often users ignore the flags in reviewing the list.) With each review of the list, you waste even more time sorting and prioritizing.

So make a habit of doing something with all e-mails on a first reading. If you don't want to read them immediately, move what can wait into a reading file for spare moments.

Set Up E-Newsletter and E-Zine Files Separately

If you have one file folder for all e-newsletters and e-zines, it will grow fat fast. With electronic newsletters and magazines proliferating at an alarming rate and increasing frequency (some even daily), one fat file will make it impossible to locate a single issue in which you vaguely recall an item of interest.

If you intend to continue receiving special-interest mailings, set up a file folder for each e-newsletter or e-zine. Then when you want to locate a back issue, you can simply select it from a list of six rather than sixty.

Archive Routinely for a Specified Period

The archive function (whether triggered manually or automatically) inspects all e-mail documents not previously saved and either deletes or saves (archives) them.

Out of fear of losing something important, users often set the archive function to retain documents for a lengthy period. No harm done—except when users actually need a file and must browse a long list of current documents to find it.

It's generally better to reverse the thinking: Set the e-mail application to archive routinely, deleting items older than a specific number of days. And in the case of extremely important e-mails that you want to keep forever and a day, put these items into a separate folder or directory from which items are never deleted.

Then routinely back up those e-mail files to disk or tape.

Set the Archive Function on a Folder-by-Folder or Document-by-Document Basis for Sensitive Situations

In lieu of keeping fat files, set your archive function to delete nonessential documents after a set number of days (typically 14 to 30 days) or to archive the keepers. You can specify the deletion or archive criteria by folder or by individual document.

For example, if you often receive e-mails relating to contracts, you may want to put those in a folder or directory for items never to be deleted. All other file folders can be set to delete or archive items automatically when they are older than a set number of days.

Don't Be Lured into Web Surfing from Embedded Links

When you hear a child begging for permission to do something because "all the other kids" are doing it, do you ever hear a parent respond with this remark: "Just because 'all the other kids' jump off a cliff, are you planning to jump, too?"?

If so, you'll understand this guideline: Just because a friend or colleague e-mails you with an embedded link to a website he or she finds interesting, it doesn't mean you have to go there.

Fight the temptation. One peep leads to another. And another. And another. At that rate, it can take you hours "to go through your e-mail."

Ignore Chain Letters

Yes, with a few keystrokes, it's easy to forward chain letters to everyone you know. But it's not just *your* keystrokes that matter. When you send the letter to the next 250 people, you're increasing their reading load. And they won't always thank you.

Break the chain. Go ahead.

Forget About Spam

The term "spam" was first used in the 1990s to describe e-mail messages not related to the topic of discussion and postings of a news group: meaningless, unnecessary, or excessive items or comments. More recently, spam has come to mean unsolicited items sent in bulk. In other words, as related to e-mail, spam has become synonymous with "junk mail" that people receive in more traditional ways.

Groups continue to debate whether spam is bad or simply an expression of free speech. According to a survey by IMT Strategies (www.imtstrategies.com), more than 60 percent of respondents said they felt negative about spam, and another 16 percent reported they felt "somewhat negative." Congress has already begun to address this issue.

In the meantime, either use a filter or just say no. Delete it. Responding with a flame only wastes your time—and confirms to the sender that he or she has your e-mail address. You *can*, however, inform the spammer's Internet service provider (ISP). If the ISP takes up your cause, the ISP can discontinue the spammer's service. ISPs would rather switch than fight. Simply remove everything in the e-mailer's address before the @, replace it with *abuse*, and forward the offending e-mail to the service provider at abuse@aol.com or another ISP address.

Check It, but Don't Be Chained to It

Many people have become almost chained to their desks or laptops by the e-mail popping onto their screen. The compulsion stems from the confusion between the urgent and the important. Few e-mails in any given week are urgent, requiring an immediate response. Instead of being constantly distracted, let the e-mails pile up and check them only once or twice a day. As a result, you can stay informed on what's happening without breaking your concentration on more important tasks.

6

BECOME SAVVY ABOUT E-MAIL MECHANICS

Guard Against a Trigger-Happy "Send" Finger

People occasionally hit the Send button prematurely or accidentally, sending an unedited or half-written e-mail. If that's a frequent frustration of yours, don't enter the recipient's e-mail address until you have the e-mail ready to go. Of course, you may need to remove it manually if the e-mail program automatically inserts it, as many do. Then if your trigger finger goes off, your e-mail is still safely in your hands.

This precaution also works with attachments, keeping you from dashing off an e-mail that refers to an attachment but actually has none.

Saving your work in a draft folder or a "send later" file also serves another function: to allow cooling-off time before sending a message about a sensitive issue. Waiting an hour or a day before hitting the Send key may save a relationship or a deal.

Limit Line Length and Fancy Features

Some fancy features are simply ignored; others produce trash. Therefore, don't depend on them for readability or clarity. Make the document text itself as clear as possible—both words and structure. Then, if the fancy features don't work, nothing is lost.

Be aware of differences and limitations in others' systems and software. For example, set your e-mail software to automatically wrap lines at

70 characters. Longer lines may wrap at the wrong places, producing continuing lines that give an odd stair-step effect down the recipient's screen.

When e-mailing *outside* your organization, avoid features and formatting (such as tables, **bolding**, *italics*, fonts, or color) that may cause other software to display gibberish.

Set Your E-Mail Automatically to Tell Senders When You're Offline

Not only is this an etiquette issue (mentioned earlier), but it's an e-mail management aid. With such automatic responses, some senders will decide to seek answers or help elsewhere. Upon your return to the office or your e-mail box, you'll find it less full than you would have otherwise.

It's amazing when people know they'll have to wait a few days for a response how often they go to someone else for the same information or figure out how to "work around" needing your input or action.

At the very least, this automatic notice builds rapport for the sake of courtesy in not setting up false expectations for a speedy response on your part.

Avoid Forwarding "Virus" Warnings Unless You Have Verified Validity

Nobody wants a virus. But we've all received so many notices that turn out to be a hoax that the false warnings have become a nuisance themselves. We ignore them as we ignore car alarms blaring in parking lots. In fact, virus hoaxes themselves are considered viruses because they can be very damaging to large organizations. The rapid and extensive forwarding of the warnings causes mail servers to crash from the overload.

Verify first by going to the websites of the most well-known antivirus companies, where you'll find a list of bona fide and hoax viruses. If you think a particular virus could be real, forward your information to your organization's systems administrator and let him or her check it out fully.

The national news media also provide almost immediate warnings after discovery. So unless your friends and colleagues don't watch TV news, listen to the radio, or read daily newspapers, be leery about sending out mass warnings.

Omit Long Lists of E-Mail Recipients That Readers Must Wade Through Before Getting to Your Message

Current e-mail software packages will now permit you to hide your recipient lists. Take advantage of that feature. Not only is reading through the list a nuisance, but it's also a confidentiality issue. Even if recipients see only first names or initials listed in the addresses, they can often make assumptions about similar groups and "borrow" the e-mail addresses for their own purposes.

An exception to this general rule is when it would be helpful for all recipients to know who else received the message. Allowing them in some cases to see the list would prevent their forwarding the e-mail to others who have already received your copy.

Be Wary About Replying to All Recipients

When hitting the Reply button, be sure that you don't carelessly hit "reply to all." Although the e-mail sender who solicited your input may think it's a good idea to update everyone on the list with shared responses, not all recipients may feel the same compulsion.

Reply selectively. Copy selectively.

Understand That Internal Monitoring Can Capture Your Confidential Statements

Even if you're protected by a firewall from outside intrusions, your e-mail may still be searchable by your organization's internal monitoring functions. In fact, there are even inexpensive software packages to help small companies monitor employee mail. They can scan up to 50,000 e-mails an hour for objectionable words (*unfair, performance review, copyright, breast, résumé, angry*) and forward those messages to a designated person.

Consider that your e-mail may be retrieved for any of the following purposes: investigating (and legally prosecuting) situations involving job termination, sexual harassment, defamation of character, assessment of promotion potential or lack thereof, charges of monopoly or price fixing, product or service negligence or other causes for liability, copyright or patent infringement—and a number of other reasons that keep people awake at night.

In the case of a lawsuit, neither you nor your organization will relish the idea of producing subpoenaed e-mail. When confidentiality is a potential issue, beware.

7

MAKE SURE YOU'RE LEGAL

Respect Others' Confidentiality and Expect Your Own to Be Nonexistent

It is considered rude to forward an e-mail without the author's permission. Having said that, don't be surprised if yours gets forwarded without your knowledge. Assume that will be the case.

Safeguard Your Own Security

Numbers and letters mixed in a combination of a minimum of eight characters increases your security dramatically.

When selecting passwords and codes, most of us are caught in a dilemma. We want to be creative enough to keep snoopers out of our mailbox, but not so creative that we can't remember our own choices. So, many people typically select personal information (birthdays, anniversaries, Social Security numbers, family names), and then for the sake of "creativity," they reverse the numbers. Such passwords and codes are easily broken. Instead, use a combination of letters, numbers, punctuation marks, or a mix of uppercase and lowercase letters. If you need a memory aid, try using the first letters of the refrain in a nursery rhyme, song lyric, or poem.

Then, after going to such trouble to be creative, don't be careless about the obvious security breaches: Keep your password secret. Don't write it down. Log off when you leave your computer unattended. Set a password on your screen saver and activate it. Remove confidential information from the hard drive (save it on removable media) when others have access to it and when you have your computer serviced. Also, you may want to consider encryption features of your e-mail program, a privacy screen, computer lock, or security plates attached to cables and peripherals.

Understand Your Liability for Personal E-Mails on Company Systems

Refer to the previous sections "Understand That Internal Monitoring Can Capture Your Confidential Statements" (p. 42 and "Safeguard Your Own Security" (p. 43)," and if you still feel inclined to court danger, understand your personal liability.

Not only is your organization liable for your e-mail misspeaks and judgment errors, but so are you. Personally. And even if you consider your e-mails will fall beneath any legal radar of interest, consider the potential damage to your career.

Let's say you're trying to negotiate with your boss for a raise and new job title by asking for additional responsibilities for correcting problems you see in your division. You may be surprised to be called into a meeting with senior executives who've been copied on your e-mail about all the "problems" and "inefficiencies" in the organization.

More than one person has lost a job because of such an e-mail.

Do Not Simply Convert Something You've Heard or Received to E-Mail and Forward It Without Verifying Ownership

If someone e-mails you a great article, newsletter, report, update, or white paper without copyright notification, beware. Just because they have cut and pasted it or attached it to their e-mail without a copyright notification doesn't mean the original writing is not copyrighted. On the contrary. It would be rare that such documents are *not* copyright-protected.

An acquaintance of mine who frequently publishes articles in business magazines and technical journals, as well as in his own newsletter, says that one of his growing streams of revenue is fines or settlement monies collected when he prosecutes people for unauthorized use of information lifted from his e-zine or from other websites posting his articles.

Ignorance is not a defense. If you forward such documents, you're liable for copyright infringement.

Respect All Copyright and Licensing Agreements

Copyright and licensing infringements are criminal acts that may result in large fines.

Many e-mail users mistakenly think their use (forwarding) of a copyrighted newsletter, article, or report is permitted under the Fair Use clause of copyright law by arguing that their use is noncommercial (meaning no one is paying them for the document).

The "Fair Use" clause in copyright law does not necessarily permit such use. Four criteria determine "Fair Use":

- Is the purpose of the challenged use commercial or nonprofit (educational, health warning, and so forth)?
- Is the nature of the work factual or someone's unique expression of the facts?
- How substantial is the length of the copied work in comparison to the whole document?
- Does the effect or result of the challenged use reduce the value of the original work to the author? In other words, would the use deprive the author of any potential income?

You cannot use the copyrighted material if your use passes only one or two of these criteria. Fair use means your use has to pass muster on *all four* criteria.

Chances are very slim that, in the typical e-mail traffic, users are legally free to forward copyrighted words. Take great care to discover who has authored the information you may be tempted to pass on. And just because you do not claim the ideas as your own, and even if you acknowledge other sources, you may be liable for infringement.

Not only will the author be on your trail, but so will others who have paid licensing fees to use the material.

Safeguard Your Electronic Signature

On June 30, 2000, U.S. President Bill Clinton signed Senate Bill 761 to make electronic signatures legally binding. Your digital signature with its unique component allows you to do business around the world without ever having had pen touch paper. As with most other computer security measures, you play a vital role in keeping your signature confidential and secure.

A Final Note About E-Mail

No doubt about it, e-mail has improved our productivity. It has increased the speed of communication and provided wider access to people around the globe and within our own organizations. It has reduced the physical effort and hard cost of paper, postage, and travel.

Use it to your fullest advantage, without abusing others' rights or offending their sense of decency and appropriateness. Common sense goes a long way in matters of etiquette.

And to compose e-mail even faster, refer to the techniques and structures in the sections that follow (Parts 3, 4, and 5). Your coworkers, customers, family, and friends will appreciate your clarity, conciseness, and courtesy. In short, you'll connect.

PART 2

THE E-WRITING CULTURE

8

COUNTERPRODUCTIVE COMMUNICATION HABITS

Collectively, e-mail and the Internet have become the biggest boon to our productivity—and bane to our sanity. E-mail alone has added an extra hour or two to our workday, cluttered our minds with trivia, tempted us to "talk" about everybody's business but our own, tried our patience in attempting to unravel stream-of-consciousness prose to come to a decision or take action, cost hours in patching up rifts caused by political minefields, added guilt-induced stress about the still "to be read" list popping onto our screen minute by minute—and threatened to serve as fodder for lawsuits in corporate embarrassments.

But e-mail has also revolutionized the way we work. E-mail helps us respond to our customers and coworkers faster. E-mail allows us to communicate when it's convenient, even if that's 2 A.M. in our pajamas 2,000 miles from home or the office. E-mail has reduced postage, paper, printer, and phone cost. E-mail has enabled the frontline staff to communicate with the executive without going through the formal chain of command.

Boon or bane? Well, it depends.

Paying the Price for Inefficiency

If you've never figured the cost of poor writing as well as the savings in good writing, calculate the time or cost for your organization with this simple model:

Reading Costs

200 words/minute	average reading time—business materials
10-page document	5,000 words or 25 minutes
salary of reader	$100,000/year or $50/hour
reading 10-page document	$20.83
reading cost per year (two documents/day)	$10,440 per reading executive

If these "reading" executives ask for revisions in half the documents submitted to them, increase the reading cost to $15,660 per year. Multiply this cost by the number of report-reading executives in your organization, and you will get an idea of the total reading cost.

Notice that this cost is calculated on the assumption that a 10-page document is necessary. If a 10-page document could be more concisely written in 5 pages, the savings would be even more substantial:

Writing Costs

salary of writer	$60,000/year or $30/hour
40 hours/10-page document	$1,200/10-page report

or:

spends 35% of time writing	$21,000 writing cost/year/writer

If you can make the necessary writing more concise, the cost goes down. A concise e-mail, letter, report, or proposal saves reading time and writing time—not to mention paper. Says one field supervisor about a notoriously bad writer, "When I see the signature, I want to throw the report in my in-basket until I have a full day to devote to it. No matter what the subject, he rambles on and on and on. I just don't have the time."

Top-management readers agree. The most frequent complaint I hear from these readers is that their staffs do not know how to get to the main points quickly; these managers continually struggle to keep up with e-mail and the print piled on their desks for review and/or approval. Conciseness enhances clarity. Conciseness helps the main points stand out rather than fade into a collage of fractured details.

> Conciseness enhances clarity. Conciseness helps the main points
> stand out rather than fade into a collage of details.

When writers habitually use the principles of good writing, they can cut writing time for most documents by 25 percent to 50 percent. For instance, if the above-$60,000-per-year writer could get a report in final form in half the time, he or she could save the organization $10,500 per year.

Simply put, poor writing costs money; good writing represents a substantial savings. But not everyone in the organization understands this concept. Some managers simply accept poor writing as part of the cost of doing business.

Paperless Offices and Other Pipe Dreams

Ten years ago if you needed an important document, you looked in the paper files. Now if you need to retrieve a document, you have three places to search: the network files, your personal computer files, and then the paper files for the printout. And chances are when you find the document, you'll begin to wonder if the version you've found is the latest iteration, thus leading to a review of all available copies to determine if they're identical.

To put it mildly, the paperless office has turned out to be a pipe dream. According to Hewlett Packard's studies, workers who say they regularly print pages from the Internet print an average of 32 pages a day.

Information Rather Than Communication

In its infancy, computer storage and web space were expensive. Today, computer storage costs only pennies and websites sprawl, limited only by available written information and graphics to dump on them.

But more is not better. Salespeople learned long ago the danger of giving buyers too many choices, choices that either baffled them entirely or stumped them with indecision.

Web writers and designers are discovering the same phenomenon. Dumping everything from your marketing and sales literature onto your customer site does not necessarily result in more sales. Likewise, dumping all your user manuals, policy statements, and training courses onto your organization's intranet does not translate to "continual learning" or better job performance.

Information—whether on the web, in an e-mail, in a brochure, or on a billboard—must be interpreted to result in clear communication. Translating difficult material into easily understood language requires much skill.

Poor Models Everywhere

Poor writing abounds everywhere—on the Internet, in books, magazines, technical journals, newspapers, and advertisements. Company databases bulge with ineffectively written documents. Too often business writers use ungrammatical constructions, inappropriate words, and a stilted or silly style, on the assumption that if a certain usage appeared in print or on screen somewhere, it must be acceptable.

Not so.

The Edit-Rewrite-Edit-Rewrite Syndrome

Hemingway said, "All good writing is rewriting." But the edit-rewrite-edit-rewrite process often substitutes for lack of up-front thinking rather than represents a penchant for preciseness.

Just because computers make it easy to revise is no reason to do it. Some writers think *as* they write rather than *before* they write. Why not? they reason. I can always go back and fix things. But asking yourself the right questions and planning your document first saves an enormous effort in drafting and revising.

Supervisors fall into the same trap. In fact, an old truism often circulates in the business world: "The greatest passion in the world is not love or hate, but the compulsion to change another person's copy." If you're asked to edit a peer's writing, make sure you know what you're supposed to be reviewing. Are you supposed to identify missing details? Comment on feasibility of solutions and ideas? Or simply spot grammatical goofs? If you don't know your purpose for review, find out before you edit.

When you're the boss, suppress the urge to edit a subordinate's writing just because computers have made it simple. Is "We'd be glad to have you visit our plant" really so much worse than "We'd be happy to have you visit our plant"? Does "Send the contract as soon as possible" sound any more urgent than "Send the contract at your earliest convenience"? Neither is superior.

Writing is a time-consuming, painstaking task. Editing should make the work more effective, not more frustrating.

No passion in the world is equal to the passion to
alter someone else's draft.
—*H. G. Wells*

Access and Response at the Speed of Touch

Consider the poor decisions made because of knee-jerk responses to an e-mail requesting an opinion. People don't think; they just hit Reply and rant. Trouble is, those rambles are replacing more seasoned thought and action. Such e-mails limit a person's career—without his or her ever knowing what struck.

A financial analyst at a mutual-fund company recently complained to me at one of our writing workshops: "I hate this compulsion people seem to have with e-mail. It's as if they feel they have to clean out the mailbox by morning—or else. I send them questions on such-and-such situation or a dilemma, wanting their thoughtful suggestions and expert opinions before I set a policy or respond to a customer. What do I get? A halfhearted attempt at some explanation or answer—covering what I already knew. When I ask somebody for an opinion on an issue, that's what I want—I want the reader to *think it over*, not just react."

On the opposite side of the coin, expectations for 24–7 availability are creating impatience and growing hostility among workers. At a writing workshop for a large software company, an attendee returned to class muttering: "Just you wait—I'm calling that guy at two A.M. to discuss his inventory problem. I'll just wake him up and we'll discuss it when it's convenient for *me*. Man, that ticks me off." The situation was that a colleague had e-mailed him, wanting an answer to a problem "as soon as possible." When the man in my workshop hadn't responded immediately because of his attendance at the training session, the coworker had sent him another e-mail and left a voice mail insisting on an immediate response. The situation had become a war of wills over the expectation of instant access.

Quick access on the web sets up the same dilemma. On the one hand, customers who know what they want can visit our site and buy from us with a click. In three to five minutes, they can deposit thousands of dollars into our account. But if those same customers can't find what they want, or become confused by our e-mail explanations, or distrust our competence because of weak writing on the screen, they never give us a chance to talk our way out of the proverbial paper bag. They simply click on to the next site, without our knowing they had money to spend.

"Anytime, Anywhere" or "No Time, Nowhere"?

Consider this directive from a sales manager to her staff: "Call the customer by noon today, or the deal is off." It goes unread until midnight, when the sales rep downloads his day's e-mail.

Many organizations advertise that they're available to provide service and information anytime, anywhere. But the reality is that that expectation disappoints coworkers and customers all too often. When front-line service agents have to wait to have a supervisor "review" what they're about to write, their customers grow impatient. In an attempt to respond quickly, organizations have various systems that automatically monitor incoming e-mail inquiries and route them to the most knowledgeable service agent available. That helps. But it is not the total answer.

Customers do have individual needs and questions that can't be answered by boilerplate form letters and e-mails. But to permit poorly written, unmonitored e-mails to go straight to the customer produces even more serious dilemmas and disappointments.

Everybody, not just the supervisors and managers, needs to know how to write.

Distribution to Everyone Who's Breathing

There's the "Someone left the lights on in the blue Cutlass in parking lot C" e-mail sent to a distribution list of 500 people, including the company's senior executives in Seoul, Korea. Then there's the announcement that all employees interested in the new insurance coverage should contact the HR department for further information—sent to a standard distribution group of 68 people, only 7 of whom are actually eligible for the new coverage. Sixty-one others waste their time and that of the person fielding the inquiries generated by the blanket note. Why? The writer thinks it's easier and quicker simply to click on the standard distribution list rather than sort and select those who actually need the information.

And how often have people intercepted dangerous drivel containing four typos, an incomplete thought or sentence, and a nasty complaint about the accounting department? At best, routinely and unnecessarily communicating to groups rather than individuals costs every reader time; at worst, it courts disaster.

Anonymity of Online Addresses and Chat Rooms

People have grown accustomed to venting their spleen on the screen. With e-mail addresses like "Jsmith3" or "we.rent2U" or "so.sez.me," writers sometimes forget that they're communicating with real people in front of the computer screen. Without a complete name attached to a recognizable organization, writers are lulled into thinking accuracy, honesty, helpfulness, and tact don't count—or that the lack of these attributes at least won't come back to haunt them. Lurking in chat rooms also fortifies writers with the feeling of anonymity. Flaming, the practice of sending hostile e-mail to those who irritate, also fosters a sense of protection across the distance. Tact doesn't even enter the sender's thought process.

This feeling of anonymity sometimes spills over into online writing to coworkers and customers. The tone is often too blunt, too brusque, or too negative. Even unintentionally, e-mail messages, by their brevity, can seem abrupt and insensitive.

Stir into the mix sensitive situations such as directives to peers, apologies, complaints, or opinions about politically explosive matters, and you understand why the tone of your writing makes a dynamic difference in the response you get.

Hedging and Jargon

Hedge words, verbosity, and jargon—diseases running rampant in the corporate world—either cover up for a lack of something to say or obscure responsibility when something controversial is written. Take, for example, these sentences from business documents:

> The efficiency with which an operation utilizes its available equipment is an influential factor in productivity.

Efficient use of equipment influences productivity. Is this such a profound idea?

> It is recognized that there may be no viable alternative to an increased return on total capitalization other than outright purchase.

Who recognizes? *May* be no viable alternative?

Rather than take a definitive stand, the writers of these sentences make vague statements in the hope that no one will understand enough to ask questions or realize that nothing has been said.

The only solution is to budget time to let your document cool off and then undergo objective editing. Otherwise, you will end up with an ill-prepared final document, and you will have to spend time on the phone to interpret or explain.

The Trade-Off Between Speed and Clarity

Speed has become the currency of e-commerce; it's the new measure of quality for companies doing business on the Internet. That explains the form letter my husband recently received about his aunt Juanita.

When she died last year at the age of eighty-three, my husband was named the executor of her estate. Shortly thereafter, he received her mail containing an "overdue bill" notice on an invoice for $28.58 from a medical lab for services rendered three months earlier. He responded by asking the lab to mail him documentation of the charges so that he could verify the expense as his aunt's before mailing payment. Instead, the lab mailed another form collection letter. It stated:

> Mrs. Dunn:
>
> Unless your payment is received by June 12, it will become a part of your credit record and remain there for a period of seven years. This information can be reported to many companies and banks upon request when you apply for any type of loan.

We laughed. But many people don't. Customers want speed, but they also want you to listen to them and respond accordingly. Speed or clarity—the choice is a common dilemma.

Writing specific, clear e-mail and letters takes time. And most people could do a faster and better job of writing if they had a well-focused day with no interruptions. Make that a good *hour*. But leisurely writing time rarely presents itself. We're torn between attending a meeting at noon or revising the report or proposal one more time.

With many writers, the first and final drafts are, unfortunately, the same. But to most professional writers, real writing is rewriting. Ernest Hemingway is said to have revised *A Farewell to Arms* 39 times. Certainly, I'm not advocating such elaborate editing and revising in business documents—unless you're proposing a merger or predicting a monsoon—but rarely does a piece of writing of any length require no editing at all.

Misunderstandings anger people, cost money, and even endanger lives. A supervisor writes, "Anyone wishing to file for these benefits should report to Room 222 at three o'clock." He then reprimands an ineligible employee who shows up at the meeting. If the supervisor didn't make clear *which* employees were entitled to the benefits, his reprimand embarrasses and angers the employee who has misunderstood.

A similar misunderstanding with a client can lose an account. "Delivery of an additional vacuum pump will be required for the project, which has been postponed, pending SOC approval." What has been postponed—the delivery, or the project?

When someone needs "8l-foot cables" but instead orders "81 foot cables," he, too, has unnecessarily decreased company profits on the construction job. Even if the incorrect shipment can be returned, consider the shipping costs and lost time involved in the error.

Similarly, instructions like the following from an actual safety manual may be the basis for a lawsuit by an injured employee:

> When motors or controllers operating at more than 150 volts to ground are guarded against accidental contact only by location, and where adjustment or other attendance may be necessary during operations, suitable insulating mats or platforms shall be provided. All belts, pulleys, chains, flywheels, shafting and shaft projections, or other rotating or reciprocating parts within seven feet of the floor or working platform shall be effectively guarded.

Can you dig out the two safety precautions to be taken? What, specifically, is "effectively guarded"? Is using the mats a choice or a company regulation? And if using the mats is a company regulation, who is responsible for guaranteeing that such regulations are followed? Operators themselves? The project supervisor? A lawsuit may be necessary to find out.

What are the odds when you trade clarity for speed? The stakes in unclear writing can run high.

The Trade-Off Between Speed and Image

In the absence of face-to-face opportunities, clients often evaluate a company's capability and dependability based on its written communications: website, e-mails from customer-service reps, year-end reports on "value added" service, user manuals, letters, and proposals.

A technical editor in a natural-gas company reported that his company's bid for a multibillion-dollar job was accepted over other bids for one reason: The client, who had learned English as a second language, was impressed that this company's proposal was the only one without grammatical errors. Unfortunately, that client's comment and bid acceptance did not get the technical editor a raise. Management chalked up the incident to a quirk in a picayune buyer.

My research, however, into this area of company image suggests that such decisions are more frequent than poor writers would like to believe. When workers are careless in their writing, how can clients know for sure that they're any more careful with data or money?

Clients notice errors. They either smile and overlook them, become vexed at what seems like little concern for their business, or get downright angry if either tone or clarity is the problem.

Poor writing not only affects company image but also limits personal promotions within an organization. According to a manager of industrial relations, "Many talented people in our organization who know the business well are overlooked for promotions simply because they cannot communicate well and influence effectively. To manage well, they *must* communicate well. It's a real problem."

Another senior executive at a major financial organization had this to say: "To me, poor writing and poor grammar mean total incompetence. Such writing conveys to me a whole attitude about the job—sloppiness and lack of concern for detail."

Like it or not, writing characterizes.

> Language was invented so that man can hide the fact that he
> doesn't think at all.
> —*Søren Kierkegaard*

Lazy Thinking or "Thinking as You Write"

Years ago, IBM's *Think* magazine ran a contest for employees to collect the "clunker" of the month—convoluted writing from internal documents. Here are two of the "winning" selections:

> You can include a page that also contains an Include instruction. The page including the Include instruction is included when you paginate the document, but the included test referred to in its Include instruction is not included.

> For a priority system based upon fixed numerical ordering of requesters, following the servicing of any given requester, a request from a lower-priority requester, if deferred due to a conflict with the just-serviced requester, shall be honored prior to honoring a second request from the just-serviced requester.

Many reports, letters, or e-mails are poorly written because writers do their thinking on paper. They have not considered a total project or body of data, interpreted it, and tailored it to the reader's purpose. Often the first few paragraphs or first few pages constitute a warm-up drill. Writers pour out everything on the paper and then come to a conclusion while writing through the details. Or, worse still, the authors never come to a conclusion but rather leave the conclusion and interpretations up to the readers.

Sometimes these problems show up in data dumps without interpretation and sometimes in convoluted sentences. Such lazy thinking and writing can be cured.

> How do I know what I think until I hear what I say?
> —*Oscar Wilde*

Poor Academic Training

Even following habits and principles held over from academic training can be at fault.

Some professors lack the knowledge or fail to understand the necessity of helping students bridge the gap from "academic" writing to business writing. For example, most academic reports begin with an introduction and lead to a conclusion. Additionally, academic writing is most often meant to impress either a professor or a peer. But in business writing, reports begin with *conclusions* and seldom need introductions. A good business writer's chief purpose is to express ideas rather than impress with an ornate writing style.

Some academicians inadvertently encourage poor writing. For instance, some advise students to avoid forms of the verb "to be"—*is, are, was, were*. Generally, that's good advice. "To be" verbs sound weak; stronger verbs add zip. But students often miss the more important point of this advice about the value of strong verbs. Instead, they learn to write awkward sentences just to avoid the "to be" construction.

Others in academia encourage students to build a large vocabulary and often give bonus points for using complex words from a weekly vocabulary list. Granted, an extensive vocabulary is to be valued for comprehension and precise expression on occasion. But a business writer routinely needs to choose words that will be widely understood by all readers.

Additionally, teachers sometimes encourage student writers to use long sentences. Their motive may be admirable—to teach variety in sentence structure. But in a proposal for a joint oil-exploration venture, this advice surfaced in the following way:

> Each company agrees that, during each accounting period after the completion date, its Company Throughput which constitutes Initial Facility Throughput, together with such company's Initial Facility Percentage of Initial Facility Throughput during such accounting period which is not Company Throughput, shall be not less than such Company's Initial Facility Percentage of the aggregate of CO_2 which will, at Universal's published tariff rates, which along with other cash resources of the partnership, will be sufficient to provide, and will actually provide, Universal during such an accounting period with an aggregate amount of cash at least sufficient to avoid a cash deficiency.

If you think this kind of writing is atypical, pick up any mutual-fund prospectus.

The advice to students to build a large vocabulary and vary sentence structure should be tempered with caution about indiscriminate use in the business world. The purpose behind many writing tips has been misunderstood, only to plague the business writer later.

Another contributor to poor writing is the tendency to assume a captive audience. College professors must read papers to give grades. Often they "read between the lines" because they are familiar with the subject and know what the student writer is trying to say. Clients and colleagues are not so accommodating.

Still another holdover from school days is equating length with quality. Who hasn't had a professor express expectations for assigned papers in the form of length rather than content? "I expect a six- to eight-page critique of your research." Certainly professors must give guidelines about the effort expected and the maximum number of pages they intend to read. But students sometimes erroneously conclude that length equals quality. The Declaration of Independence set up a whole new concept of freedom in fewer than 1,400 words. Students rarely practice or experience the impact of brevity.

Temper any such prior training with careful attention to purpose.

The Declaration of Independence set up a whole new concept of freedom in fewer than 1,400 words.

Writing to the Tune of a Team

An administrative assistant at one of the nation's largest oil companies once confided to me that she'd just entered changes on the tenth draft of a 30-page policy statement. Here was the scenario: Her boss gave her a rough draft, which she keyboarded and he edited. She input his changes and then sent it to three other members of the policy committee, each of whom made comments for changes. She revised the document accordingly. Then, as a team, they sent their draft to the manager, who made extensive changes before the administrative assistant was asked to revise it yet again. When that manager was satisfied, he passed it to his boss, who also asked for changes before sending it out to other divisions for their comments.

Ten drafts.

The upside is that the team saved travel time to meet face-to-face. The downside is that they all continued to print out copies, make handwritten changes, and send the document around for others to "offer comments."

Despite software that allows simultaneous online editing, the process just described represents writing by committee the hard way. It's still done ad infinitum today.

Completed Staff Work by Telecommuters in Virtual Offices

In current commerce, where careers have given way to jobs and jobs have given way to projects, workers assume control of their own future. They are encouraged to consider themselves self-employed—whether or not they're on someone else's payroll. The theory advocates continual learning and self-development, empowerment, and accountability.

In our environment of telecommuters and virtual offices, the "completed staff work" idea requires closer scrutiny than it did twenty years ago in brick-and-mortar headquarters. In essence, "completed staff work" means that when a subordinate is given an assignment, he or she should not bother the boss or the client with questions until the project is completed and ready for sign-off.

Where writing is concerned, the concept translates to something close to the following: An employee begins with a problem, investigates the options for solutions, decides on the best course of action, prepares all the necessary documents required to initiate that action, and then submits his or her work to the boss or client so all that remains to be done is for the boss or client to "sign off" to put the solution or agreement into force.

Although it sounds good in theory and works well in the decision-making, problem-solving phase of a project, completed staff work wastes considerable time in the writing phase of a project. Why should someone spend 40 hours putting together a proposal or report, only to send it to the boss or client and hear, "That's not exactly what I had in mind"? Then both writer and reader must spend additional time discussing the answers to questions they both should have discussed long before the drafting stage.

With the speed of current technology, there's a better way: A worker will do well to e-mail an outline to the boss, client, or others who have input and veto power, giving them opportunity for feedback *before* committing ideas to paper or screen in final form.

Thorough thinking, proper planning, and collecting pertinent data to combine into the appropriate format is part of the writing process. Thinking and writing in the right order save both writer time and reader time.

> Writing is not hard. Just get paper and pencil, sit down, and write it as it occurs to you. The writing is easy—it's the occurring that's hard.
> —*Stephen Leacock*

Poorly Designed Forms—Online and on Paper

I recently completed and returned a registration form on a software package. A week later it came back to me inside an envelope with a handscrawled note across the top: "What product did you buy?" Sure enough, on the line of the form that read "Product Purchased," I had written the name of the store where the product had been purchased. Why the confusion? The line above it asked for the date and city, so I assumed the "Product Purchased" phrase referred to *where* purchased—which store, catalog, or website. It never occurred to me that the manufacturer would enclose a registration card with no reference or code whatsoever to identify the specific product on the bounce-back card.

What's the company's expense in returning such forms to confused customers? Guess.

Often the same people who have difficulty designing clear paper forms are putting them online, creating the same frustration for users. Flashing a message that says "Invalid entry. Registration cannot be processed until complete" does not help the situation. As in so many other cases, the usefulness of the medium is dependent on the clarity of the message.

Manager-Misfits Who Generate Unnecessary Writing and Excess E-Mail

So how do manager-misfits handle their insecurities with the latest technology?

Some don't want to be held accountable for anything. Therefore, they establish elaborate controls and systems for everything done in their department. They *document* in their database every phone conversation and meeting attended. They also request that their subordinates send them enormous volumes of paperwork and copy them on e-mail to "keep them in the loop" on everything said or done. All this to prove that these managers aren't responsible if things go wrong.

Some manager-misfits *delay*: They record all thoughts in e-mail or database records and then copy everyone upward and laterally to get help and possibly to get someone else to make the decisions before they're forced to do so. Another tactic is to delay responding to their own e-mail until the decision is overcome by events and someone else has to act or go down with the ship.

Still other manager-misfits *delegate*: They send e-mail downward, asking subordinates to gather more and more information and send more and more reports to keep them busy analyzing the situation and crunching the numbers until "all the facts are in." The trouble is that all the facts rarely ever do come in. But as long as everybody below is busy, thinking that the reason for delays is his or her own long-awaited information or analysis, then no one has to risk taking action and making a mistake.

Delegating managers also tend to be overly impressed with jargon-spouting "experts" on their staff. Much of what these experts say is unintelligible, but their manager-misfit asks no questions; they are so impressed with the "technically correct" report that it's passed up the chain of command without question. Of course, if someone else up the ladder does ask questions, the manager is not responsible—he or she has the subordinate's "misleading" report and is holding that subordinate "completely responsible."

On the other hand, those supervised may resist a manager's attempt to get comprehensible information. A Ph.D. data-processing analyst at a public utility company jokingly "complained" when he enrolled in one of our workshops: "My boss took this course a few months ago. Things have been kind of tough on me since. Yeah, I used to give him all these technical explanations, and he'd just accept what I said and send the reports on. Now that he knows that's not good writing, he makes me put everything in plain English. And he argues with my conclusions now that he knows what I'm saying!"

He laughed. The VP nearby didn't.

Some manager-misfits *do*. They act and then record what they've done as an afterthought. They ignore most of the information that comes to them, therefore making uninformed decisions on the basis of gut reactions. At least they can't be accused of not taking action—or not "managing." But their staff grows more and more frustrated by information requested of them and then ignored.

The solution: self-confidence, accountability, management know-how, the expectation for good writing, and a commitment to eliminate unnecessary gobbledygook.

Websites That Inform but Don't Communicate

Writing on websites must pass the same tests as writing on paper: You have to know your purpose, your audience, and your core business. Websites can provide scads of information, but bad websites will be unable to motivate visitors to take action. The websites may also communicate a disregard for what customers actually wants to know. For example, text-rich sites may overwhelm visitors and create confusion rather than comfort.

Websites That Communicate but Don't Inform

Customers get annoyed fending off flashing messages, slow-to-load graphics, and silly sounds that communicate a superfluous message. In an effort to grab surfers' attention, some websites weave in so many extraneous choices and diversions that visitors can't even figure out what the organizations do. I have even had webmasters tell me they've been intentionally vague and cagey on their websites, so as to obscure specifically their line of business until they usurped market share and made their "official" debut.

Most are simply blithely uninformative. They've read their own website so long and are so familiar with their business that they can't remember what it was like to be unknowledgeable about the product or service.

Another frustration is visiting websites that lie—even if unintentionally. For example, a website announces that "Download takes 8 minutes at 28.8 Kbps," when in reality downloading takes 30 minutes at 38.8 Kbps, communicates a disregard for the truth and the visitor's time.

If visitors to the site have to wait too long to find their information, they leave. If they become confused, they leave. If the writing is bloated, they leave. Your job is to make them stay. To communicate with customers who have increasingly short attention spans is a never-ending challenge for all of us.

To write simply is as difficult as to be good.
—*Somerset Maugham*

PART 3

WRITING ON PAPER
OR ONLINE

Effective business or technical writing requires training; success comes by method, not chance. You can reduce your writing time, improve clarity, and achieve your objective—whether to inform, persuade, or simply create goodwill—by following five key steps. Let's overview them initially. Then we'll proceed to fill in the details.

Step 1: Consider Your Audience for the Proper Approach. Decide how your readers will use your document, and narrow your message to suit their interests. Choose details to be included on the basis of the audience's experience, biases, uses, and knowledge of your subject.

Step 2: Anticipate Special Reader Reactions. If you think your audience will be skeptical because of the data you cite or the policies you advocate, or if you foresee a personality or situational problem in the reader's accepting your message, anticipate those reactions, and plan to minimize or overcome them by selecting the appropriate details and tone. Usually this consideration means refuting alternatives and supporting your conclusions with additional evidence and authority.

Step 3: Outline Your Message Functionally in the MADE Format™. Think before you write. Summarize your entire message in two or three sentences at most (*M = Message*). State what action your reader needs to take or what action you plan to take (*A = Action*). Answer the *who, when, where, why, how,* and *how much* details (*D = Details*). Next, mention any optional enclosures or attachments you're sending to make the message or action more authoritative or clearer (*E = Evidence*).

For longer documents, expand this basic MADE Format™ into some logical order: most to least important, point-by-point comparison, problem to solution, goals and steps, categorical, chronological, geographical, or some other arrangement. Give your reader the conclusions and recommendations first. Follow with a discussion of the details of your conclusions and recommendations (usually the *hows* and *whys*). Last, attach supplementary information in an attachment or appendix.

Then query your supervisor, client, or teammates about your writing plan. If these others involved have additional suggestions, make the necessary changes in this planning stage—*before* you write a complete draft.

Step 4: Develop the First Draft Quickly. Follow your plan. Compose the e-mail, letter, report, or proposal in one sitting, if at all possible. The faster speed will improve the tone and give you momentum in capturing your ideas. As you develop this first draft, do not stop to edit and polish grammar; instead, concentrate on the logical flow of ideas.

Step 5: Edit for Content, Layout, Grammar, Clarity, Conciseness, and Style. Use the following checklists as guides for producing a polished, well-written final document:

Edit for Content and Layout (Step 5 Expanded)
- Focus on the reader's interest up front.
- Make sure your elaboration of details matches the intended emphasis.
- Check accuracy and completeness.
- Add authority.
- Eliminate repetitious details, but retain first-choice words.
- Paragraph by idea and eye appeal.
- Use easy-to-skim lists where appropriate.
- Add informative headings, adequate spacing, and other typographical effects to make information quickly accessible.
- Design and use charts and graphs effectively.

Edit for Grammar (Step 5 Expanded)

- Keep related words together.
- Don't dangle verbals.
- Avoid unintentional fragments and run-on sentences.
- Use parallel structure.
- Make pronouns agree with their antecedents and functions.
- Make verbs agree with their subjects.
- Be consistent with tenses and moods.
- Avoid commonly misused words.
- Spell correctly—be careful with possessives, plurals, prefixes, and suffixes.
- Capitalize only when valid, not randomly.
- Punctuate precisely.
- Proofread with a purposeful plan.

Edit for Clarity (Step 5 Expanded)

- Measure readability.
- Position ideas for the proper emphasis.
- Link to show proper relationships.
- Use clear transitions.
- Use clear references.
- Prefer concrete words and phrases.
- Know when to use and avoid jargon.
- Avoid unnecessary foreign words and phrases.
- Eliminate gaps in logic.
- Maintain a consistent viewpoint and voice.

Edit for Conciseness (Step 5 Expanded)

- Prefer active-voice verbs.
- Dig buried verbs out of noun phrases.
- Avoid adjective and adverb clutter.
- Eliminate redundant words, phrases, and ideas.

Edit for Style (Step 5 Expanded)

- Strive for a style somewhere between stuffed-shirt writing and T-shirt writing.

- Prefer a personal, conversational tone.
- Prefer directness and brevity with tact.
- Vary sentence pattern and length.
- Revise weak verbs.

The most difficult part of writing is getting a handle on the project. Every time I tackle a new book, I feel as if I'm looking at a flopping catfish at the end of a fishing line. The fish just hangs there, flopping back and forth, daring me to catch and unhook it without getting finned. Hovering in exactly the right position, I have to pin the fins firmly to its sides before working the hook out of its mouth and feeling it's all mine.

So it is with writing. A well-written e-mail, letter, report, proposal, or manual produces great satisfaction, but the process is usually the pain.

Following this step-by-step plan will give you a handle on any writing project. Every step has a reason. If you decide to take a shortcut, you'll find the omission will cost you much more time later in the writing process.

9

STEP 1: CONSIDER YOUR AUDIENCE FOR THE PROPER APPROACH

When writing any document, always make the reader's interest central. And remember, for the most part, readers don't care about your trouble, only your results.

Bad reports and manuals get written not merely because the authors don't have adequate control of style, but because they don't select, interpret, and write for people.
—*Russell Ritter*

Will There Be a Single Reader or Multiple Readers?

Name names. Most reports and many letters and e-mails go through several people for approval. And even if the document doesn't need the approval of others, it is often passed on simply to inform them.

When writing to a mixed audience, first rank readers in importance. Then broaden your document to include all levels of readers and their diverse interests in your subject. List names or at least groups of readers your work needs to satisfy: top management; general professional staff, such as engineers, accountants, and geologists; specialists in a particular field such as inspectors, machine operators, auditors, and so forth.

After you have pinpointed and ranked each reader or group of readers, give the most important readers their information first. When writing to only one person, focus solely on *his or her* interests, likes, dislikes, expectations, or needs.

What Are the Interests of Your Audience?

Management readers will be interested in answers to the following questions: What is the significant, bottom-line message? Have we made some major technological advance? What's the profit picture? Are we in compliance with a particular governmental regulation? What company image are we projecting? What actions should we take? Who should take these actions?

Note that this kind of information is usually headed "Conclusions and Recommendations." The majority of managers will read no further into your document.

General professionals will be interested in answers to the following questions: Why was the project undertaken? Why was the policy reevaluated? How did you carry out the research? Under what conditions did you investigate? Are there exceptions to your message? Note that this information is usually given in the "Body" or "Discussion" part of a document.

Specialists will be interested in your detailed evidence—the actual sales statistics, expense forms, flow charts, area maps, chemical formulas, equipment specifications. Note that this information is usually given in the "fine print" of the text details or in an attachment or an appendix.

With the proliferation of e-mail and long distribution lists, it is becoming increasingly difficult to know exactly who may be reading your document. You may have intended your document to address the needs and interests of one specific reader but learn later that your message has been forwarded to seventeen others.

The complexity of focusing on the reader's interest doesn't lessen the need to do so. For this reason, simply consider the "layered" reading phenomenon. Understand that your document may need to provide details to many different people, without cluttering the path for primary readers who have a specific need and interest. More about that later.

How Will Readers Use Your Information?

The answer to this third question will help you decide what details to include. Will readers use the report as the basis for a decision? If so, should the facts be presented persuasively to win their cooperation?

Is the information meant merely to keep them informed of some advance in their field or on some project? If so, you will give a broad description of the problem or discovery and zero in on the significance of the new information for other projects or decisions.

Will your readers need to duplicate or build on your work? If so, give them directions—all the *if*s, *and*s, *what*s, and *how*s.

How Much Do Your Readers Already Know About the Subject?

Will the readers understand the significance of your research or work? Will they understand the technical, human, and economic implications of the conclusions? Will your readers understand all the jargon, acronyms, abbreviations, and symbols? Your assessment of the readers' background knowledge will greatly influence your decisions about which details to include and which to omit, about the overall document structure, and about the overall writing style.

Do not spend time telling readers what is obvious, but be sure to give them enough background on the problem so they understand the solution. Avoid jargon for those readers who are outside your specific field.

For example, consider the term "working interest." The term refers to investment interest on property, equipment, or research; an organization may have "sole" or "joint" interest in a particular project. Accountants handling expenses usually use the term to mean *net* working interest—interest *after* royalties, taxes, or other specified expenses. But accountants dealing only with revenue use the term to mean *gross* working interest—interest *before* royalties, taxes, or other specified expenses.

An engineer calling the Accounting Department to find out the company's working interest on the Upton Project may get two different answers from two different accountants. Or, more perplexing, the engineer may talk to an accountant who handles both revenue and expenses. "Do you want *net* or *gross* working interest?" the accountant asks.

"Uh . . . I don't know," the engineer may stammer. "What's the difference?"

As a general rule, the fewer the acronyms the better. Not unlike other organizations, the IRS uses so many acronyms that even experts get confused. According to a recent *Wall Street Journal* story, an IRS specialist sat through a discussion of the IRS's Art Advisory Panel, which values taxpayer gifts of artworks. The puzzled expert grappling with all the new acronyms turned to ask his boss, "What does 'art' stand for?"

Writers who fail to consider their audience before using unexplained and variable terms court misunderstanding.

And even if your audience understands all the concepts and terms you use, readers may need more detail because of noninvolvement in the problem or project. For instance, if you've been collaborating daily by phone with your readers, you may not need to explain the particular significance of certain test results. If, however, you mentioned the significant test results only briefly two months earlier, you may need to remind your readers again of the significance for the decision at hand.

How much your readers know dictates *how much* detail and *what* detail you must include in *which* sections of your document. It's far better to err by giving too much detail than too little—as long as you structure the document so readers can skim over what they don't need.

Select One of Three Ways to Handle Multiple Readers

So what about all those secondary readers, those who will read your e-mail, report, proposal, or manual simply to be informed or to take assigned action rather than to make a decision? You can address their needs with one of three options, always keeping in mind not to dilute or bury your message to your primary reader.

Write multiple documents. Create each document to meet the needs of a particular reader or group of readers. That's the logic behind most transmittal letters or e-mails. The items of interest to the senior decision-maker—conclusions and recommendations—appear in the transmittal. The full report then presents the details that will satisfy other technical professionals.

Design different document sections for different readers. An informative table of contents and descriptive headings will take decision-makers immediately to the executive overview or the conclusions. Geologists can go directly to "Test Results" to find details about the six contaminated samples at the well site. Or software designers can skip to the details they need to identify the changes necessary in their new program code.

Arrange ideas in the need-to-know format. A third option to help readers find the information of most interest to them is the need-to-know arrangement. In journalism circles, this is called the inverted pyramid. The headline presents the most important information—the message that is of interest to all readers. Some readers will stop after that headline. Others may read the first paragraph for the "who," "what," "when," "where," "why," and "how" details. Still other readers may stay with the story to discover all the details.

This need-to-know arrangement, with the most important information up front, satisfies all readers by permitting them to control their own reading. As soon as each person's need to know is satisfied, he or she can stop.

In technical reports, we can accommodate various levels of interest in much the same way. The executive summary tells all readers the most important facts. Some readers may stop reading there. Those who want details continue into the body of the report or skip to a particular section.

The same need-to-know principle applies to manuals. Suppose a user wants only to install software X onto a hard disk. In that case, she can stop reading after the installation procedures. If the user wants to learn how to do only one budgeting procedure, she refers only to the appropriate section of the manual. On the other hand, if the user wants to learn the entire spreadsheet package, she continues through each section.

After a thorough analysis of your audience, you have one last chance to stop the writing process—before you get started. Are you sure that your reader and purpose can best be served by a formal document? Would a meeting or phone call accomplish the same objective?

Will your information be used for reference over a long period of time? If so, design it with informative headings so that readers can easily skim or relocate specific information.

Will your information be used by a reader (perhaps your immediate supervisor) to persuade someone else up the line to take action? If so, include adequate detail and don't rely on past explanations of your research. Give your immediate reader all the background and explanation necessary to understand your conclusions thoroughly enough to defend them to others involved in the decision.

Will your reader distribute various parts of your information to different readers? If so, be sure each piece of information—transmittal, attachment, data sheet—is independent of the remainder of the document.

On occasion, the form the message takes may be as important as the message itself. A document that looks too perplexing to read may condemn your project to oblivion. On the other hand, an informal e-mail may not get proper attention.

To sum up this first step: Identify your reader or readers. Focus on the main interests of each reader or group. Decide how your audience will use your information and what your audience already knows about the subject. Finally, determine which of the three ways you'll provide information for your audience—whether you need to write one or several documents, or simply "layer" your details into one document.

Thinking is hard work.
—*Thomas Edison*

10

STEP 2: ANTICIPATE SPECIAL READER REACTIONS

From time to time in your business career, you will have to write to a reader who, despite all the facts, will habitually respond: "But I still think . . . " If you know you're dealing with such a person or group, anticipate reactions, questions, and alternatives; don't just cross your fingers and hope for the best. Plan how you will overcome, or at least minimize, any negative reaction.

It's more fun to arrive at a conclusion than to justify it.
—*Malcolm Forbes*

Will There Be Skepticism?

Are you refuting existing data? Has your past work damaged your credibility? Is your product or service unusually expensive? If so, why? Will you need to convince the reader of a need or a problem?

If skepticism is involved, you'll need to document your conclusions and recommendations more heavily than you ordinarily would. Or perhaps you'll need to refute the validity of existing data or the feasibility of alternative solutions. You can't simply hope that the reader will overcome a skeptical attitude and give you the benefit of the doubt. You have to stamp out reservations aggressively.

Is There a Personality or Situational Problem?

Will your reader have to lose face to accept your recommendations? Will she get pressure from a superior because of your message? Will you create extra work for her? Do you and the reader have a personality clash? Do you want to fire your reader's brother-in-law?

Here are some of the most typical negative reactions in a business setting:

- Skepticism about the information, data, or message
- Loss of the writer's credibility because of a prior mistake
- Loss of face on the part of the reader or others if they agree with or accept your message, information, or data
- Personality clash or a habitually disagreeable nature or negative attitude
- The creation of what others perceive as unnecessary extra work
- Short deadlines and heavy workloads
- Reluctance to comply because of the difficulty of a task
- Low priority to the reader
- Resistance to change
- Money (too much, too little, unplanned, unbudgeted)

If you uncover a personal or situational problem, you'll need to make a conscious effort to be as tactful and objective as possible. Find a way to let your readers save their dignity. If you can't, you'll need to overwhelm them with supporting evidence. If your message makes your own past decisions circumspect, you'll need to detail why your past decisions were logical at that time, or why you were misinformed, or why the picture has changed. If you're creating extra work for someone, you'll need to impress the reader with the importance of your request or directive.

For example, consider the following situation: Every month you send an e-mail to all departments, requesting statistics about work in progress, statistics you will incorporate into your own report to be presented at the monthly board of directors' meeting. Your e-mail reads:

> Monthly reports should be submitted to my office no later than April 14 so that my staff can prepare the final report for the board of directors' meeting, to be held April 28.

Perhaps you have a special problem in that many of your readers fail to submit their reports to you by the specified date—in this case, April 14. A few even hand-deliver them only a day or two before the board meeting. Their delay then causes your staff to have to work overtime to prepare the final report.

Why are these people late with their reports? Perhaps because you've included the date of the board meeting, they know that they have a "grace" period, the time you've allowed yourself to prepare the final report. By anticipating this special procrastination problem, you could omit the board meeting date in your e-mail, thereby eliminating the "double due date" effect.

Specifically, when you're writing to persuade your readers, anticipate whether their reactions will be positive, negative, or neutral. That bias will affect which details you select and how you arrange them. If, as a proposal writer, you know the client already likes your approach to the problem, it may be unnecessary to outline all the alternatives. If, on the other hand, you know the reader will react negatively to your suggestion to use weld-over sleeves and instead favors the use of a smaller-diameter pipe, then you will want to address both options. You will present and refute other alternatives, detailing the reasons why your proposed solution is best.

Rarely do writers find unbiased readers. That is, most readers have a stake in the subject matter of your writing. Determining the strength of your readers' biases may make the difference between accomplishing and not accomplishing your purpose.

If your audience is neutral, you will be as thorough and persuasive as you think necessary to move your readers from inertia into action. Can you interest them by dangling a new product possibility in front of them? Can you quantify the savings in your project plan? Can you show them what the competition may decide to do?

Reader bias always affects acceptance of ideas. Don't ignore it; instead, let that bias help determine the structure, tone, and detail of your document.

Of course, you can never be sure you have overcome all negative reactions to your message or information, but be aware that such issues may exist and plan how you will address these reactions from the outset.

STEP 3: OUTLINE YOUR MESSAGE FUNCTIONALLY

We have two kinds of drivers in the world: those who look at a map before they leave home and those who "drive until they find it." When it comes to surfing the web, we have two kinds of web-heads: those who go directly to a specific website and those who surf randomly from one link to another until they find something intriguing.

Similarly, we have two kinds of writers: those who plan what they want to say before they write, and those who write while they decide. If given a choice, most readers will try to avoid the latter.

Planning the structure *before* you write makes you focus on the central message without spending words "working into" each new topic:

Mike:
I received your July 9 e-mail in which you requested information concerning the status of the Veta project with regard to the feasibility of establishing a new plant in . . .

Instead, with a plan, you already know where you're going, and you can simply cut to the chase:

Mike:
I have decided to proceed immediately with the Veta project. . . .

Have a plan. Follow a structure. You'll eliminate most of the drudge work of writing.

Speaking or writing without thinking is like shooting
without aiming.
—Arnold Glasow

Structure Ideas in the MADE Format™ for Most Documents

A common tendency is to structure documents in the once-upon-a-time format—to start at the beginning of a situation and write to the end of the information you have about the subject. In other words, we tend to tell a story from beginning to end as a recap, thinking we are providing "background" so that the reader can understand our point, conclusion, or action.

Just the opposite is true. People will rarely understand your background information until they have the "punch line." The traditional formal document of twenty years ago followed the academic format, varying slightly from organization to organization (see Figure 1).

Traditional Formal Report or Proposal Format	
Summary	Overview of entire report or proposal
Body	Introduction: history, problem, scope
	Discussion: methods, details
	Conclusions and recommendations: test results, suggested actions
Appendixes	Tables, maps, charts, forms, questionnaires, brochures, and so forth

Figure 1. Traditional Report or Proposal Format. Items of most interest to readers are buried.

The problem with this traditional ascending format is that the items of major interest to the most important audience—management or customer decision-maker—are buried in the last sections of the report, proposal, or e-mail.

Understanding a message written in this ascending format is an uphill climb (see Figure 2). The details gradually unfold as the reader trudges toward the top of the hill: the message.

If you organize your proposal, report, letter, or e-mail in the ascending order, you have failed to consider your audience's point of view. Instead, you have written the document from *your* point of view: why you started the study, what you found out had already been done in related fields, how you computed figures, and what results you finally discovered. For the most part, the management reader is not interested in your activities, but rather in your conclusions and recommendations.

So, the first reason to restructure the document with the punch line up front is clarity. Readers understand the information, conclusions, or actions more clearly from the start.

Reading experts have done study after study on which to base their advice that readers should skim a report's or book's headings, illustrations, and summary sections before reading for details. Different experts may call this "previewing" or "prereading" the material, but the effect on comprehension is the same: When readers know from the beginning where they're going, they can better understand and remember the details.

Certainly, the ascending structure has a use—for novels, movies, jokes, and anecdotes. In these, the writer creates the atmosphere, gives background, and adds suspense to whet the appetite for the final thrilling scene or climax.

We as writers are most tempted to use the ascending order when we think the conclusions or recommendations are going to displease our readers. We're tempted to paint the picture slowly and hope the evidence along the way will convince readers to adopt our conclusions by the time we get around to stating them. But even here, the ascending order is dangerous. By the time readers get to our conclusions, they may have reached different conclusions or have a strong case built against our interpretations all along the way. Figures 3 and 4 illustrate the danger of division at the decision line.

For the most part, business and technical writing should be straightforward, not suspenseful.

On December 9, 1941, President Franklin D. Roosevelt addressed the nation with these opening remarks: "So far, the news has all been bad. We have suffered a serious setback in Hawaii. Our forces in the Philippines,

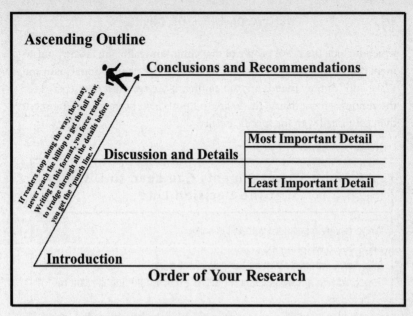

Figure 2A. Ascending Document Diagram

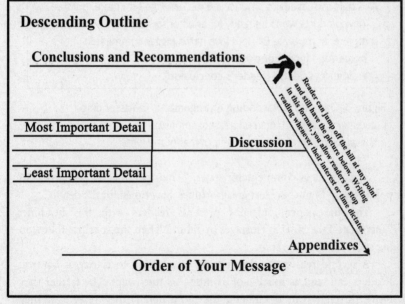

Figure 2B. Descending Document Diagram. The ascending format creates mystery; the descending format informs quickly and clearly about what follows.

which include the brave people of that commonwealth, are taking punishment but are defending themselves vigorously. The reports from Guam and Wake and Midway islands are still confused, but we must be prepared for the announcement that all these three outposts have been seized." Roosevelt then continued with the specific details.

Ascending Arrangements Can Lead to Division at the Decision Line

We're having a problem with Bill in sales.

Bill is bored with his job.

Bill's administrative assistant bungles client calls.

We could hire a new assistant for Bill, but that would not alleviate his boredom.

We could expand Bill's sales territory to challenge him more, but John would get angry.

We could increase Bill's product line to challenge him more, but the new products won't be ready for another six months.

Therefore, to motivate Bill, let's give him a bigger commission percentage [your conclusion].

Therefore, let's fire Bill [reader's conclusion].

Figure 3. Dangerous Ascending Arrangement. The ascending presentation can lead to an unpleasant surprise: The reader may come to a completely different conclusion from that of the writer.

The TV news commentator states, "The stock market plunged 1200 points today. Many have lost great fortunes. Stay tuned for the details."

The newspaper journalist presents readers with this headline: "Terrorists Take 50 U.S. Hostages in Tahiti." Then the specifics follow in the succeeding paragraphs.

A second reason for this format, in addition to clarity, is control. Readers can read as much—or as little—as they want. The farther they move through your document, the more details they receive. If they decide to stop reading before the end of the document or the end of a section, they haven't missed any buried key points. As a nation of web surfers, we have become used to controlling what we read, when we read

Ascending Arrangements Keep Readers in the Dark

STATEMENT	READER'S RESPONSE
1. A complete report on the status of all blivit arms will be presented July 10.	Why?
2. Metallurgical analysis showed normal structure.	Analysis of what? So what?
3. The fillet radius was .040 of an inch smaller than design requirements.	?
4. The fracture originated in the arm/body fillet.	Fracture? What fracture?
5. The blivit arm failed due to metal fatigue.	What blivit arm?
6. Inspection procedures have been revised to prevent a recurrence of the problem.	What problem? What procedures?
7. The Mark V press failure was caused by a broken blivit arm. All Mark V's have been shut down pending inspection. Full production will resume Monday, July 1.	*@!!**#!

Figure 4. Confusing Ascending Arrangement. This arrangement typically exasperates readers because details are unclear until the end, causing readers to grow impatient.

it, and how much time we want to devote to it. Your document format has to accommodate that preference and impatience.

That same control issue surfaces in all other media. We've become accustomed to reading newspapers that summarize all the key stories on the front page, "headline news" in a minute, and one-word billboards. Readers want information in capsule format as quickly as possible because they are inundated with paperwork. In addition to hourly e-mail, reports of all kinds arrive on their desks—feasibility studies, research reports, statistical analyses, trip reports, marketing survey results, status reports, and investigation reports. Needless to say, they can't read everything in full detail. Whether watching TV, the computer screen, or reading hard copy, the mind-set is the same: Have remote, will surf.

Whether watching TV, the computer screen, or reading hard copy, the mind-set is the same: Have remote, will surf.

Your job as a writer is to make that kind of reading possible by presenting your most important information up front and allowing readers to decide how much or how little detail they want. This descending arrangement allows readers to control their own reading according to the need-to-know principle.

Even technical specialists reading your document prefer this descending arrangement. Although they may be as interested in the detailed discussion of the test procedures as in the conclusions, they will understand those details more quickly and more easily with the conclusions presented up front (see Figure 5).

Compare the two report outlines in Figure 6. This expansion outlines a service problem report written to a client who has had equipment failure. In the ascending-order outline, notice the buried message of primary interest to the most important readers: management. But in the descending-order outline, the message comes at the beginning of the report. From reading the first section, the manager has a "photo" of the entire report findings. He can stop reading anywhere along the way that time or interest dictates and get on with the necessary repairs to his equipment.

The second section of the descending-order outline (the "why" and the "how" details) adds to a reader's understanding of how the writer arrived at the conclusions and recommendations about the equipment failure.

The third section of the descending-order outline (the Appendixes) is for the manager who wants more evidence and discussion of the details and for the specialist who will actually correct the problem by pinpointing the hydrogen leak.

Notice in the descending-order outline that the introduction is missing. Frequently, most information in introductions is already known and/or

Descending Arrangements Give Readers Control

STATEMENT	READER'S RESPONSE
The Mark V press failure was caused by a broken blivit arm. All Mark V's have been shut down pending inspection. Full production will resume Monday, July 1.	Okay.
Inspection procedures have been revised to prevent a recurrence of the problem.	Excellent!
The blivit arm failed due to metal fatigue.	I'm not surprised.
The fracture originated in the arm/body fillet.	Uh-huh.
The fillet radius was .040 of an inch smaller than design requirements.	I see why it broke.
Metallurgical analysis showed normal structure.	Okay.
A complete report on the status of all blivit arms will be presented July 10.	Good.

Figure 5. Descending Arrangement. This arrangement of information makes details clear and allows readers to control how much or how little elaboration they want.

Comparison of Ascending and Descending Outlines

ASCENDING OUTLINE

I. Introduction
  A. Past equipment failure
  B. Present couplings failure
II. Methods
  A. Metallurgical analysis
  B. Torque-turn analysis
  C. Field investigation
III. Discussion
  A. Metallurgical analysis
    1. Hardness results
    2. Iron sulfide
  B. Torque-turn analysis
    1. Bottom turns incorrectly monitored
    2. Incorrect torque setting
  C. Field investigations
IV. Conclusions and Recommendations
  A. Conclusions
    1. Causes of failed couplings
    2. Torque-turn unit not calibrated
  B. Recommendations
    1. Investigate causes of embrittlement
    2. Pinpoint hydrogen leak
V. Appendixes

DESCENDING OUTLINE

I. Conclusions and Recommendations
  A. Conclusions
    1. Causes of failed couplings
    2. Torque-turn unit not calibrated
  B. Recommendations
    1. Investigate causes of embrittlement
    2. Pinpoint hydrogen leak
II. Methods and Findings
  A. Metallurgical analysis
    1. Hardness results
    2. Iron sulfide
  B. Torque-turn analysis
    1. Bottom turns incorrectly monitored
    2. Incorrect torque setting
  C. Field investigations
III. Appendixes

Figure 6. Comparison of Ascending and Descending Outlines. The descending outline presents key ideas first.

boring. Any necessary background explanation can be woven into the discussion section as explanation in the "why" and the "how" of your message.

To elaborate further on this descending arrangement, let me introduce you to the ready-made outlining structure we call the MADE Format™. This four-part basic format will work for 90 percent of all the e-mails, memos, letters, proposals, reports, and manuals you write.

M = Message: What's the Message?

Begin your document with a summary of the most important question or issue: We should open a new manufacturing plant in Houston. We should expand the Atlanta warehouse. We have perfected a new excavation tool that will be 20 percent more economical than what we're now using. Your operators don't know how to monitor such-and-such machine. Your year-end reports contain two discrepancies. We held a pre-award meeting with the vendor and are hesitant to sign the contract. Our competitors have a new product ready for market that's $10 cheaper and more reliable than ours. Bill Grimes wants to hire two additional software designers in his department.

Whatever the situation, overview it first before plunging into the details.

You expect this same summary daily in informal conversation. For example, you arrive home late at night after a hard day's work and you're ready to shower and relax. You ask your spouse, "What about the shower leak?"

"Oh, that. I thought I'd never get a plumber out here because there's been an emergency in the northeast part of town and—"

"Is it repaired? Can I take a shower?" you cut in.

"Yes. After a real hassle. First, he—"

"How much did they charge?" you interrupt again.

"Ninety-eight dollars."

You roll your eyes upward and head for the shower. Now that you have the most important message, you're willing to listen to all the "who," "when," "why," and "how" details.

Do the same for your readers: Give them what they want to know at the beginning, and do so briefly. If you can't summarize your "bottom-line" message for most proposals, reports, letters, or e-mails in about two or three sentences, you don't have the focus narrow enough.

With the message up front, your readers can pay attention to your details with enlightened purpose.

A = Action: What Action Next?

Based on that narrowly focused message, fill in the second section of the basic MADE Format™. What are your readers supposed to do about your message? Should they assign someone to begin a new project? Should they buy the land? Should they discontinue testing the system? Should they modify their computer program? Should they turn the case over to the Legal Department? Should they refund your money and send shipping instructions to return the damaged merchandise?

When your readers know what action you want them to take, they can listen more intelligently to the details about how to do it.

Or perhaps you yourself need to take the next action, and you merely want to inform your readers of your plans: Will you begin a survey of all employees about their options and needs in training? Will you assign someone else in your department to follow up on your present study? Will you write a contract with a new service company? Will you fire an accountant who has continually refused to work overtime? Will you send another progress report in two months?

Again, if your readers first know what you plan to do, they can read the details about your action more intelligently.

D = Details: Who, When, Where, Why, How, and How Much?

Next, give the necessary details; omit the obvious. Usually the "why" and the "how" will be the essential details of your message. *Why* have you discarded the old policy? *How* will you put the new policy into effect? *Why* have you hesitated in awarding the contract? *How* will you solicit new bids before the construction deadline? *Why* did this equipment become obsolete so soon after purchase? *How* do you propose to avoid this obsolescence in future purchases?

Of course, more of these details must be answered when the answers are not obvious to your readers: *When* will you require employees to begin using the new ID badge? *Where* will the new spray be most success-ful? *Who* will oversee the marketing plan for the new widget? *Who* will arrange for advertising the new consulting service? *How* are the question-naires to be distributed and collected?

Often, the "who," "when," and "where" details are necessarily included in the message or action summaries at the beginning of your document. If they need elaboration, however, expand on such details, as necessary, in the third section.

If a thing goes without saying, let it.
—*Unknown*

Remember that any obvious details should be omitted. For example, if you want to save money for the organization, you don't need to explain *why*. Such unnecessary details merely add length. On the other hand, if your targeted audience will not understand the implication of the changes you're requesting or will be skeptical that such changes are necessary, you may need to elaborate extensively on *why*.

E = Evidence: Optional Enclosures or Attachments

Finally, you will enclose or attach any optional material you need to support your conclusions, recommendations, and discussion details. Figure 7 presents a summary of the MADE Format™.

The MADE Format™	
M: Message	State the bottom-line message of interest to your readers. (conclusions)
A: Action	Make recommendations or state any follow-up actions you want from readers or that you plan to take. (recommendations)
D: Detail	Elaborate on the necessary details: who, what, when, where, why, how, how much? (discussion)
E: Evidence	Mention any attachments or enclosures you're sending to make the message clearer or more authoritative or the action easier. (forms, tables, charts, graphs, copies of past correspondence, and so forth; appendixes, attachments, enclosures)

Figure 7. The MADE Format™. Readers have the most important information up front. Time and interest dictate how much or how little they read.

Business reading is done on the run. Billboard advertisers know this; brochure designers know this; webmasters know this; even your kids know this. They leave a note on the kitchen table: "Please leave me twenty dollars for school tomorrow—will explain later." Business readers demand that you get to the point quickly.

For help in applying the first three thinking steps presented here to your own specific writing tasks, we recommend that you use a Document Plan Sheet like the one in Figure 8.

Document Plan Sheet

Step 1: Consider Your Audience

Reader(s)?   Bottom-Line Message of Interest?

Step 2: Anticipate Special Reader Reactions

Reader(s)?   Reactions or Concerns?

Step 3: Outline Your Message in The MADE Format™

⟨M:⟩ **Message**

⟨A:⟩ **Action**

⟨D:⟩ **Detail**

        Who?

        What?

        When?

        Where?

        Why?

        How?

        How Much?

⟨E:⟩ **Evidence (Optional enclosure or attachment)**

Figure 8. Document Plan Sheet. Use a plan sheet to focus your thinking during the first three writing steps.

Review Figures 9–18 to compare the differences in clarity, control, and reading time.

Once-Upon-a-Time Format	
XYZ depreciates general properties at an annual rate of 30 percent. Most of the computer equipment is basically in this general-properties category. An exception to this depreciation schedule is some of our video Lexitrons, depreciated at a 40 percent rate.	*So what?*
I suggest that we review our 30 percent rate for the depreciation of this equipment. We are in the process of purchasing some major items for the sales group, and the technology in this field changes rapidly and could affect the market value of the equipment drastically.	*So why now?*
If you agree with this review, please let me know and I'll move ahead on the project next week.	*Oh.*
	What did you say about how we do things currently?

Figure 9. Once-Upon-a-Time Format. Readers must read blindfolded while the writer moves through background information.

The MADE Format™

We are in the process of purchasing some major equipment for the sales group. I suggest that we review our 30 percent rate for depreciation of this type of equipment because rapid technological advances in this field could affect the market value of our equipment drastically.	*Message: Good.* *Action: I agree.*
XYZ typically depreciates general properties at an annual rate of 30 percent, and most of our computer equipment is basically in this general-property category. An exception to this depreciation schedule is some of our video Lexitrons, depreciated at 40 percent.	*Details: How?* *How much?*
If you agree with this review, please let me know and I'll move ahead on the project next week.	*Sure thing.*

Figure 10. The MADE Format™. Prefer the functional MADE Format™ for documents.

Once-Upon-a-Time Format

Kim:

Enclosed is a packet of materials to be used in revising, improving, and revitalizing our budget-planning process for next year. Included in the packet are the following: Ten Standards, Schedules A and B, the Annual Planning Package, and the regional P & L forms.

Why do I need these?

You are cordially requested to be a member of the Goals and Budget Planning Committee for this upcoming year. Please evaluate these enclosed materials before attending the committee meeting at the Houstonian from noon, Tuesday, April 14, through the afternoon of Thursday, April 16. If you have a serious schedule conflict or otherwise believe you cannot participate, please call me now so that a suitable replacement can be arranged.

Oh? Requested? Is this a command performance, or do I have a choice?

We hope to come out of the meeting with an improved planning product. We will evaluate the printed materials, the process itself, and the underlying assumptions and general goals. It is necessary for you to formulate your thoughts in a well-organized manner to be able to express your supporting reasons effectively and concisely.

Why? How?

Don't I usually do this?

Additionally, as the meeting agenda is developed, I will be calling you to get ideas and to make assignments of specific responsibilities to be carried out prior to and at the meeting.

Oops—some help in preparing after all. Okay, so what's in that package you mentioned?

We appreciate your participation in this project.

Figure 11. Once-Upon-a-Time Format. The reader must read the document blindfolded while the writer moves through background information.

The MADE Format™

Kim:

You have been selected as a member of the Goals and Budget Planning Committee for this upcoming year. As a committee member, you will need to attend a meeting at the Houstonian from noon, Tuesday, April 14, through the afternoon of Thursday, April 16.	*Message: Okay.*
If you have a serious schedule conflict or cannot serve on this committee for other reasons, please call me now so that we can find a suitable replacement.	*Action: Okay.*
Additionally, as the agenda of the meeting is developed, I will be calling you to get ideas and to make assignments of specific responsibilities to be carried out prior to and at the meeting.	*Action: Good.*
We hope to come out of the meeting with an improved planning product. We will evaluate the printed materials, the process itself, and the underlying assumptions and general goals. As you prepare for this meeting, please keep in mind the necessity for everyone to formulate all thoughts and data in a well-organized manner, with supporting reasons effectively and concisely stated.	*Details: Why? How?*
Enclosed is a packet of materials for your use in helping us revise, improve, and revitalize our budget-planning process. Included in the packet are the following: Ten Standards, Schedules A and B, the Annual Planning Package, and the regional P & L forms.	*Attachments: Should be helpful.*

We appreciate your participation in this project.

Figure 12. The MADE Format™. Prefer the MADE Format™ for clarity and quick reading.

Once-Upon-a-Time Format

Geri,

Revenue brought an invoice to me that
they don't know what to do with.   *So what?*
Apparently, Blendwold billed us for   *What's this all about?*
$154.05 for a joint-venture payout
correction on Baytree #1. I had Sandra   *Why are you telling me?*
check on this, and she couldn't find this
billing in October or November. Accordingly,
Blendwold did not get paid, so they
subtracted this amount from the revenue.
It took Blendwold two checks to do that
(see August and September billings).

Revenue wants us to make an entry to   *Oh.*
get it off our books.

Can you see if this bill was ever paid? If   *Now, what were the*
not, can you have it approved and   *details again?*
sent back to me so that I can make an
entry? If you have any questions, let me
know. Thanks.

Sam

Figure 13. Once-Upon-a-Time Format. The ascending format forces
people to reread to understand the point.

The MADE Format™

Geri,	
Blendwold Company did not get paid for a joint-venture payout correction billing (Baytree #1) dated December 19 for $154.05, so they deducted this bill from our revenue checks. Revenue wants us to make an entry to correct our books.	*Message.*
	Okay.
Would you please check to see if this bill was ever paid? If this bill has not been paid, please have it approved and sent back so that I can make an entry to clear Revenue's books.	*Action:* *Yes, I can do this.*
	Detail: Why.
I had Sandra check on this, and she could not find that the invoice had been paid in either October or November. Because this bill was a correction, it could have been sent further into the year. It took Blendwold two checks to make the correction: August and September. I have faxed copies of the bill and other documents showing the expenses subtracted from revenue.	*Detail: How it happened and how to trace the problem.* *Evidence: I'll review these if I need to.*
Sam	

Figure 14. The MADE Format™. The descending arrangement makes the details understandable on first reading.

Once-Upon-a-Time Format

Jason,

Rosita Gonzales called yesterday to say that she couldn't get by here until the end of the week to show us the samples for the new storage bins. I told her that this was the fourth time that some some salesperson from her office had canceled or postponed an appointment. Frankly, I'm getting tired of dealing with these people. If you ask me, their product is no better than what we've been using, and I'm sure their price is going to be higher—although Rosita insists that with their volume discounts (a big mystery until we talk) we can save a bundle.

Who's she?

So why tell me? I thought you were arranging the meetings with these people.

Do you have some overriding reason to try to deal with this company? If so, let me know. Otherwise, I'd prefer to stick with the vendor we have on the storage bins. In any case, let me know if you're available to meet with Rosita on Friday, or if we should cancel the appointment altogether. I told her when she called that I'd have to check schedules with you. Let me know. See ya.

No.
Okay. Why didn't you say so?

Oh, I need to respond about the meeting. Now, what's the deal again with these people?

Tony

Figure 15. Once-upon-a-Time Format. Such formats confuse readers and waste their time.

The MADE Format™

Jason,

I'm still having difficulty getting a   *Message.*
representative from Universal to keep an
appointment with us to show us their
storage bins. Unless you have an overriding
reason for dealing with this company, I'd
prefer to stay with the vendor we
currently use.   *Oh, I see.*

Let me know your preference on this   *Action: Okay.*
and if you want to try to reschedule our
appointment with the rep for Friday.

What prompted this conclusion on my   *Details:*
part is that Rosita Gonzales called today   *So that's why.*
to say she would have to cancel our
appointment Wednesday and couldn't
get by here to show us the samples
until the end of the week. That's the fourth
time someone from her company has
canceled or postponed. No one will share
pricing information over the phone, and
I don't think Universal can beat our   *Well, I agree.*
current prices.

So do you want to meet with Rosita on   *No.*
Friday, or forget about it?

Tony

Figure 16. The MADE Format™. Readers understand the message as they
read through the document the first time.

Once-Upon-a-Time Reports and Proposals

To:
From:
Subject: KEW De-oiling Heater Options

Attached are calculations showing the cost of a *So? What do*
serious de-oiling heater problem. The pressure drop *you want me*
through the KEW de-oiling heater has caused *to do?*
operations to bypass the heater and go to the soft-
wax recovery surge drum to prevent dewaxing filter
boots from overflowing. According to my calculations,
the old boot pumps can run 8,590 BPD at 320 feet *So?*
of head with new impellers. New impellers from
Huffmaster are available on 26-week delivery. These
impellers have a capacity of 9,860 BPD at 390 feet
of head. On certain blocks it would be necessary to
run 1,150 BPD at 215 feet of head, so new pumps
would definitely help overcome the pressure-drop
problem.

The control valve is oversized and does not *So?*
contribute to the pressure-drop problem. The
de-oiling heater has plenty of warming area, but the
treated water side is fouled and needs cleaning.

There are 4 permanent solutions to the problem: *Which one is*
  1. Replace the de-oiling heater with a larger *best?*
     one.
  2. Add another heater in parallel.
  3. Replace the boot pumps with a surge drum
     and two large pumps.
  4. Replace the impellers in the boot pumps.

We recommend the surge drum and new pumps *Oh, I see.*
mentioned in the Process Duty Specification. We
also recommend that the de-oiling heater be
carefully designed with a high fluid-flow velocity
because melting product wax adversely affects
filtering.

As you know, this procedure is costly because part of the bypass material is product wax. We need your decision about either replacing or adding another de-oiling heater. Please call me with any further questions.

Now, what were the options and differences?

Figure 17. Once-Upon-A-Time Reports and Proposals. Readers must read to the end of the document before the details make complete sense and the recommendations become clear.

The MADE Format™ for Reports and Proposals

To:

From:

Subject: KEW De-oiling Heater Options

Due to the pressure drop through the KEW de-oiling heater, product wax is bypassing to the soft-wax recovery surge drum. This problem leads to a loss of approximately $10,000 annually.

Message

To correct this problem, we recommend the purchase and installation of a new surge drum and pumps to replace the dewaxing boot pumps. This change will solve the problem permanently without causing damage to the wax crystal. We also recommend a de-oiling heater with a high fluid-flow velocity be installed because melting product wax reduces filtering efficiency and increases pressure drop.

Action

The total cost of these changes will be $4,200. The project can be completed by September 1, with total downtime of three days or less.

Details:
How much?

The other 3 possible solutions are:
- Replace the de-oiling heater with a larger one.
- Add another heater in parallel.
- Replace the impellers in the boot pumps.

Details:
How else?

The old boot pumps can run only 8,590 BPD at 320 feet of head with new impellers. Larger impellers have a delivery wait of more than 26 weeks, a delay that will mean the problem cannot be corrected before winter. Furthermore, the maximum capacity of the existing pumps is 9,860 BPD at 390 feet of head, and on certain blocks it will be necessary to run 1,150 BPD at 215 feet of head. Thus, new pumps will be necessary anyway.

I understand.

Additionally, new pumps will definitely help overcome the pressure-drop problem.   *Makes sense.*

The control valve is oversized and does not contribute to the pressure-drop problem. The de-oiling heater has plenty of warming area, but the treated water side is fouled and needs cleaning. This cleaning will be done during downtime for modifications.

As you know, the present situation is very costly because part of the bypass material is product wax.

Attached are calculations detailing the cost of the problem.   *Evidence*

Figure 18. The MADE Format™ for Reports and Proposals. With the message and action statements up front, readers can understand the details as they read.

After you become familiar with this functional MADE Format™, you can organize in your head most simple proposals, reports, letters, or e-mails. Rarely will major revisions be necessary.

> Drowning problems in an ocean of information is not
> the same as solving them.
> —*Ray E. Brown*

Distinguish Between a Purpose Statement and a Message Statement

One final note about the MADE Format™: A message statement differs from a purpose statement. A message statement informs; it summarizes the key points of the entire document. A purpose statement is like a prose table of contents; it merely promises to tell readers something later—if they keep reading. You should generally prefer a message statement rather than a purpose statement.

Review these purpose and message statements to cement the difference in your mind:

Purpose: In our audit of the Tesa branch operations, we have discovered some serious problems.

Message: In our audit of the Tesa branch operations, we have discovered two serious problems: falsification of payroll checks for three employees, and two unapproved personal loans ($5,000 each) to the branch managers.

Purpose: This memo is in response to your request to provide further information about the NTA convention expenses.

Message: I have reviewed the trade-show opportunities at the NTA convention May 9–11 and estimate our total exhibit and travel expenses to be approximately $15,500.

Purpose: The purpose of this letter is to outline some of our plans in the marketing efforts to be directed by John Lynover.

Message: The Model 409TZ marketing efforts to be directed by John Lynover include a direct-mail campaign, free public seminars, and a rebate coupon packaged with the product. We've outlined below. . . .

Purpose: We have had problems in delivery of the vacuum pump at the Octobron field site. We need your approval on a decision that will affect our completion date.

Message: We have been unable to get delivery of a vacuum pump at the Octobron field site because of the vendor's worker shortage. We need your approval to change suppliers from Abbott Fielden to Bletz International.

Purpose: This report will outline several major problems that occur during the continued recycling of lithium negative electrodes.

Message: Three major problems that occur during the continued recycling of lithium negative electrodes are dendritic growth, film formation on the electrode surface, and dimensional instability.

Only rarely do you need both a purpose statement and a message statement.

Consider the Ascending Format Only for Biased Readers

On rare occasions, the ascending arrangement may be useful for presenting conclusions and recommendations against which your readers are strongly biased.

For example, consider the jaded TV viewer who's about to change the channel to find something more intriguing during the on-the-hour station break. Quickly, the producer slides into a teaser: The suburban housewife finishes her phone call, kisses her husband good-bye, and walks out to the car parked in the garage. The garage door rises as she presses the button. From out of the shadows, a gruff voice demands that she keep her mouth shut as brutish hands claw at her throat. She gasps for breath, then slides limply to the garage floor.

Commercial. The rest of the movie circles back to let us guess "who done it."

If you use this ascending arrangement for most information, you purposefully try to keep your readers blindfolded, forcing them to follow your reasoning slowly and deliberately. If we did X, then Y would happen. If we tried to do A, then B might happen. If we then tried option C, then D might ruin us. Therefore, it follows that EFG appears to be our best course of action. With this suspenseful format, you as the writer completely control how much or how little you want to reveal to the readers, and in what order.

Needless to say, the arrangement usually annoys busy management readers and clients or customers who want to control their own time. Their reaction quite often is: "Tell me what your main point is, and I'll decide if I want to hear more."

If you think your readers, however, are so biased against what you have to say that you have to sneak up on their blind side, then you might well choose the ascending format. You hold up the reader's first cherished idea, then refute it. Next, you hold up the reader's second most cherished idea, then knock it down. Finally, you present the only remaining option—your conclusions and recommendations—and hope you have left the reader no alternative but to accept your position.

Sometimes it works and sometimes it doesn't. Sometimes readers bow to your reasoning and let you lead them down the primrose path. On other occasions, readers refute your ideas each step of the way and arrive at a conclusion totally different from yours.

Unless your document is so short or of such great interest that all readers will feel compelled to read every single detail, avoid the ascending arrangement. Novelists and screenwriters get away with such a structure, but most business writers create far less intrigue.

Identify the Exceptions and Variations to the MADE Format™

In our more than twenty years' experience of conducting business and technical writing workshops for corporate clients, we've found that about

90 percent of all documents (proposals, reports, e-mail, letters) should be arranged in the MADE Format™.

But, of course, there are exceptions to any general rule or format. Primarily, the exceptions or variations to the MADE Format™ fall into these general categories:

- Directives (when the tone is important)
- Transmittals (because the attachment or enclosure *is* the message)
- Requests for voluntary action (because you must motivate readers to act)
- Negative responses (because the "no" may sound overbearing, blunt, intimidating, or discouraging)
- Complaints (because of the negative tone when you need corrective action)
- Apologies (because readers are already upset)
- Procedures (because the message is the series of actions)

For special guidelines and models of these exceptions and variations, refer to Part 5 for your specific interest.

Expand the Basic MADE Format™ for Longer Documents

For routine e-mail and short documents, the MADE Format™ will be the only outline you need. But when your message is complex (such as in a lengthy report, proposal, or manual), you will need to expand the basic MADE Format™ into a more detailed plan to accommodate more complex information. Writing workshop participants frequently confess, "I was one of those students who always wrote the paper first and afterward prepared an outline to hand in to the professor." Those people, perhaps unknowingly, miss the real shortcut to writing a final document. They view the outline as a final product rather than as an effective means to an end.

To the writer, the word *outline* often brings to mind the drudgery of high school or college English courses, where outlines had to be written in parallel form—either all sentences or all topics, never mixed. If the first word in Point A was an adjective, points B, C, D, and E had to begin with an adjective. If Point II had an "A," it also had to have a "B."

Let me state from the outset that I advocate *functional* outlining, not the rigors just mentioned. Topic-sentence outlines can help you remember exactly where you are going with each point. But if the details in the paragraphs can be summed up in a topic phrase on your outline, that's functional. The outlining process should be as short or as long as necessary for you to turn out a well-organized document.

Why not just skip the outline and write a draft? Time.

Someone has aptly questioned: "If you don't have time to do it right the first time, how will you ever find time to do it over?" That observation was never more appropriate than for the task of writing. Working without an outline almost always ensures a rewrite or time on the phone interpreting what you meant to say.

First, outlining organizes your message. Outlining lets you see logical relationships and visualize major and minor ideas. **Second, outlining speeds up the drafting process.** The hardest part of writing is beginning. Once you have summarized the main points in sentences or phrases in an outline with details to support each idea, half the work is done. Your draft is simply a matter of filling in the flesh around the skeleton.

Third, outlining long documents eliminates major revisions in the editing step. Without a plan, you often have to do a cut-and-paste job of editing—for example, moving page 4 to the middle of page 2. Then that move calls for a new transitional sentence to keep the logical flow of ideas and a new paragraph conclusion to bridge the gap to the following idea. Getting the order right the first time precludes later major revisions.

Finally, an outline functions much as a bookmark does. It helps you keep your place in the project through interruptions. No matter how many phone calls, appointments, drop-ins, or holidays interrupt your writing task, an outline will show you where you've been and where you're headed.

All of the preceding are good reasons to outline. Remember them when you're tempted to skip this step to "save time." Here's how you will use your outline:

To gather your information. An outline indicates what points you plan to cover and helps you decide what figures, tables, or artwork you will need to support each point. If you wait until you draft the report or proposal to determine what support you may need, you will be hopelessly behind schedule in your writing project. You'll be forced either to omit the additional information or graphics or delay the writing. Neither is a good option.

To visualize and overview the final document design. Just as engineers design prototypes of new products, writers benefit from seeing what the end document will look like while there's still time to alter the writing plan. With an outline in hand, you can see where the main emphasis falls in your document. Are you getting mired in minutiae? Are you devoting more time to specifications than to benefits, or vice versa? That is, have you spent too many words on *how* something works rather than on *why* readers should do what you want?

With this outline in hand, you can often avoid the need for major rewrites by asking supervisors for their comments on your writing plan. Have you covered all the key issues? Do they agree with your interpretations? Do they want to add a key point to your plan here or there? Getting this prewriting approval on your outline will often keep you from turning in a completed report, proposal, or manual, only to hear your supervisor, client, or teammate respond, "This isn't exactly what I had in mind. Now, when you rewrite this. . . . "

To discover missing or incomplete information. An outline points out deficiencies in your thinking and in your data. As you plan, you may list points to make and then realize you have no evidence or information to support them. This discovery puts you back on the data-collection trail before time runs out.

To eliminate repetition. Those who don't plan are doomed to repeat themselves needlessly. When you see overlapping ideas and details in your structure, you can make immediate decisions about where to include such information and where to eliminate it.

To set schedules and deadlines. Many people claim to work better under pressure. Often they're making a false assumption; it's only that they have no basis for comparison. For some people, every document they produce must be completed "under pressure," and they never have an opportunity to see how much more effective they could have been had they devoted the proper time to their writing.

With an outline, you have the trail before you, making it very difficult to tell yourself there's just another "hour or two" of writing to go before completion. Realism sets in. You can time yourself to estimate how many hours or days you need to compose each section of the document, and then plan your schedule and the interim deadlines accordingly. Supervisors and other colleagues who may be involved will also appreciate receiving a realistic schedule of deadlines from you.

To conduct meetings and work with cowriters. You'll also find it much easier to break the writing project into portions and assign them to colleagues. All those involved will know what others are doing and what structure and format they're following. The result will be a more cohesive document. When you and your colleagues meet to discuss various phases of the writing project prior to completion, a working outline will answer questions and help you anticipate and circumvent problems.

To prepare progress reports. The meat of your progress reports comes from your outline. You can skim the writing plan for data and details as they become available. The outline becomes your tickler file for reporting in the interim until the project is complete.

Organizing your thoughts into a writing plan saves time, produces a better final document, and alleviates much of the pain in the process.

The Formal Outline

So how do you design an outline that isn't an afterthought? You have three methods available. Of these, the most time-consuming and least effective is the formal, academic-style outline.

Formal Outline

I. Introduction—pipelines installed
  A. Trunk lines
  B. Connections from new fields to existing systems
  C. Infield lines connecting platforms to central facility
II. Problem issues
  A. Hazardous diving
  B. Difficult repairs
  C. Complex tie-ins
III. New pipe-laying techniques
  A. Welding techniques
    1. Friction welding
    2. Flash-butt welding
    3. Laser welding
    4. Electron-beam welding
  B. Lay-barge procedures
    1. Laying
    2. Inspection
    3. Piggybacking
  C. Tow methods
    1. Bottom tow
    2. Off-bottom tow
    3. Control-depth tow
  D. Trenching
    1. Jet sleds
    2. Plows
    3. Mechanical trenching machines

Figure 19. Formal Outline. Such an outline can be counterproductive to the writing effort. It is useful primarily when you already know what you want to write.

The formal outline (Figure 19) is not a thinking tool. It is helpful only when you already know exactly what you want to say. If you decide to use this traditional outlining method, you can use either words and phrases or complete sentences.

If you use only words and phrases, be complete enough so that you don't forget what point you want to make. For example, does "torque-turn analysis" mean that you plan to tell why such an analysis is significant, or will you be explaining the procedure for such an analysis? If you list only "New York sales," when you get ready to write the corresponding paragraph you may have forgotten what you were going to say about New York sales. If, instead, you write "Compare New York sales to Boston sales," you'll remember immediately where you are headed with the paragraph. Complete sentences leave a clear trail to follow when you are writing your first draft.

The Random List

A second outlining technique is to generate a random list. That is, you don't worry about what should come first, second, third, and so on. You don't even stop to consider which are major points and which are minor points. You simply list ideas as they come to you. Then after you have the idea list in front of you, you arrange the items into some logical order.

Such a random list makes use of the brain's ability to pull ideas from many sources. Putting ideas down on paper or screen without sorting or evaluating them helps keep the ideas flowing quickly. Later, with the entire "database" captured in front of your eyes, your brain can sort and file.

If you want to include three details in an e-mail or letter, you have a choice of six ways to arrange those three details. If you have four details to include, you can choose from twenty-four combinations. The reason many writers stare at a blank screen trying to decide how to begin is that they are trying to visualize all the possible combinations of major ideas or details and choose the best arrangement. To examine mentally all the possible combinations of even three or four details (without seeing something on paper or on-screen) is virtually impossible.

Skip the staring stage and begin with a random list of ideas as they come to mind.

In the random listing, also be sure to add all the details, illustrations, or figures that come to mind. Everything you put down in the outline will save you time later.

The Idea Wheel

We recommend the third outlining method, what we call the idea wheel, for speed and efficiency. Other writers refer to a similar technique in other ways—"branching," "brain writing," "clustering," "mind-mapping," to name a few. Although the diagrams do look similar to these other methods, there are three major distinctions with idea wheels: structure, subordination, and sequence. The idea wheel quickly allows you to distinguish major points from minor points and to sequence the spokes on the wheel in a specific order.

As with the random-list method, the technique lets you capture your thoughts randomly as quickly as you can and then reorder them easily as you move along with your first draft.

Here's how the technique works: Start with your key concept written inside a circle (or wheel hub) in the center of the page. As you think of ways to break down that broad concept, draw spokes from the hub. For subpoints, draw spokes from the spokes. When you see repetition, you can immediately make a decision, for example, whether to discuss a particular detail under spoke A or spoke B. Rearrange the details immediately. When you run off the page, simply turn the spoke into another wheel hub and start the process over in order to break down your ideas further. After you have captured all your ideas on the page, then go back and add letters and numbers (from the traditional outlining system you learned in school) to show the sequential order in which you plan to include the ideas in your document draft.

Don't worry about starting off "right" with ideas on each spoke. If you knew exactly what to put on each spoke as you began the process, you wouldn't need the idea-wheel technique. Just begin with any two or three ideas that you want to include in a document or document section. If absolutely nothing comes to mind, start off with "who," "what," "when," "where," "why," "how," and "how much" on the wheel spokes. Then go from there. If every detail seems to spin off the "why" spoke, then start over with another idea wheel, using "why" in the hub of your wheel.

After a few false starts, you will gradually—then quickly—have all your ideas in front of you to arrange into a more logical, usable format. Study Figures 20–23 to see how this outlining technique works.

Use Idea Wheels for Planning Longer Documents

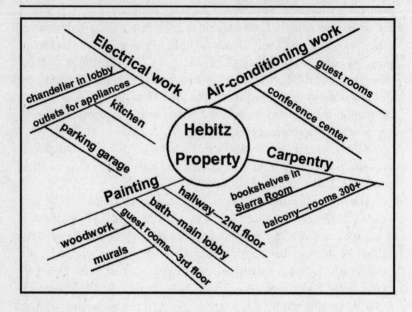

Figure 20. Idea Wheel. Use idea wheels for planning key concepts in a complete document.

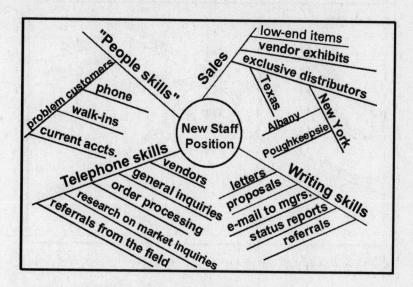

Figure 21. Idea Wheel. Use idea wheels for reorganizing ideas as the document structure "evolves."

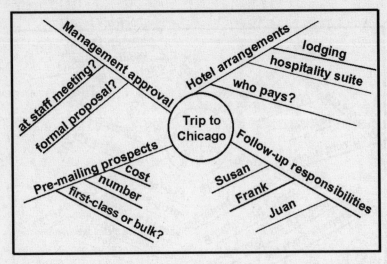

Figure 22. Idea Wheel. Use idea wheels for expanding one section of details.

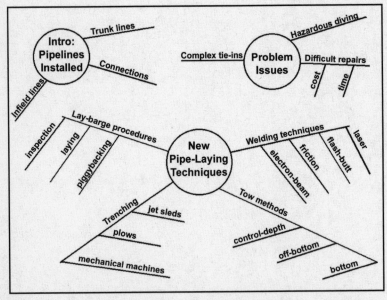

Figure 23. Idea Wheel. Use idea wheels for generating ideas to include in your document.

Arrange the Random List or Idea Wheel in Logical Order

If you are describing a process, you will probably shuffle ideas into chronological order. If you are evaluating two vendor contracts, you may shuffle ideas into a point-by-point comparison. If you are persuading management to move a warehouse, you may arrange your argument from the strongest to the weakest reasons.

Some ideas will lend themselves to more than one logical arrangement. For example, let's say you are writing to a vendor about your dissatisfaction with a software package. You might arrange the letter or e-mail chronologically: dates and description of problems as they developed, dates of unanswered or delayed service calls, dates and details about phone calls to ask questions about the equipment capabilities.

Or you could arrange the details in order of significance of the problems: equipment features that do not accomplish your objectives, two ignored service requests, one delayed service call, rudeness of maintenance personnel.

Or you could arrange the details of your dissatisfaction by category: features you need but that the equipment can't perform; features the equipment has but that you do not need; costs of initial purchase, maintenance, and supplies; overall appearance, such as bulkiness and unsightly cables strung over the office.

Investigate several logical arrangements and choose the most appropriate one for your purposes. The following guidelines offer extra help in frequently used logical arrangements.

Instructions:

(Policy manuals, user manuals, department procedures, investigative procedures) (Also, see "Procedures" in Part 5.)

- Explain reasons for changes in the old method, if cooperation is a problem.
- List materials, forms, or equipment needed.
- Mention any safety precautions and repeat them again before the step in which the precaution should be taken.
- Give steps in chronological order, stating each step in a separate sentence.
- Write sentences in the imperative mood. ("Monitor these machines for . . . "—not "These machines should be monitored for . . .")

- Give examples when possible and place supporting tables, drawings, or illustrations as close as possible to each step.

Processes:

(Investigative research and progress reports) (Also, see "Accomplishment or Status Reports" in Part 5.)

- Overview the objectives of the process, project, or research.
- Pinpoint and mention the number of stages involved.
- Explain any equipment, materials, or terms the reader will not understand in the details to follow. (Details to be covered here depend on what you discovered when you "considered your audience.")
- Explain the process chronologically.

Definition or Description:

(Job descriptions, project overviews, equipment or service brochures)

- Overview the object's or person's function.
- Describe the equipment's appearance or organizational structure, if necessary. In describing equipment, begin with internal parts and move to the outer. In describing an organization, begin from the bottom up or from the top down.
- Describe the operation or functions in detail.

Question/Answer:

(Analysis of data, ideas, attitudes, policies)

- Pose unknowns or problems.
- State your hypothesis or answer.
- Present your support in descending order of significance in most presentations.
- Address and refute any alternative hypotheses or answers.
- Restate briefly your answer or hypothesis.

Comparison/Contrast:

(Comparison or contrast of equipment, processes, people, policies, plans of action and so forth)

- State that two things are primarily similar or dissimilar, or state that one is superior to the other for your purposes. (Unless your

readers are strongly biased toward an option you don't plan to recommend and when you don't want to go into great detail about options you're not recommending, prefer to use the persuasive format for most contrast purposes.)
- Overview the criteria used to come to the above conclusion.
- Arrange the details by criteria. Explain how each option measures up against the criteria for decision (see Figure 24). (Tabular presentations of criteria and options often convey information to be compared or contrasted better than paragraph arrangements.)
- Briefly, restate your conclusion: Both will serve your purpose, neither will serve your purpose, or one will best serve your purpose.

Persuasive—Unbiased Internal Readers or Interested Outsiders:
(Internal proposals and suggestions to your management or outsiders)

- State your conclusion/recommendation in terms of the decision-maker's interests.
- Explain your reasons, benefits, or criteria (most to least important).
- Include a cost analysis and implementation plans.
- Refute objections and address alternatives.
- Restate briefly your major conclusion/benefit/recommendation.

Example:
Our field tests indicate that the new machine has the capacity to . . . , and I recommend . . .

Important test #1 showed . . .

Less important test #2 revealed . . .

Test #3 also verified that . . .

The costs will involve . . . and we should begin the first phase of implementation in the second quarter under the direction of . . .

Earlier questions (problems) that can now be put aside are . . .

Persuasive—Uninterested Outside Readers:
(Unsolicited proposals to clients and customers, sales letters) (Also, see "Proposals" in Part 5.)

- Draw attention with a startling statistic or quote, a prevalent problem or issue, a benefit statement, a striking question, the name of a mutual acquaintance, or a shared experience or situation.
- Offer your message, conclusion, or recommendation.
- Elaborate with an explanation of benefits or reasons.
- Call for action.

Comparison and Contrast Documents

LESS EFFECTIVE	PREFERRED
Machine A	Cost
Cost	Machine A
Ease of operation	Machine B
Delivery schedule	Machine C
Machine B	Ease of operation
Cost	Machine A
Ease of operation	Machine B
Delivery schedule	Machine C
Machine C	Delivery schedule
Cost	Machine A
Ease of operation	Machine B
Delivery schedule	Machine C

Figure 24. Comparison and Contrast Documents. For most situations, arrange information by criteria, not by options. Otherwise, the information about any single option cannot be completely evaluated until all the details on all options are presented.

Example:
Our newest machine can save you 38 percent on . . .
The equipment's primary function is to . . .
The most important benefit is . . .
A second saving involves . . .
A third consideration will be . . .
We can install it in 48 hours for x dollars . . .
Neither the X machine nor the Y machine equals the precision of the one I'm recommending because . . .

Persuasive—Biased Internal or External Readers:

- Raise a striking question or pertinent problem.
- Suggest and then refute alternative explanations, conclusions, and/or recommendations.
- Present your conclusions and/or recommendations.
- Outline the cost and implementation plans.

Example:

Is it possible to improve our rating on X?

The most obvious answer seems to be . . . but that won't explain the problem with . . .

Another plausible solution would be to . . . but neither will that overcome the issue of . . .

A third course of action might be to . . . but that will cause serious difficulties with . . .

Therefore, my proposal is to . . .

The project will require x dollars as we begin the renovation project, which involves four steps . . .

If you do not attempt to control the reasoning of readers but instead simply present your facts, they may agree with each fact you present and still arrive at a totally different conclusion. Persuasive writing requires structuring your document around your audience's interests and biases.

Putting pen to paper lights more fire than matches ever will.
—*Malcolm Forbes*

In some documents, of course, you will combine several of the previous formats and guidelines. Choose any logical arrangement that fits your material and your reader's purpose; that arrangement should be evident as you review your random list or idea wheel and see relationships among major and minor ideas.

If the body of your document does not fall into place naturally, chances are that you have the wrong arrangement of ideas. Shuffling your outline into a different order is much easier and quicker than rearranging an entire draft.

* * *

To repeat: Your ideas will not automatically come to mind in a smooth framework. Don't worry. Simply use one of the previously mentioned organizational methods (random listing or idea wheel) to capture your thoughts. Then, when you have all the details at hand, you can structure them into one of the suggested document frameworks.

Review Your Outline or Structure

Have you stayed with the appropriate focus all the way through your document? Have you dealt with any special problems identified in Step 2? Have you refuted skepticism and alternative suggestions? Is your message presented in descending order—the conclusions and recommendations up front, the discussion and details following? Have you gone off on tangents that have no bearing on your main focus? (If so, delete those ideas from your outline and don't waste time writing the paragraphs that will have to be cut later.) What examples or supplementary information could you attach to make the message more complete or easily understood?

Check with your supervisor or team about your writing plan. A professional writer rarely considers writing a complete article or book without a prior go-ahead from an editor. When a magazine writer gets an idea for an article, she ferrets out an unusual angle and then does a brief outline to send to an editor for approval. If the editor answers "Sounds great," the writer can prepare her manuscript with confidence that she'll make a sale. The editor may respond, however, that the writer's angle doesn't fit the magazine's readership and that the writer should try a new angle. Or the editor may respond, "I like your angle, but leave out the part about the mushrooms in Gawangatan." In either case, the writer has profited. If the beginning focus is wrong, she has saved herself a major revision or a flat turndown.

Your time is no less valuable. Make sure your supervisor or peers who will have to approve your final document agree with your criteria, your interpretations of the data, and your conclusions and recommendations. They may also point out skepticism or other special problems they foresee down the line—problems you should deal with the first time around.

You may want to use the checklist of questions in Figure 25 as a guide for reviewing your document structure. These critical questions will guide you to ask the decision-maker or team in any given situation about the document structure before composing a complete draft. Prewriting approval provides peace of mind. Writing a first draft is much easier when you know that you'll not be rewriting a document from a completely new perspective.

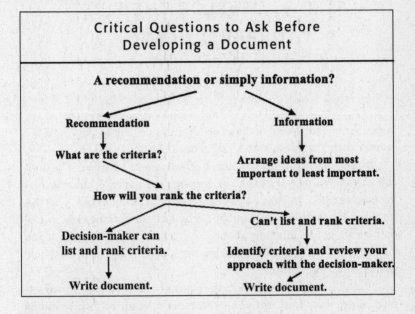

Critical Questions to Ask Before Developing a Document

A recommendation or simply information?

Recommendation

Information

What are the criteria?

Arrange ideas from most important to least important.

How will you rank the criteria?

Can't list and rank criteria.

Decision-maker can list and rank criteria.

Identify criteria and review your approach with the decision-maker.

Write document.

Write document.

Figure 25. Critical Questions in Document Review. Ask these critical questions of the decision-maker reader *before* you draft to reduce the chances of having to do a rewrite.

12

STEP 4: DEVELOP THE FIRST
DRAFT QUICKLY

If you write only e-mail or short documents, feel free to skip from this point to Step 5. But if you write longer documents, stay tuned.

By the time you reach this step, half your work is finished. The difficult part of writing is thinking: considering your audience and anticipating their reactions to your message and their interest in details. That upfront thinking will require about 50 percent of your writing time. Actual drafting should require only about 25 percent of the total effort. If you have followed the preceding planning steps, developing the draft should go quickly and smoothly.

If at all possible, plan to write the entire document in one or two settings. Otherwise, you'll spend an enormous amount of time rereading and "working into" your subject again each time you begin the project.

Also, don't feel as though you must start drafting "at the beginning." To gain momentum, you may begin the document with any section, preferably the easiest sections. Having an outline ensures that you will not "lose your place" if you decide to start writing about Benefit #2 instead of Benefit #1.

Manage a Major Writing Task

Writing a draft is one of the later stages of the overall project, not the beginning. With a long, complex writing task, take the project-management approach to writing. As the primary writer on a team project, you must take charge of information collection, deadlines, and coordination of all group writing efforts.

Normal sequence of product design:

1. Management announces the product.
2. Technical writing publishes the manual.
3. Engineering begins designing it.
   —*William Horton*

Let's backtrack for a moment. To begin the writing project, set deadlines for yourself for each phase. Then work backward from your due date. Depending on the length of the document, of course, you should plan on several days (several weeks would be better) between completion of the first draft and the final document. The interim cooling-off period between first and final drafts allows you to approach the revision stage objectively with a fresh eye.

After you've counted backward from the final due date to the first-draft deadline, continue to count days until you have set interim deadlines for all phases of your work. Your planning calendar should include deadlines for the following:

- Calls to all people supplying information
- A completed outline
- An outline-review meeting with any other writers involved and with the supervisor
- Requests for artwork to be prepared by others
- First drafts from all writers of sections
- The compilation of a complete first draft
- Comments on the first draft from all reviewers
- An artwork review meeting
- The revision of the document
- Final manuscript preparation
- Final proofing and submission

Assuming you've marked your project calendar with all these deadlines, don't count on all coworkers to meet them automatically. Make additional notes on your calendar for such things as follow-up phone calls to remind others involved of their upcoming deadlines.

As far as your own part in the writing effort is concerned, you may find useful the following tips collected from numerous professional writers.

Mull over your writing project while you are still doing the preliminary work. Don't wait until you actually begin drafting a long document. Fifty percent of any writing effort is thinking. While you're performing tests or visiting clients, you can begin to analyze your audience and decide how you want to approach the writing. Your subconscious will do wonders while you are going about your other activities.

Suppose you are an engineer conducting a test to determine the effects of a machining process on the final surface finish. You are measuring the root-mean-square smoothness of various pieces and compiling data that will form the basis of your conclusions. You will make graphs and tables to summarize and support your findings. But think how much more impact your report would have if you include photos of the surfaces using low-angle light. Such photos would give readers a much better "feel" for the conclusions, especially if they don't speak RMS.

Who among us has not sat down to write a report, only to say, "I wish I'd got that data point . . . or that photo"? How many times have you sifted through that stack of "snapshots" of your test apparatus, looking in vain for the one that shows exactly what you want to convey?

Sometimes you can redo your work. Often, however, it will be impractical to restart your experiment or test. The conditions aren't right. Money is not available. The apparatus has crumbled to dust.

As you gather and evaluate data, you begin to form conclusions. Like any good technical professional, you ask yourself, "What new data do I need to satisfy myself that this conclusion is valid?" Then you collect more data until you're satisfied. What we're suggesting is that you, too, from the very beginning of the project, ask yourself: What photo, data point, measurement, slide, table, or other graphic will increase the value of my final written presentation?

Keep notes. Don't ever rely solely on your memory. As ideas come to you about points to include, facts to state, arguments to present, or artwork to use, jot them down and toss them into a file. When you get to the drafting stage, much of your outline work will come from these bits and pieces.

Plan each section of the document. If you don't have time to organize your thoughts, how will you ever have time to revise the draft once it's written? And that's exactly what you'll have to do if you string your information together without forethought.

Set aside blocks of time to write. You lose time and continuity in "getting into" a project each time you temporarily put it aside. If you cannot devote full days to the writing effort, at least faithfully devote two to three uninterrupted hours each day.

Use prime time to write, and putter around only in off-peak hours. If you're a morning person, write the first two to three hours of your workday. If you're more energetic in the afternoon, set aside a few hours then. Thinking and writing require high-energy time.

Psyche yourself out of procrastination. Break the writing project into small sections and then do the easy parts first—perhaps write the introduction or the section on procedures or compile a list of charts and graphs to include in the document. As your "finished" pages or screens grow, you will gradually pass the halfway mark and become motivated to finish the more difficult parts of the writing task.

Inspiration comes only to prophets. The rest of us have to tackle writing just as we do any other project—with planning, determination, and coordinated effort.

A deadline is negative inspiration. Still, it's better than no inspiration
at all.
—*Rita Mae Brown*

Collect and Assemble Data

Assemble your data from Internet or other published research, interviews, experience, observations, or tests. If some of your research is hard to handle because of odd physical size, simply note on your outline a summary of the available data. This reminder will help you remember to relocate the oversized flowchart or copy the data from another computer file when you're ready to write that particular section of the document.

Basic research is what I am doing when I don't know
what I am doing.
—*Wernher von Braun*

Next, label any printout according to its subject matter in the upper *left-hand* corner. Use short, informative labels such as "Stress analysis test results" or "Reasons for low mercury levels." Now, with an eye to your outline, label each item in the upper *right-hand* corner with a corresponding outline number. Then sort into piles by outline item.

During this labeling step, you may uncover major weaknesses in your previous research. If your primary point is that a piece of equipment is too expensive, you may discover that you have little support for that opinion. In that case, you should postpone writing until you've collected more supporting information—perhaps statistics on costs of all other alternative equipment.

On the other hand, while matching data to your outline, you may discover that you have unnecessary information. Avoid the temptation to include all the extra data simply because this represents time-consuming work. Spare your readers all the details of your failures and miscellaneous adventures. Such irrelevant material damages the thrust of your overall report.

Keyboard or Dictate with Voice-Recognition Software

Fewer and fewer people dictate their documents to a human anymore. The speed of keyboarding and the ability to see immediately how your document looks makes voice-recognition software the tool of choice for many writers of long documents.

Today, talking to your computer will be a sign of intelligence, not insanity.
—*Headline in ad for IBM's ViaVoice, speech-recognition software*

If you decide to learn to dictate, dictating long documents may prove awkward at first, but with practice you will quickly improve and save yourself valuable time. A good expanded outline helps you move from point to point without pause. Don't worry that your sentences will not be polished; you can always correct grammatical errors or sentence structure in the editing step.

The computer takes advantage of the speed of dictation, the ease of reviewing hard copy, and the ease of editing clean copy. Whichever method you choose for composing, after you have a first draft, 75 percent of your writing project is finished.

Allow a Cool-Off Period and Then Reread

Never send out an important document without allowing time to give it a fresh reading. Allow a cool-off period of at least a few hours and preferably a couple of days. Otherwise, you'll simply read over what you thought you wrote.

Your time-management skills come into play here. When you are planning your work schedule, plan with this cooling-off period in mind. Take up a new project in the interval. Then come back to editing the first draft. This break lets you approach your earlier work with more objectivity to catch inconsistencies not apparent when working with fresh material: gaps in logic, missing details, irrelevant information, awkward constructions and transitions.

In short, at this point you're ready to edit your work to bring it to its final near-perfect form. (I say "near perfect" because no professional writer of my acquaintance ever feels that his or her work is perfect. If you don't believe it, just ask any best-selling book author.)

Now let's move on to Step 5, the most enjoyable step. The pain is over; the process leads to progress.

In any type of writing, no sentence can be both accurate and grammatical when written after 4:30 on Friday. However, the error will be obvious by the first coffee break on Monday.
—William Horton

PART 4

STEP 5:
EDIT FOR CONTENT AND LAYOUT, GRAMMAR, CLARITY, CONCISENESS, AND STYLE

Editing is to a document what polish is to shoes. Much business and technical writing fails because this final step is hurried or nonexistent, especially when the writing project has been short and relatively simple. And some writers confuse editing with proofreading, which is merely checking for typographical and grammatical errors. Editing, although it includes such errors, involves paying attention to much broader flaws.

Because the major work is over and you have an almost-finished product before you, editing can be the most rewarding and enjoyable step in the entire writing process. To edit on computer or hard copy? That's a key question. The complexity of editing on screen grows with the length of the document. By all means, do all you can on computer. For a final read-through, edit hard copy.

As you edit hard copy, use the standard editing symbols shown in Figure 26. If both you and your team use them, you can eliminate much miscommunication in this editing process. In my earlier book *Send Me a Memo,* I presented an editing checklist (see Figure 27). You may find it helpful in reviewing your document with supervisors or team members so that you can discuss writing issues with common terms and agree on changes to be made.

Proofreading and Editorial Marks

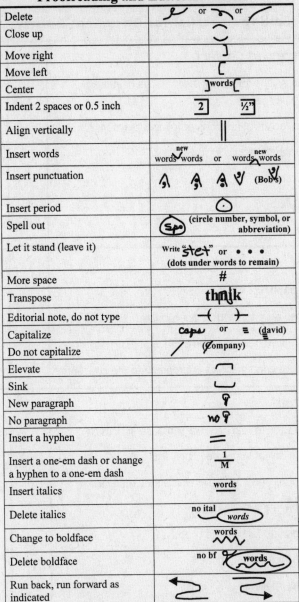

Delete	
Close up	
Move right	
Move left	
Center	]words[
Indent 2 spaces or 0.5 inch	2 ½"
Align vertically	
Insert words	words ∨ words or words ∧ words
Insert punctuation	(Bob's)
Insert period	
Spell out	(circle number, symbol, or abbreviation)
Let it stand (leave it)	Write "stet" or • • • (dots under words to remain)
More space	#
Transpose	thnik
Editorial note, do not type	
Capitalize	caps or ≡ (david)
Do not capitalize	(Company)
Elevate	
Sink	
New paragraph	
No paragraph	no ¶
Insert a hyphen	=
Insert a one-em dash or change a hyphen to a one-em dash	1/M
Insert italics	words
Delete italics	no ital (words)
Change to boldface	words
Delete boldface	no bf (words)
Run back, run forward as indicated	

Figure 26. Editing Symbols. Use these standard editing symbols on your hard copy as a shortcut method to flag changes to be made to your final document. Consistent editing symbols improve clarity and save time.

Editing Checklist for Document Review

Structure and Content	Yes	No
Begins with summary of the message of interest to readers?		
Clear recommendations or follow-up actions?		
Appropriate details included?		
Accurate?		
Complete?		
Authoritative?		
Layout		
Paragraphing for eye appeal?		
Easy-to-skim lists where appropriate?		
Informative headings and subheadings?		
Well-designed graphics appropriate to the concept?		
Grammar		
Clear, easy to read, correct sentence structure?		
Parallelism of ideas, headings, lists?		
Pronouns agree with the words they replace?		
Verbs agree with subjects?		
Appropriate tenses and moods?		
Word choice?		
Correct spelling?		
Capitalization?		
Punctuation?		

Clarity	Yes	No
Readable sentences (averaging 15 to 20 words)?		
Important ideas positioned for emphasis?		
Linking words appropriately show relationships between ideas?		
Clear transitions?		
Clear references (*which, it, they, this, that*)?		
Concrete words and phrases?		
Absence of unnecessary jargon or foreign words and phrases?		
Logical development of ideas?		
Consistent viewpoint?		
Active voice?		
Conciseness		
No irrelevant information?		
No buried verbs, hidden subjects, redundant words or phrases?		
Style		
A personal, conversational tone?		
Positive approach and language?		
Direct and clear, yet tactful?		
Variety in sentence pattern and length?		
Strong verbs?		
Appropriately informative or persuasive?		

Figure 27. Editing Checklist for Document Review. Review documents for structure, content, layout, grammar, clarity, conciseness, and style.

13

EDIT FOR CONTENT AND LAYOUT

The beautiful part of writing is that you don't have to get it right the first time, unlike, say, a brain surgeon.
—Robert Cormier

The web makes us impatient with anything we can't skim. Quick access to information mandates that readers understand the layout of your document so they can pick and choose, sort and file, as they read. Consider your own impatience:

- How do you feel about being put on hold when calling a support line?
- Do you find standard online tutorials helpful?
- Do you relish the thought of having someone send you a 67-page report to read and then spending 45 minutes in a meeting telling you what the report said?
- Do you grow angry when trapped on a malfunctioning airplane, parked only 20 yards away from the terminal gate?
- Do you like being caught in a hospital waiting room in front of a TV that's preset with only one channel option?

Your readers react similarly. Give them quick access to what they want and need.

Focus on the Reader's Interest Up Front

Any writer's first interests are usually self-interests. But remember that the first step in writing must be to consider the interests, experience, and knowledge of your readers. If their interest is money, did you sidetrack to tell them about the prestige involved in owning the new product? If readers are interested primarily in speed of operation, don't let the body of your document trail off onto the economics of the new system you're proposing. And even when you're addressing readers' interests, have you told them too much of what they already know? Move the "extra" information to an attachment for the less knowledgeable secondary readers, or eliminate it altogether.

Make Sure Your Elaboration of Details Matches the Intended Emphasis

Proportion suggests importance and emphasis. Have you used a large portion of the space to justify a minor action? Have you expended too many words in telling your readers *what* you did, while using too few words to explain *why* you did it?

Graphs, charts, and tables can make your document look out of proportion. Here is a good rule of thumb for their placement: If the figures are necessary for the discussion at hand, include them in the body of the document as close to the text reference as possible. If they are merely secondary, optional material that you can summarize in the text, put them in an appendix.

To sum up: Make sure the proportion of the text devoted to a particular idea matches the importance of that idea.

I believe more in the scissors than I do in the pencil.
—*Truman Capote*

Check Accuracy and Completeness

Recheck all graphs, tables, and figures. If readers find even one error, they will often doubt everything else in the document. One workshop participant related that he had investigated a job-related injury and wrote his report of the accident to his superior. Top management decided to go to court to fight the lawsuit filed against the company for damages. But to the report writer's chagrin, the company's attorneys reversed the decision after reading his report.

Why? The investigator had stated that the accident took place on October 16 rather than October 15 (simply a typo, he assured me). Because of that one inaccuracy, his supervisors pointed out, the plaintiff would question every other detail of the investigation. His company settled out of court.

Is it really necessary to emphasize accuracy and precision to technical professionals? A story from a systems engineer should suffice as an answer: "When I first came to work for this company, I was asked to sit in on a meeting in which my boss was making a big presentation to his executive team. On about the fifth slide, one of the VPs in the group said, 'Back up. That figure doesn't agree with the one you had on the second slide.' My boss went back to the previous slide and found the discrepancy. The VP's comment was, 'Sit down. Everything you say from now on will be totally invalid for me.' I remember thinking at the time that he was awfully harsh and rude about that kind of mistake. But . . . I don't know. . . . I see his point, now that I'm a manager myself. I get so tired of seeing reports with errors—just carelessness and sloppiness. They really affect credibility."

Similar stories about technical inaccuracies surface frequently.

Consider another area for inaccuracy: Check the spelling of company names and individuals' names, and use correct titles. People get offended when you don't consider them important enough to verify correct spelling and titles.

Now for completeness: Would a case study or illustration (such as the two I just used) help? Novelists and playwrights make abstractions like greed and loyalty understandable by showing how these attitudes destroy or strengthen a particular family. Rather than quoting farm-price indexes, the President tells of a specific Iowa farmer's crop failures. Rather than merely giving cure rates for leukemia, the journalist interviews victims about their hopes for recovery.

Recently, a speaker at a civic luncheon group put things in perspective for "those in Washington who don't really know what one billion dollars is."

- One billion seconds ago, the first atomic bomb had not been exploded.
- One billion minutes ago, Christ was still on Earth.
- One billion hours ago, people were still living in caves.
- Yet one billion dollars ago, in terms of government spending, was yesterday.

Business writing as well as business speaking benefits by such illustrations; the bare facts do not always illuminate the whole story.

Be accurate, be complete, be sure.

> It is much easier to be critical than to be correct.
> —*Benjamin Disraeli*

Add Authority

What's involved? In a nutshell, avoid vague, unsupported generalizations. Identify subjective statements as such. Use numbers, statistics, and symbols with care, omit unnecessary auxiliaries or conditional words (*can, may, would, should, might*), and be as technically precise as necessary for your intended audience.

In 1944, former Texas congressman Maury Maverick coined the word *gobbledygook* to express his distaste for the pompous prose of bureaucrats. According to Maverick's way of thinking, such writing and double talk resembled the self-important gobbling sounds of the male turkey. Researcher Jack Z. Smith used this former tidbit of history in his *Fort Worth Star Telegram* article to add validity to his point about corporate babble. Yes, it took a little time to research that information, but his purpose was well served. The remainder of his column rang with authority because of that effort.

We should do no less when our mission is to sound authoritative.

Consider using quotations. Concerning authority, any time you can find an expert to underscore your conclusions, or can survey to substantiate majority opinion, or can research other sources to find documentation, you will have added weight to your arguments.

Use an exact quotation when: 1) the idea is not generally accepted; 2) the idea is original with a particular person; or 3) the thought is particularly well phrased. Quotes should be short and to the point; a four-line quote gets more attention than a twenty-line quote. Paraphrase the context and qualifications; use ellipses when necessary; then quote only the pithy statement.

> Stronger than an army is a quotation whose time has come.
> —*W. I. E. Gates*

Avoid vagueness; quantify when you can. Be precise and diligent in presenting the details and statistics necessary for your intended audience and for your purpose. Vagueness can lead to misunderstanding and may cast doubt on all your research.

Not: Several prior studies . . .
But: Three prior studies . . .

Not: A large number of well completions . . .
But: Almost 1,200 well completions . . .

Not: We spent several weeks investigating whether . . .
But: We spent 24 days investigating whether . . .

Not: A majority of our lab samples . . .
But: Eighty percent of our lab samples . . .

Not: The hotel is several blocks from the stadium.
But: The hotel is six blocks from the stadium.

Beware of unsupported generalizations. Have you overstated the case anywhere? Prefer understatement to overstatement. Overstatement begs readers to be skeptical. Consider this comment from a stranger: "I heard the funniest story yesterday—you won't believe it. You really won't." Your first thought usually is, "Oh, really?" And after he or she tells the story, there's always the letdown—the that-wasn't-so-funny feeling. Give readers the facts; let them tell you how impressed they are.

When you feel the need to make statements such as the following, beware of the tendency to write your "facts" rather than research them. Assume the skeptical thinking presented in the parentheses.

As leading experts have noted . . . (Who? Where?)

Few will doubt . . . (If that's true, why point it out?)

Few will argue with the fact that . . . (An attempt to keep me from arguing?)

Most users prefer . . . (What survey?)

The vast majority of engineers today . . . (Agree? You've got to be kidding.)

Several professors at major universities . . . (Your graduate adviser and who else?)

Interpret facts. Facts rarely speak for themselves. After stating a fact, answer the "so what?" about the fact so that readers arrive at the same destination as you have. Salespeople, particularly, know they can't assume readers will understand the reasons behind all the features of their product or service. So they must focus on benefits, turning their facts into reasons for buying. Any persuasive writer must do the same. Facts are not reasons. They may be the basis for reasons, but interpretation is the key to making them authoritative.

Identify subjective statements as such. When writers pile fact upon fact, readers may become lazy; they may accept unsupported, subjective statements along with the rest. Therefore, it's the writer's responsibility to warn readers when there could be other plausible interpretations of a finding or other conclusions drawn from test results.

Use direct statements to identify subjective, controversial comments rather than hedge words and phrases:

Although others may differ in their interpretations of these findings, I believe . . .

Although some may argue that . . . , I propose . . .

It is my opinion that . . .

I think . . .

In my estimation, the results show . . .

While there are other feasible alternatives, my work suggests that . . .

Use numbers, statistics, and symbols with care. If there's one common characteristic in most technical writing, it's a document chock-full of jargon, symbols, abbreviations, and numbers. If the subject is already a complex one, the numbers and symbols add to its complexity. Therefore, handle all numbers, statistics, and symbols with care.

Some of the most insidious misuses of "statistics" show up in television commercials. Unlike ad writers, technical professionals seldom purposefully mislead. But carelessness with statistics can confuse readers.

In the testing and procedural sections of a document, of course, you will give numbers that are appropriately precise because readers of these sections will need to know specifics. But when you summarize the major conclusions in an executive overview, be cautious about statistical overkill. Rounded numbers are easier to grasp quickly and to remember ("about 50 percent" rather than "51.1 percent").

Keep these additional guidelines in mind:

- Express decimal numbers using significant digits—and no more. (For example: We decreased print cost 26% last year [not 26.24%].)
- Always use the same basis for comparisons. (For example, compare all land measurements either in miles or acres or lots rather than switching back and forth.)
- Always specify the base in any expression of percentages. (For example: We surveyed 22% *of the managers* and of these managers 68% *of those based in Chicago* said . . .)
- Introduce acronyms and symbols before using them. (For example: Quality assurance [QA] is . . .)
- Define symbols unfamiliar to any of your readers.
- Follow grammatical rules to fit symbols substituting for words into a sentence.
- Center equations on separate lines in the text and keep all fractions and signs on the same level. (Exceptions, of course, include numerators, denominators, and exponents.)
- Express units of measurement by using words or standard symbols, not informal abbreviations.

How authoritative is your document? If you have to tell someone how authoritative it is, it isn't. Be definite, specific, concrete.

Get your facts first, and then you can distort them as
much as you please.
—*Mark Twain*

Eliminate Repetitious Details, but Retain First-Choice Words

Cut out details or paragraphs that say what you have already made obvious. Repetition can be a problem, particularly when you make "Procedures" a separate section from "Discussion." Repetition also becomes a problem with a lengthy introduction or summary. It's better to begin with the summary, the conclusions, and the recommendations, omitting an introduction altogether. Most necessary background information can be woven into appropriate parts of the body of the document.

Don't worry, however, about repetitious words. In school, you may have been given this advice: Instead of saying *evaluation* over and over, write *survey, opinion,* or *analysis.* The motive was to add variety and to build your vocabulary.

The holdover to that advice in business writing is something like the following:

> In order for all parties to have incentive to cancel these arrangements and enter new ones, subsequent contracts should qualify for the maximum lawful price. (Does *arrangements* mean *contracts* or other working arrangements?)

> Table I summarizes the production values at each site; the evaluation does not include the Malcolmson project. (Is Table I the same thing as the evaluation, or are they two different items?)

Avoid repetitious details, but stick to your first-choice words; repetition is always preferable to miscommunication.

Editing your own work is like removing your own tonsils—possible but painful.
—Anonymous

Paragraph by Idea and for Eye Appeal

Consider coherence. Does the paragraph flow logically? Are irrelevant details buried in the middle of an otherwise organized paragraph?

Consider length. Generally, a paragraph should complete the subject at hand. One idea, one paragraph. However, the paragraph must also have eye appeal; long paragraphs tire readers and make the material look too complex. On the other hand, short, choppy paragraphs cause readers to lose the thread of a discussion.

In general, continue a paragraph until you finish a thought; if, however, length becomes a problem, break the paragraph at a logical point. If you're giving five reasons why the new software is inadequate and the paragraph becomes too long, you can put three reasons in one paragraph, two in the following. Or if each reason will require a three- to four-sentence explanation, devote one paragraph to each reason.

There is no minimum or maximum paragraph length. Do unto your readers as you would have them do unto you.

Use Easy-to-Skim Lists Where Appropriate

Lists draw immediate attention to the ideas they present. Did you skim through this book before buying it? If so, your eyes probably were immediately drawn to the lists on the pages you skimmed. The list format is like a red flag, stating: "This is important, reader."

Therefore, use lists to do the following:

- Highlight major ideas in your reports, proposals, manuals, letters, or e-mail
- Break complex information into smaller, more manageable chunks
- Overview key information quickly
- Review key information quickly

On the other hand, the misuse of a list for unimportant information confuses readers. If they find minutiae too often in a list format, readers become distrustful of all your lists.

To number or bullet the list—that often becomes the pressing question. Bulleted items do not necessarily constitute an exhaustive listing and may represent separate ideas altogether. Numbered lists, however, are helpful for reference purposes, such as in a long contract or request for proposal, when you want to respond to specific clauses by corresponding numbers. Enumerated lists also convey a chronological sequence, such as a sequence of actions. Choose which you need deliberately.

But be careful not to overuse the list format. Sometimes writers fall into the habit of writing everything as a series of lists. When documents begin to look like an expansive grocery list, listing has become a nuisance rather than an aid for understanding the connection between points.

Add Informative Headings, Adequate Spacing, and Other Typographical Effects to Make Information Quickly Accessible

When you're writing long documents (more than half a page or screen), provide informative headings and subheadings so that readers can skip to the essentials. Headings allow readers to preview the entire document quickly to decide what they need to read immediately, then review the information for later reference.

Think newspaper headlines. In general, make your headings state your key points. Headings such as "Introduction," "Discussion," or "Justification" tell readers very little unless you add more specific subheadings underneath them. Prefer specific, informative headings, not vague, general ones. Examples: "Torque-Turn Test Results," "Schedule for Transferring Permanent Records," "Upward Sales Trends in Chicago," "National Meeting Scheduled for Third Quarter."

Finally, don't forget to leave adequate blank space between document sections. A crowded page or screen makes written material look too complex to read. But adequate space tempts the reader to wade into the water because it promises time to come up for breath before the next lap.

Blank space on screen or paper adds to the readability of what remains.

Additional formatting techniques such as bold printing, repetitive characters to produce a divider line, and italics also make information more accessible for skimming readers. Review Figures 28–30, paying particular attention to layout techniques such as these. Keep in mind, however, that if you're sending e-mail and the recipient's software doesn't support these formatting techniques, they produce gibberish on the screen. Blank space always works. Be sure that the message remains clear and the information easy to skim with those formatting techniques available to everyone. Finally, remember that any technique for emphasizing—whether listing, **boldfacing**, <u>underlining</u>, or *italicizing*—loses its effectiveness if overused.

Special Effects: Informative Headings, Listings, Graphics, Typographical Effects, Blank Space, Color

TRX proposes the following plan to finish repairing all the Type 4 sites on the Belco-Gilmer pipeline system. This plan will ensure that, at a minimum, **60 percent of the pipe wall is remaining.**

- **Dolphin Section:** Replace 9 sections (620 feet) of pipe where Type 4 internal corrosion exists.

  Proposed completion: ***Second quarter***

- **Little Williams Creek Bottom:** Add one block valve on either side of the Little Williams Creek bottom. This section of the pipeline has the lowest elevation of the entire system (150 feet compared to 450 feet).

  Proposed completion: ***Third quarter***

- **Mt. Montgomery and Grayson Stations:** Install scraper traps. This installation will allow monthly scrapers to be run in the remaining sections of the system, with fewer corrosion problems than any other section.

  Proposed completion: ***Fourth quarter***

Figure 28. Easy-to-Skim Layout. Special effects such as informative headings, boldface, italics, underlining, and adequate blank space guide readers to key points.

Intimidating, Once-Upon-a-Time Format

Ming:

For the last month, we have been gathering information pertaining to your question about how much time it takes a check to clear if drawn on Challenge Bank and deposited in one of the 12 cities most representative of your disbursement needs.

This information wasn't communicated earlier because of the hesitancy over how the new law might affect clearing times in the cities where business is conducted. A clear decision from the Federal Reserve was promised weeks ago but still has not been made, and given the difficulty in getting any direct communication from the Fed, we should feel fortunate that our own financial people knew about the impending legislation. Otherwise, we might have done the study and made far-reaching conclusions, and you might have had to revise your collection procedures again needlessly once the Fed made a ruling on the issue. The answer from the Fed should be here by Monday. On the whole, the volume of checks clearing through Dallas is quite insignificant.

In conducting the study, we discovered that a number of factors influence these clearing times. The best collection time seems to be 2 days in Nashville, and the most inefficient collection time seems to be 5 days in Seattle. We also found a few exceptions to these times in each city during the data-collection period, but these lapses were not uniform in all cities, which could be a problem if you intend to rely on this information for your final decision. However, a number of checks took up to 10 days to collect in a couple of cities. Our data show that the average collection time is 3 days in the 12 cities. I hope this answers your question completely.

Don

Figure 29. Unappealing Once-Upon-a-Time Format. Don't make your readers become sleuths to find answers and details. Readers are put off by long paragraphs of text without headings and other typographical reading aids.

The MADE Format™ in an Easy-to-Skim Layout

Ming:

For the last month we have been gathering information pertaining to the time it takes a check to clear if drawn on Challenge Bank and deposited in one of the 12 cities most representative of your disbursement needs. Our data show that the average collection time is **3 days in the 12 cities.**

Clearing Times Vary

In conducting the study, we encountered four factors that influence these clearing times:

- bank hours
- lock-box arrangements
- deposit procedures at the branches
- state regulations

The best collection time seems to be 2 days in Nashville, and the most inefficient collection time seems to be 5 days in Seattle. We also found a few exceptions to these times in each city during the data-collection period, but these lapses were not uniform in all cities. However, a number of checks, particularly those of more than $10,000, took up to 10 days to collect in New York and in Atlanta. On the whole, the volume of checks clearing through Dallas is quite insignificant—less than $1,000 each month.

Pending Federal Reserve Action

We have hesitated to communicate this information to you until we could get a clear decision from the Federal Reserve about how the new law will affect clearing times. The answer from the Fed should be here by Monday.

Don

Figure 30. The MADE Format™ in an Easy-to-Skim Layout. Even in short documents, provide easy access with informative headings, lists, boldface, and italics.

Clarity in layout equals clarity in content because the process
requires clarity of thought.
—J. Hartley

Design and Use Charts and Graphs Effectively

Finally, if you have not done so already in the planning or drafting steps, consider what ideas and data you should present graphically. Remember that a poorly designed visual is much worse than no visual at all.

The higher one looks in administrative levels of business,
the more one finds decisions are based on tabular or
graphic formats.
—Norbert Enrick

Know When and When Not to Use Charts and Graphs

Charts and graphs are both the message and the medium. Correctly used as a message, they displace text and explain ideas better than words themselves—simplifying, clarifying, and summarizing. On occasion, you may decide to use redundant text and graphics to reinforce difficult concepts or explain complex information. Charts and graphs highlight key points and create high-impact pictures that remain in the reader's memory. The goal is to use text and graphics together for an effective whole.

Many people "digest" a report simply by reading the abstract or executive summary and then by looking at the tables and figures. If readers can grasp the important ideas with such little effort, why shouldn't they? Why should they have to read tedious textual passages when they can understand the significant information with a quick glance at a graphic presentation? Visuals require much less conceptualizing time for readers.

An additional benefit of charts and graphs is that they make facts or statistics more explicit and memorable by showing relationships. They tell readers how to interpret the data—what the facts or numbers mean.

Consider the impact of graphics this way: How effective would advertisers be if they presented their new products by rolling paragraphs of text across the TV screen?

On the other hand, some writers approach the question of charts and graphs haphazardly and wind up adding far too many, simply because they find them easy to create with their favorite software package.

Use the following checklist to cull unnecessary graphics from your documents:

- Does the chart or graph emphasize trivial or irrelevant information?
- Can the information be included in another graphic without cluttering it?
- Does the information confuse rather than clarify?
- Has the information already been included simply and emphatically in the text?

Select Charts and Graphs Appropriate to the Concept

To be effective, each chart or graph should have one primary purpose; that purpose dictates the most appropriate design. Many writers, however, tend to select repeatedly the same graphical designs. Yet because there are so many ways to present data graphically, the challenge is to decide which is the most effective choice for which concept (see Figure 31). Choosing the wrong chart or graph to present your information is like wearing a tuxedo to McDonald's.

People, including managers, do not live by pie charts alone—
or by bar graphs or 3-inch statistical appendices to
300–page reports. People live, reason, and are moved by symbols
and stories.
—*Tom Peters*

Charts and Graphs Based on Concept

VISUAL	BEST ILLUSTRATES
bar or column chart	relative quantities
line graph	trends to be compared over a long period; to emphasize movement rather than amounts
circle graph	proportions of a whole
flowchart or time chart	a process through steps or stages
map	locations
line drawing	a simple phase of a process or an enlargement of physical detail
step chart	a procedure
diagram	how something looks or works
network	how events or persons are related
table	body of data
pictorial	comparison of units
organizational chart	relationships between positions
decision tree	steps involving actions or decisions
cluster	related ideas within a whole
matrix	comparisons
cartoon	abstract ideas
photo	how something looks

Figure 31. Charts or Graphs Based on Concept. Choose charts or graphs appropriate to your concept and purpose.

Let's look in detail at some of the most common charts and graphs.

Bar or Column Charts

A bar chart has horizontal bars (see Figure 32); a column chart has vertical bars (see Figure 33). Such charts best show data groupings and percentages. They also add impact to high/low comparisons. Data can be sequenced in a variety of ways: numerically, chronologically, geographically, qualitatively, or progressively. Data in vertical bars can be more easily compared than data in horizontal bars. Additionally, vertical columns also provide more room for labels. Prefer vertical columns to show change over time; prefer horizontal bars to compare items during a fixed time frame.

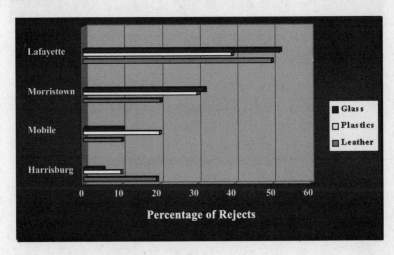

Figure 32. Horizontal Bar Chart. Such a chart allows quick understanding of multifaceted comparisons.

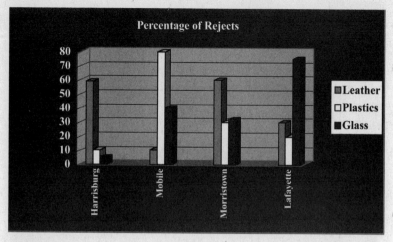

Figure 33. Vertical Column Chart. Such a chart emphasizes high/low comparisons.

Bar or column charts are meaningless, however, when the differences between quantities are small. Newspaper editors are fond of splitting the vertical scale on column charts (or the horizontal scale on bar charts). This split makes the absolute difference between quantities much more apparent. Technical writers should avoid this practice because it often creates a graphic that misrepresents relative differences, which, after all, is what you're trying to show with a bar or column chart. If you must use a split scale, make sure to point out that fact clearly on the graphic.

Line Graphs

A line graph (see Figure 34) emphasizes movement and change over time. Generally, the independent variable is shown on the horizontal axis, and the dependent variable is shown on the vertical axis. Line graphs quickly become cluttered when you try to convey too much information or present too much variation.

Line graphs are not often useful for presenting quantitative data, but they are unsurpassed for showing trends.

Line graphs intended to show the results of data measurement should usually show each data point so readers can draw conclusions about the precision of the relationship being shown. Line graphs showing trends need not show individual data points.

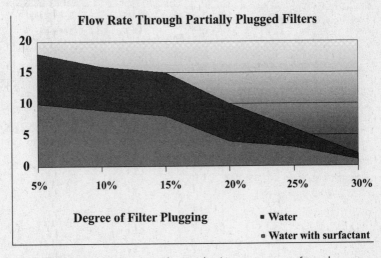

Figure 34. Line Graph. These graphs emphasize movement of trends more than actual amounts.

Circle Graphs

A circle graph (see Figure 35) conveys data quickly and makes abstract percentages immediately visual as parts of a whole. A circle graph has little value in showing a large number of small percentages. Such graphs can present only a limited amount of data, and no part of the information can be updated without restructuring the entire graph.

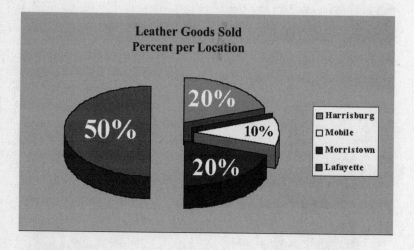

Figure 35. Pie Chart Circle Graph. Circle graphs best illustrate relationships of parts to a whole.

Flowcharts

Flowcharts (see Figure 36) illustrate specific procedures, activities, or events as they proceed through often overlapping stages. The primary emphasis is on the movement, the interaction, and the sequence between stages. Cause-and-effect relationships can be presented quite effectively here. Unlike the circle graph, the bar or column chart, and the line graph, the flowchart looks complex and requires more concentration and time from readers.

Procedure for Monthly ERP Entries

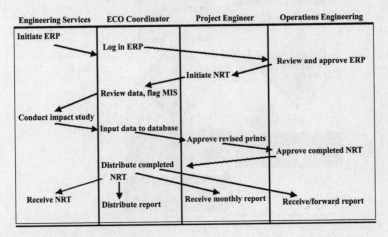

Figure 36. Procedure Flowchart. These flowcharts emphasize interaction and cause-and-effect relationships.

Logic flowcharts (see Figure 37), which can show events, decisions, and alternate paths, are extremely useful in planning. Their primary use is in organizing completed activities, not necessarily in presenting specific schedules. Such charts also help ensure that all important points are addressed.

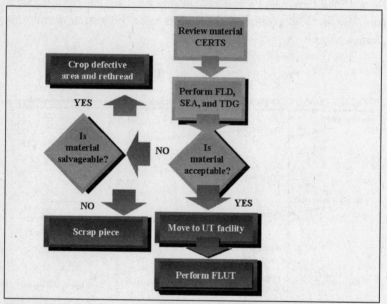

Figure 37. Logic Flowchart or Decision Tree. These flowcharts show not only sequential events, but also alternative paths that depend on the outcome of events. Rectangles indicate a process or activity, diamonds show where a decision must be made, and arrows indicate flow.

The Gantt flowchart (see Figure 38) was developed by Henry L. Gantt as a project-management tool to display effectively the schedules of complex interactive and sequential events. In a Gantt chart, one axis shows output and the other axis shows units of time.

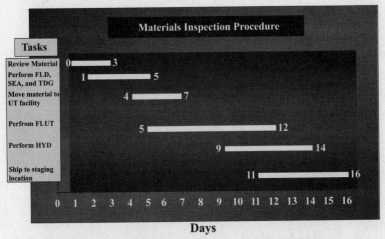

Figure 38. Gantt Flowchart. These flowcharts effectively show schedules as well as interactions.

Maps

Maps, of course, show location, but unless the preparer adds other effects (see Figure 39) to emphasize and highlight, readers may miss key points. Dots, symbols, pictures, shading, color, arrows, concentric circles, and spot blow-ups all add variety to maps and convey information easily and quickly.

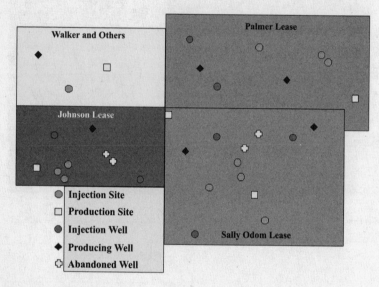

Figure 39. Map. Add variety to a map for quick grasp of data.

Drawings

Drawings may be more effective than photos to show the physical appearance or the inner workings of equipment or to illustrate a process (see Figure 40). You should not try to show everything in a drawing; instead, a drawing should be as simple as possible so it does not hide the key ideas you want to present. Informative labeling also helps readers grasp major ideas quickly.

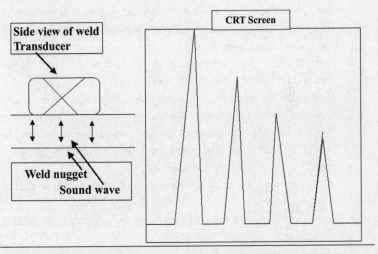

Figure 40. Line Drawing. Line drawings can be more effective than photos to illustrate simple processes or the inner workings of equipment.

Follow Graphic-Design Guidelines to Improve Clarity and Eye Appeal

The following guidelines will help you improve your charts and graphs within a document:

- Provide a reference in the text for every graph or chart.
- Place a visual that highlights new or significant information as close to its text reference as possible.
- Place a chart or graph containing reference data (that is, data of interest to only a few secondary readers) in an Appendix, where it is easily accessible but does not clutter the text.

- Group "lost" text passages (scattered text of only a few lines), placing multiple large visuals together at the end of a document or in a particular section.
- Arrange on a single page charts and graphs that are part of a series.
- Retain the standard margins of the text.
- Balance each visual on the page.
- Never place a chart or graphic so that it is upside down when the reader holds it in the normal reading position or when the "gutter" (white space separating two bound pages) is at the top. If the visual must be placed sideways, the reader should turn the page clockwise to see it.
- Set off each chart or graph from the text by adequate blank space, borders, or typeface changes, or with separate pages.
- Use color for emphasis, but limit colors to two or three in any specific document. Rather than simply adding color because new technology has made it possible, use color for a specific effect: to link equivalent points, to create a mood, to improve readability, to highlight key ideas.
- Give enough information within each chart or graph so that it can stand alone.
- Make wording on a visual consistent with the wording in the text reference.
- Number charts and graphs consecutively. Place them in the order in which they are referenced in the text.
- If possible, present no more than one concept in each visual.
- Give each chart or graph an informative title or caption that sums up the key idea. Many readers will read only the captions and then just skim the text. Explain in the caption what the visual illustrates (for example, not "Close-up of Fatigue Crack," but "Fatigue Crack at 1,000X shows transgranular propagation and planar shape").
- Label all axes and columns.
- Place labels in a straight and horizontal plane.
- Be accurate and precise in the use of scales of measurement and in the wording of labels.
- Place labels on or near graphics.

- Use common language on labels; try to avoid abbreviations and cryptic phrasing unless limited space mandates such shortcuts.
- Make labels and legends visually distinct from other chart text.
- Arrange headings so the major classifications for ultimate comparison will be in vertical columns, not horizontal rows.
- Use vertical lines for the strongest emphasis.
- Express fractions as decimals.
- Prefer standard symbols.
- Give the sources of all data that are not your own.
- Place legends, sources, or references within the body of the visual itself, unless doing so would make the visual too cluttered.

Always ask yourself: Can a chart or graph replace a thousand words? If so, use it. Visuals save reading time, simplify text, make abstract terms understandable, emphasize key points, summarize facts and trends, and present ideas creatively so that readers remember them.

In summary, to edit for content and layout, follow these guidelines: Throughout the document, focus on the information of major interest to your reader. Make sure the space devoted to each idea indicates the importance of that idea. Recheck all figures for accuracy. Clarify and add impact to your ideas with illustrations or examples when necessary. Add authority to your proposals or arguments with support from the experts and other research. Avoid repetitious details from section to section of a document, but retain your first-choice words. Paragraph by idea and for eye appeal. As a courtesy and "teaser" to your readers, use informative, correctly placed headings and lists, as well as plenty of white space. Design visuals effectively and use them judiciously.

People don't read today; they flip.
—*John Lyons*

14

EDIT FOR GRAMMAR

Grammar rules are not static; they reflect usage, changing as lifestyles change. A few strict grammarians still insist that *advise* cannot mean *inform*, as in "advise me of any change of plans." *Advise* traditionally has meant to give counsel or advice. But the above business usage has been so common that dictionaries now give *inform* as one meaning for *advise*. When grammar and common usage clash, common usage always wins over the course of time.

This acknowledgment of change is not meant to discount grammar rules. Appropriate grammar is a matter of both clarity and image. Business writers frequently smile at grammatical blunders in the work of colleagues and competitors and on this basis classify the authors, sometimes unjustly, about their expertise in other areas. But even more serious than creating an unfavorable personal or company image, grammatical errors muddy your message.

To refresh your memory of grammatical structure, review the basic sentence elements presented in this chapter. One more caveat: This section is not meant to be a comprehensive treatment of grammar and usage. Our focus will be limited to the most common errors and issues in business and technical writing.

With sixty staring me in the face, I have developed
inflammation of the sentence structure and a definite
hardening of the paragraphs.
—*James Thurber*

Identify the Major Elements of a Sentence

The major elements of a sentence are the subject, the verb, the object (direct or indirect), and the complement (subjective or objective).

The *complete subject* names to whom or what you are referring. This who or what is usually a *noun* or a *pronoun* plus the additional words that describe or limit its meaning. The *simple subject* is the person, place, thing, or idea without the descriptive or limiting words. Examine the following examples, in which the simple subject is *boldfaced:*

The **employee** hired last	will make the trip.
Los Angeles and the **surrounding areas**	offer the most attractive clientele for our purposes.
The company-owned **equipment**	has been depreciated at an annual rate of 10 percent.
Cost-center **budgeting**	is the process of identifying individual managers with their performance.

The *complete predicate* tells something about the subject. The major word in the predicate is the *verb*. This verb tells what the subject does, has, or is. For example:

Ivan Blosnik	*signs all the contracts.*
The client	*infuriated our webmaster.*
That hotel	*looks old and dilapidated.*
Our lab technicians	*participated in the investigation with renewed determination.*
The first construction project	*consisted of three 80-ft x 750-ft piers.*
The major recommendations	*include the interconnection of technologies through telecommunications.*

A sentence may be complete with only a subject and a verb:

Activities slowed.

Jennifer disapproves.

Temperatures stabilize.

Trade shows will disappear.

Bids have been submitted.

Winners were selected.

The problem with verbs is that they are often confused with verbals (infinitives, gerunds, and participles).

An *infinitive* is the word *to* plus a verb, serving as a noun, adjective, or adverb in the sentence. For example:

To complete these tables is a waste of time. (noun) (*Is* is the verb of the sentence.)

The tables *to show* income have been altered. (adjective) (*Have been altered* is the verb of the sentence.)

He altered the facts *to prove* the experiment a success. (adverb) (*Altered* is the verb of the sentence.)

A *gerund* is a verb plus *-ing,* serving as a noun in the sentence. For example:

Drilling is going slowly. (noun, subject)

Brown hates *compiling* these quarterly reports. (noun, direct object)

A *participle* is a verb plus *-ing* or *-ed,* serving as an adjective in the sentence. For example:

These graphs *illustrating* our project are being questioned by the programmers. (adjective, modifying *graphs*)

This *completed* audit has been challenged by all parties who have an interest in the override. (adjective, modifying *audit*)

Finishing the two-week project early, James Duncan rescheduled that new assignment for mid-June. (adjective, modifying *James Duncan*)

Never confuse a verb with one of the previous verbals, or you may write a fragment rather than a complete sentence.

The *direct object* receives the action of the verb or shows the result of the action. For example:

> Jim shipped the *box*.
>
> They reduced construction *time* by pile-driving.
>
> He placed the *cage* outside the longitudinal holes.
>
> Technicians assembled the *equipment* in functional order despite the previously discussed layout.

Notice that the direct object always answers *what?* about the verb. Jim shipped *what?* They reduced *what?* He placed *what?* Technicians assembled *what?*

The *indirect object* names the receiver of the direct object. The indirect object is used with verbs of asking, giving, or telling. (In the following examples, the *indirect objects* precede the *direct objects*):

> My assistant brought *me* the accumulated balances as of March 31.
>
> We sent *their representative* an ultimatum and are waiting for their response.
>
> Send *me* the shipping instructions to return the material as soon as possible.

The *subject complement* follows a linking verb and tells something about the subject of the sentence. Linking verbs are verbs incomplete in themselves—(*is, are, were, been, appear, become, seem, look,* and so forth). You can never say "My client seems" and express a complete thought as you can with a complete verb, such as "My client approves." For example:

> Their manager becomes *disgruntled* with every mention of the promotional rally scheduled for next summer.
>
> These policies seem more *outrageous* with each revision.
>
> The basic consideration of that budget is the detailed expense *classification*.

The *objective complement* tells about the direct object of the sentence. For example:

He considered the project a *waste* of time because of a lack of financial commitment to the follow-up activities.

The preliminary draft kept the boss *preoccupied.*

Mr. Weymeyer proved the precautionary measures *unnecessary* because the temperatures decreased without artificial stimulus.

These four elements—subject, verb, objects, complements—form the skeleton of all sentences in the English language. You may or may not have objects or complements, but you must have a subject and a verb to express a complete thought.

Identify the Secondary Elements of a Sentence

Adjectives and adverbs, two secondary elements of a sentence, represent the flesh around the bones.

An **adjective** modifies (describes, points out, numbers, or limits) a noun or a pronoun. For example:

Those slim black cell phones remain *our* most *popular* model.

Spiral reinforcement will be *the same quality* steel.

All qualified employees should report to *this first* meeting.

This lengthy procedure has been detailed once again for *obvious safety* reasons.

An **adverb** modifies (describes or limits) a verb, an adjective, another adverb, or the sentence as a whole. An adverb tells *when, where, why, how,* or *to what extent* something was done. For example:

Frank Broughton rechecked each graph *extensively before* forwarding it to the Editorial Department.

Our engineers *blatantly* refused to take on the project, insisting that the reassigned funds would be a problem.

The *much*-publicized policy has eliminated tardiness.

Candidly, I cannot fulfill the obligations within his time frame.

Word carpentry is like any other kind of carpentry—you must join your sentences smoothly.
—*Anatole France*

Isolate Clauses and Understand Sentence Patterns

English sentences usually follow four basic patterns. The building blocks of these sentence patterns are clauses.

An *independent clause* contains a subject and a predicate and expresses a complete thought. For example:

> We have paid drilling advances to all producers in the South Padre Island area.

> Juan Gonzales attended the trade show last week.

> The software glitches caused problems all day long.

A *dependent clause* contains a subject and a predicate but does not express a complete thought. It depends on the main (independent) clause to complete its meaning. For example:

> *Although the samples were contaminated,* he recorded all the results.

> *If I knew the answer,* I would suggest a resolution.

> Jill decided to fire Cary *while he was traveling abroad.*

> The documentation needs to be rewritten *because it will also serve as an addendum to the contract.*

A clause can serve as either a major or a secondary sentence element. For example:

> *Whoever wants the project of coordinating the collection efforts* may volunteer. (The italicized dependent clause serves as the subject of the independent clause.)

> Please tell his assistant *that he will not be in today.* (The italicized dependent clause serves as the direct object of the independent clause.)

> Tell anyone *who enters the warehouse* about the contamination. (The italicized dependent clause serves as an adjective limiting the meaning of *anyone* in the independent clause.)

Sentences are composed of clauses. Sentences with one clause are *simple.* Sentences with more than one clause are categorized as *compound, complex,* or *compound-complex.*

Simple sentences. Simple sentences contain only one independent clause. Simple sentences are usually direct and easy to read.

Simple (one clause):

His manager retired in June.

The water keeps rising in the low areas.

Tseuko Fong rechecked and relabeled all the bar graphs from each survey.

The hotels in our city improved their services after the tax increase back in the spring.

We estimated the radial position of the waterfront by planimetering the contact area.

The unadorned declarative sentence is one of man's noblest architectural achievements. But it is one of the rarest.
—*George Ball*

Compound sentences. These sentences have two or more independent clauses. They divide the readers' attention and force consideration of two or more ideas at once. Readers, therefore, must slow their pace to concentrate on both.

Compound (two or more independent clauses):

Anita signed the checks, and then she left for vacation.

The Universal reps seemed confused; they had not read the e-mail sent earlier.

Ivana Hyde thinks the decision is inconsistent with company policy, and she wants to calculate retroactively the interest on all such payments.

We estimated the radial position of the waterfront by planimetering the contact area; however, the accuracy of this determination depends on the model grid.

Complex sentences. These sentences have one independent clause and one or more dependent clauses. This structure adds peaks and valleys. Listen to the writer raise and lower her voice throughout the following examples. Complex sentences add variety to writing and help emphasize the most important ideas.

Complex (one independent clause; at least one dependent clause):

If you fly home early, we can leave Wednesday.

I don't understand why Melanie Peabody resigned.

We can offer a discount if you buy 1000 boxes.

Because McWayte had mentioned the mistakes earlier, he rechecked and relabeled all the bar graphs from each survey.

Although the slumping problem manifests itself most visibly in the enhanced gas recovery (EGR) predictions, it is also present in the primary depletion case.

Compound-complex sentences. The compound-complex sentence pattern has at least two independent clauses and at least one dependent clause. Compound-complex sentences really slow the reading pace. Readers have to follow the peaks and valleys, while also concentrating on two equally important ideas. Many compound-complex sentences are too long for fast, easy comprehension.

Compound-complex (two or more independent clauses; at least one dependent clause)

If you have time, let me know which color you like best, and I'll order that chair.

Fred Turpin included the applicable interest, and then he modified the conflicting policy, which seemed outdated.

You can tell the homeowner that it's too late to accept the offer because the date on the contract has expired.

Because the optimal timing for ending water production will be very sensitive to aquifer description, the best opportunity will appear late in the project life; therefore, we should revise our timing estimate after we have evaluated aquifer response to water production.

The last few pages have summarized the fundamentals of English grammar. (For additional help with the basic rules and terms of English grammar, see Appendix A: Grammar Glossary pp. 363–68.)

After more than twenty years of reading corporate documents, we've noticed a definite pattern of confusion and mistakes. The next section focuses on the most common grammatical errors and questions from participants in our writing workshops.

Keep Related Words Together

Place descriptive or qualifying words, phrases, and clauses as close to the words they describe as possible. Misplaced words, phrases, and clauses obscure meaning. The most frequently misplaced words in business or technical writing are the adverbs *almost, only, nearly, just,* and *even.* Such words inserted incorrectly can completely change sentence meaning. Notice the difference in meaning in the following sentences when the word *only,* a particularly troublesome adverb, is moved around:

Only the operator altered the table in his report about the company's inefficiency.

The operator *only* altered the table in his report about the company's inefficiency.

The operator altered *only* the table in his report about the company's inefficiency.

The operator altered the table *only* in his report about the company's inefficiency.

The operator altered the table in his report about the company's *only* inefficiency.

The adverb *just* also has the power to alter your sentence meaning by limiting what follows it:

Just Joseph Holland has the authority to revise the specifications for the couplings. (No one else has the authority.)

Joseph Holland *just* has the authority to revise the specifications on the couplings. (He has authority only, not any ability or expertise in design.)

Joseph Holland has the authority *just* to revise the specifications on the couplings. (He has authority only to revise.)

Joseph Holland has authority to revise *just* the specifications on the couplings. (He can revise the specifications only; he cannot revise anything else, such as a brochure, pertaining to the couplings.)

Joseph Holland has authority to revise the specifications on *just* the couplings. (He cannot revise specifications on items other than the couplings.)

Almost can cause the same problems:

Almost all manufacturers' protectors were able to meet our test criteria in all these areas.

All manufacturers' protectors were *almost* able to meet our test criteria in all these areas.

All manufacturers' protectors were able to meet our test criteria in *almost* all these areas.

Misplaced clauses also create havoc with sentence meaning:

The aluminum housings have been favorably compared with stainless-steel inserts, *which experience abrasive wear at the entrances and exits.* (The inserts experience the wear.)

The aluminum housings, *which experience abrasive wear at the entrances and exits,* have been favorably compared with stainless-steel inserts. (The aluminum housings experience the wear.)

The poron cellular urethane, *which must be specified in the client proposal,* warrants further consideration as the preferred product. (Poron cellular urethane must be specified in the proposal.)

The poron cellular urethane warrants further consideration as the preferred product, *which must be specified in the client proposal.* (Whatever product we prefer must be specified in the proposal.)

In the previous examples, all meanings may be logical in a given situation. So it's up to the writer to make sure the writing accurately conveys the meaning.

Confusing: There are discrepancies in some of the data which we are trying to recheck. (Are they rechecking the discrepancies or all the data?)

Clear: There are discrepancies, which we are trying to recheck, in some of the data.

Confusing: Is there nonproprietary documentary information that would help distinguish these samples from possible future ones that we could have? (Is the writer asking to be sent information? Or is he asking if there is information available to help them distinguish these samples from future samples they may uncover? If he doesn't get the information, he shouldn't be surprised!)

Clear: Is there any nonproprietary documentary information that we could have to help distinguish these samples from future ones?

Confusing: Packing for the upper and lower stems on all valves must be installed with a special fixture witnessed by Arabomo, Inc.

Clear: Arabomo, Inc., must witness the installation of packing for the upper and lower stems on all valves. This installation requires a special fixture.

Even if an idea is clear, keep the subject and verb of a sentence together when possible. Interposing a phrase or clause inappropriately between the subject and verb interrupts the smooth flow of the main idea.

Interrupted: Most of the engineers in our building, if you consider the supervisors in this group also, have special payroll deductions for their dues to professional organizations.

Smooth: If you consider supervisors also, most of the engineers in our building have special payroll deductions for their dues to professional organizations.

Interrupted: Van pools, if they're well-organized, can save employees money.

Smooth: Van pools can save employees money if they're well organized.

A modifying word, phrase, or clause naturally seems "attached" to the closest noun or pronoun; make sure that this close noun or pronoun is the one you intend to describe. Then create a smooth-flowing sentence.

Don't Dangle Verbals

A participial verbal phrase serves as an adjective and tells more about a noun or a pronoun. An introductory participial phrase usually attaches to the first noun that follows in the main clause. For example:

Incorrect: As instructed in our phone conversation on March 21, his order was increased to 400 pocket binders. (This sentence says that *his order* was instructed on the phone.)

Passive voice is the culprit most of the time; it brings a host of problems (as you'll see before you finish the editing step). Passive voice means that the subject of the sentence *receives* the action of the verb. With an active-voice sentence, the subject *does* the action of the verb:

Active: Management rejected our plan.
Passive: Our plan was rejected by management.

Active: All parties signed the contracts.
Passive: The contracts were signed by all parties.

You can correct dangling-verbal errors on most occasions by an active-voice construction:

Incorrect: As instructed in our phone conversation March 21, his order was increased to 400 pocket binders.
Correct: As instructed in our phone conversation March 21, we have increased his order to 400 pocket binders.

Incorrect: Having secured all windows and doors, the storage facility was vacated for the night. (The storage facility secured its own windows and doors?)
Correct: Having secured all windows and doors, the workers vacated the storage facility for the night. (The workers secured the windows and doors.)
Correct: The storage facility, with all windows and doors secured, was vacated for the night.

You can also correct danglers by rewording the sentence to eliminate the verbal (notice the previous corrected sentence):

Incorrect: Assuming the previous values then, the revised cooling rate is given in Table 8. (The revised cooling rate assumed the previous values?)

Correct: Assuming the previous values then, we have revised the cooling rate as given in Table 8.

Correct: The revised cooling rate based on these assumed previous values is given in Table 8.

Don't be confused when the same error occurs at the end of the sentence:

Incorrect: Security is inefficient when deliveries are made leaving doors open for long periods of time. (Deliveries leave doors open?)

Correct: Security is inefficient when delivery people leave doors open for long periods of time.

Although most readers will understand your meaning when you have a dangling verbal, the error may embarrass you, as in this example: "Dangling free over the hole, the work crew attached the wire rope to the drum." (The work crew dangled free? Probably not.)

Consider the following sentences as a final review of the dangling verbal:

Incorrect: While gathering information for my résumé, the position was filled. (The position was gathering the information?)

Correct: While gathering information for my résumé, I discovered that the position had been filled.

Correct: While I was gathering information for my résumé, the company filled the position.

Incorrect: Being injected directly into the veins, the doctor monitored the patient around the clock. (The doctor was injected into the veins?)

Incorrect: Being injected directly into the veins, the doctor monitored the effects of the medicine. (The doctor was injected into the veins again?)

Correct: Monitoring the patient around the clock, the doctor injected the medicine into the veins.

Correct: Being injected directly into the veins, the medicine caused an immediate reaction.

Just remember that a verbal needs to link to (describe) a specific word in the sentence, the closest noun or pronoun to the verbal phrase. The meaning or link can't simply be implied.

Avoid Unintentional Fragments and Run-On Sentences

Fragments are word groups rather than complete sentences. Usually, these word groups are fragments because they contain no verb for the subject in the main clause. For example:

Fragment: The policies which have proven inadequate in the past and have even infuriated some employees. (*Have proven* and *have infuriated* are verbs of the dependent *which* clause. *Policies* has no verb.)

Fragment: Although there is no clear authority for any of these procedures outlined in the manual. (The subordinate conjunction *although* introduces a dependent clause. This dependent clause cannot stand alone as a complete sentence. If *although* means *on the other hand*, the writer must separate it from the rest of the clause with a comma.)

To correct these fragments, either add a verb or connect a dependent clause or phrase to an independent clause. For example:

Fragment: The lease should be maintained. Although there is no clear Texas authority for doing so.

Revised: The lease should be maintained, although there is no clear Texas authority for doing so.

Fragment: We do not think it would be economical to consider a used spectrometer. Because the cost is not much less than for a new one.

Revised: We do not think it would be economical to consider a used spectrometer because the cost is not much less than for a new one.

On the other hand, two independent sentences that run together can be equally confusing.

Run-on: André wrote that he was aware of the situation it has been a problem for several months. (To correct, add a semicolon or period before *it*.)

Run-on: Elian has authority to sign the form however he's out of the country for six weeks. (To correct, add a semicolon or period before *however*.)

Writers particularly tend "to write as they talk" in their e-mail. The benefits of an informal "talking" style include a conversational tone and word choice. But the negatives show up in rambling prose. Instead of using periods, writers often fall into a confusing habit of linking rambling thoughts with *which*:

> I e-mailed my broker about the problem with the duplicate entries on my IRA account, which he said was fairly common when you make two years' contribution with the same check, which I did this January, including a contribution for the previous year along with the contribution for the current year, which is, of course, expedient for my purposes but not for the broker. They've made several errors recently, which is why I had to resend the last paycheck deposit twice, which is becoming a problem for our own Payroll Department, which is responsible for stopping payment on checks and reissuing them when there's a problem, which is what I had to ask them to do this past payroll period.

Speakers often punctuate with *which* and a breath. Writers should not.

Use Parallel Structure

Parallelism refers to like structure of words, phrases, or clauses within a sentence or list. Unparallel parts of a sentence can lead to confusion. For example:

Unparallel: One of the benefits of the call-forwarding system is that the initiator has complete control of when it can be done, to whom it can be forwarded, and for any length of time.

Parallel: One of the benefits of the call-forwarding system is that the initiator has complete control *of when, to whom,* and *for what time* the forwarding can be done. (The three equal ideas are equal in construction—three prepositional phrases.)

Unparallel: When I phoned McConnel, he asked me to review those calculations, to select 15 VPL contracts for his review, the purchase agreements with OSD, and to verify the volumes and prices. (What about the purchase agreements with OSD? Are they to be reviewed by the writer or selected for McConnel's review?)

Parallel: When I phoned McConnel, he asked me to review those calculations, to select 15 VPL contracts for his review, *to discuss* the purchase agreements with OSD, and to verify the volumes and prices.

Any parallel form (all adjective phrases, all clauses, all infinitives, or such) will work as long as equal ideas are given equal weight in the sentence:

Unparallel: Technologists with good experience and knowledgeable . . .
Parallel: Technologists with good experience and knowledge . . .
Parallel: Technologists who have experience and knowledge . . .
Parallel: Experienced and knowledgeable technologists . . .

Even lists sound better when parallel. Note the difference in the following two examples:

Unparallel (Some items begin with the noun phrases; others don't.):

   Fuel-air ratio out-of-balance
   Insufficient pin and bushing lubrication
   Lubrication of cylinder insufficient
   BTU's too high
   Maintenance procedures not followed
   Ignition malfunction
   Peak balance was improper

Parallel (The descriptor comes first, then the noun or noun phrase.):

   Out-of-balance fuel-air ratio
   Insufficient pin and bushing lubrication

Insufficient cylinder lubrication
High BTU's
Improper maintenance procedures
Malfunctioning ignition
Improper peak balance

Unparallel sentences and lists grate on the ear, make skimming diffi-cult, and they often obscure the meaning and slow the reader's pace.

Make Pronouns Agree with Their Antecedents and Functions

Pronouns must agree in number with the nouns they replace: A plural pronoun (*they*) must refer to a plural noun (such as *chairs*). A singular pronoun (*it*) must refer to a singular noun (such as *chair*). An agreement error, usually a careless one by a writer who knows better, also leads to clarity problems. For example:

Unclear:	These tools arrived with the later order. Therefore, we were unable to use it to perform those tests. (He couldn't use the tools or the entire order? If you were working in the Shipping Department, what would you return to the sender for a refund?)
Revised:	These *tools* arrived with the later order. Therefore, we were unable to use *them* to perform those tests.
Unclear:	Each supervisor should inform his employees of the new procedures. They should also develop a checklist for monitoring the equipment. (Who should develop the checklist? *They* in the second sentence may refer to *employees*, but the word *also* in the second sentence suggests that the writer is still talking to each supervisor.)
Revised:	*Supervisors* should inform their employees of the new procedures. The *supervisors* should also develop a checklist for monitoring the equipment.

A couple of decades ago, writers rarely made this pronoun mistake; they simply wrote *he* whenever they needed a singular pronoun because they feared someone slapping them on the wrist for writing "*everyone* should tell *their* own story." The problem: The English language does not have a singular pronoun that refers to both genders. Today, most people consider such writing that refers only to the male gender exclusive, particularly when writing procedures or job announcements.

Confusing: The authorized person approving the entry is indicating that they have knowledge of the corresponding data. (Who does *they* refer to—the authorized person or some other group such as the department employees?)

Therefore, select one of the following ways to include both genders, while being grammatically correct and clear.

- Replace the pronoun with *a*, *an*, or *the*—or omit the pronoun altogether.

    An authorized person approving the entry is indicating general knowledge of the corresponding data.

- Use plural nouns and pronouns.

    Authorized *persons* approving the entry are indicating that *they* have knowledge of the corresponding data.

- Use second-person pronouns.

    When *you* authorize the entry, *you* are acknowledging general knowledge of the corresponding data.

- Use noun substitutes.

    The authorized *person* approving the entry is indicating that *the reviewer* has knowledge of the corresponding data.

- Use *he or she* or *he/she* or alternate between the two genders, if doing so will not confuse readers. (Use this last alternative only when the other alternatives do not work well in your situation.)

    The authorized *person* approving the entry is indicating that *he/she* has knowledge of the corresponding data.

Some of these ways work better than others in various sentences. Whichever you choose, let clarity rule.

A second consideration in proper pronoun usage is that pronouns have "case." That is, different kinds of pronouns serve in different ways in a sentence. You remember that sentence elements include subjects, verbs, direct objects, complements, and so forth. Therefore, for pronouns to match their function appropriately means that only objective pronouns can serve as objects—objects of prepositions, direct objects, indirect objects. And only nominative (subject) pronouns can serve as subjects of a sentence or clause. To sum up, the pronoun "case" has to be appropriate to how the pronoun functions in a sentence.

Pronouns that serve as subjects:

I you he she it we they who whoever

Pronouns that serve as objects:

me you him her it us them whom whomever

Incorrect:	Just between you and I, the project is doomed.
Correct:	Just between you and me, the project is doomed. (*Me* serves as the object of the preposition *between*. An objective pronoun always replaces an object.)

Incorrect:	Harry, Susan, and me were all aware of the problem. (*Me* can't serve as a subject.)
Incorrect:	Harry, Susan, and myself were all aware of the problem. (*Myself* can't serve as a subject.)
Correct:	Harry, Susan, and I were all aware of the problem.

Incorrect:	He told the managers and I the good news. (*I* can't serve as a direct object.)
Incorrect:	He told the managers and myself the good news. (*Myself* can't serve as a direct object.)
Correct:	He told the managers and me the good news.

Here's a tip to help you select the correct pronoun. Read the sentence, leaving out the other people's names; your ear will help you choose correctly. Possessive and reflexive pronouns complete the list of pronoun "cases," but we'll leave those for a basic grammar book.

> When *whom* is correct, use some other formulation.
> —*William Safire*

Make Verbs Agree with Their Subjects

A singular subject calls for a singular verb; a plural subject calls for a plural verb. Remember that to make most *nouns* plural, you add an *s*. But to make most *verbs* plural, you remove the s. For example:

The experiment proves our theory.
The experiments prove our theory.

In short, with simple sentences you can usually depend on your ear for typical subject-verb agreement rules. However, long sentences with complicated structure may cause problems. Study the following 12 sentences and select the appropriate word. Then refer to the section of correct answers and explanations that follow the sentences.

Sentences

1. The group of employees that recently became eligible for these benefits (have, has) steadily grown in the past two months.
2. Also helpful in this analysis and related to the study of adjacent support (is, are) cases involving underground water rights.
3. Management (meet, meets) on Friday to exchange data.
4. Neither Wayne Brown nor his two associates (have, has) given us the go-ahead for the project.
5. None of the tools used for the job (was, were) accurately serviced before the workers began.
6. Data (show, shows) that the project is doomed from the beginning.
7. One-third of the samples (has, have) been sprayed.
8. A person who is liable under the rule stated in Subsection G is also liable for harm to artificial additions that (result, results) from each subsidence.
9. This is one of the accounts that (is, are) frequently paid late.

10. Bad weather, together with faulty tools, (complicates, complicate) the analysis and sample-taking.
11. The trial balance (is, are) the debits and credits.
12. Ten dollars (is, are) too much to pay for that item.

Answers and Explanations

1. *(has) Group* is the subject. Don't be confused by words, phrases, or clauses coming between the subject and the verb of the main clause.
2. *(are)* Watch out for inverted sentence order. Writers of English sentences most often use the subject-verb-object construction, but don't be confused with a less frequent construction.
3. *(meets)* In business usage, collective nouns take singular verbs.
4. *(have)* When you have the conjunctions *either-or/neither-nor*, treat them as separate units and make the verb agree with the closest subject. If the subject of both units is singular, use a singular verb: "Neither Pierre Trudeau nor Beth Smith has transferred out of the office." If, however, one of the units happens to be plural (as in sentence 4), place the plural unit last and make the verb plural.
5. *(were) None* is an indefinite pronoun; that means it can be either singular or plural. Some writers incorrectly insist that *none* is a contraction for *not one; none* can, however, have either of two meanings: *not one* or *not any*. Make your choice according to the pronoun's referent. In this case, none refers to *tools*. But you would write: "None of the nitrogen *is* missing." "All" and "some" follow the same rule. You would write: "Some of the cake *is* missing," but "Some of the coins *are* missing." Speaking of a painted wall, you might write: "All of it has been scratched"; but speaking of people, you would write: "All of them are leaving tomorrow."
6. *(show, shows)* Either is correct, depending on meaning. Actually, *datum* is the Latin singular, but common usage states that *data* can be either singular or plural. *Data show* means that you are referring to more than one piece of information. *Data shows* means that you are referring either to one piece of information or to the body of information as a single unit.
7. *(have)* With fractions, the context gives meaning. When referring to the samples individually (as in this case), use the plural. But when referring to the samples as a collective unit, use the singular: "One-

third of the shipment goes to Baltimore, and one-third stays here."

8. *(results)* You must decide on the referent for *that—harm* or *additions*. In this case, *that* probably refers to *harm*, because the sentence talks of liability for damage. But a reader could build a strong argument for *additions* as the antecedent for *that*. Again, grammar and clarity go hand in hand. Only the verb choice tells the reader your meaning.

9. *(are)* With *one of those who . . .* and *one of those that . . .* constructions, focus on the sentence in two halves: The first half focuses on the singular individual or thing; the second half focuses on the group or class of people or things. Make the second verb plural because the second pronoun refers to the plural noun naming the class or group.

10. *(complicates) Together with faulty tools* is a parenthetical element—like an appositive. Don't be misled by asides and additional explanatory material. Locate the real subject—in this case, *bad weather.*

11. *(is)* Always make the verb agree with the subject of the sentence, regardless of whether the subject complement is singular or plural. Many such sentences read better if reworded: "The trial balance is the total of the debits and credits."

12. *(is)* When referring to an amount of money (or any total) as a collective sum or unit, use the singular. When referring to individual pieces of money, use the plural.

When determining subject-verb agreement, keep one overriding caution in mind: Many people write by ear—that is, they do not consciously ponder verb choice. The danger of error is most prevalent in sentences containing *that* or *which* clauses, because your ear will make the verb after *that* or *which* agree with the noun immediately preceding it. And that noun may or may not be the correct reference. In addition to being aware of dangerous *that* or *which* clauses, note the differences in meanings determined by verb choice in sentences such as 5 and 6.

Your verb choice may be the reader's only clue to your meaning.

Be Consistent with Tenses and Moods

Switching tenses and moods, like making an error in subject-verb agreement, is rather common. But unnecessary switches mislead readers. For example:

Unclear:	The term "use" is *defined* broadly and *would include* sales, processing, and manufacturing. (Fact or opinion?)

Let's say the writer of the previous sentence is explaining to his supervisor the contents of Document A. Is the term "use" only broadly defined in the document, and is the writer adding his own opinion that "use" includes sales, processing, and manufacturing? Or does Document A specifically mention that "use" refers to sales, processing, and manufacturing? When writers slip into the subjunctive mood (*would*), their comments sound like opinion rather than fact.

Clear:	The term "use" is defined broadly to include sales, processing, and manufacturing.

Be careful about switching to the conditional mood carelessly. Take a moment to refresh your memory about verb tenses:

Present:	We *analyze* the samples each day.
Past:	We *analyzed* the samples yesterday.
Future:	We *will analyze* the samples tomorrow.
Present perfect:	We *have analyzed* the samples each day this week.
Past perfect:	We *had analyzed* the samples before he called last week.
Future perfect:	We *will have analyzed* the samples before he calls tomorrow.

Indicative-mood verbs make declarative statements of fact or ask questions:

We *analyze* each sample.
Did Marianne *analyze* the samples?

Subjunctive-mood verbs state ideas or events that are contrary to fact, are conditional, or express strong wishes:

We *would analyze* the samples if we had the right chemicals.
The managing partners *would give* you a raise if they had the budget.

Imperative-mood verbs give commands:

Analyze the samples.
Forget the raise.

Be particularly careful about changing tenses unnecessarily when you are writing procedures or reporting on your work. For example:

The gas *was analyzed* by injecting water and withdrawing gas with a calibrated syringe. A carrier gas *transports* the sample through the column, which *separates* the gas components before they *reach* the detector.

Has the gas mentioned in the first sentence been analyzed at a time prior to the present procedure in the second sentence? The tense mix suggests that. Or perhaps the second sentence represents a pause in the procedure and is merely an explanation of what is happening at this point in the process. Unnecessary tense changes confuse readers.

Clearer:	The gas *is* analyzed . . .
Clearer:	A carrier gas transported the sample through the column, which separated the gas components before they reached the detector.

Of course, some tense changes are necessary. If you are referring to two different time frames, then by all means, change tenses to reflect the appropriate time.

Our company *initiated* the process in the 1990s; each employee *has* since *reaped* the benefits. We *will continue* to see benefits well into the future.

Here is another passage illustrating the proper use of present and past tenses in the same document, separating existing conditions from experimental work. Notice the clarity of a complicated report. The verbs distinguish correctly between past work and current reports.

The Chemstrip bG Test Strips *were tested* by the procedure listed on the container label. Results *were determined* by a comparison of the reacted and wiped strip to the color chart on the container label. The results *were selected* from a list of interpolation levels composed of the color-block levels and three equally spaced levels in between the color-block levels. The results of this study *are described* in three figures. Figure 12 *presents* a comparison of the two testing products. . . .

Don't be lax about tense and mood changes.

Avoid Commonly Misused Words

Study the meanings of the frequently misused words and phrases shown in Figure 41. Edit such errors from your work.

"When I use a word," said Humpty Dumpty, "it means just what I choose it to mean, neither more nor less."
—*Lewis Carroll*

Commonly Misused Words and Phrases	
accept	(verb—to receive)
except	(preposition—not including)
adapt	(to adjust)
adept	(proficient)
adopt	(to choose)
addition	(something added)
edition	(particular version of a publication)
adverse	(unfavorable)
averse	(to be opposed to)
advice	(noun—counsel)
advise	(verb—to give counsel)
affect	(verb—to influence; to involve)
effect	(verb—to cause; noun—a result)
affluent	(prosperous)

effluent (adjective—flowing outward; noun—a stream flowing outward)

aggravate (verb—to add to; to make a bad situation worse)
irritate (verb—to vex or annoy)

allowed (permitted)
aloud (audible)

altar (noun—a structure)
alter (verb—to change)

alternate (noun—substitute; verb—to switch between two things; adjective—a choice between two things)
alternative (incorrect as an adjective, such as an *alternative approach;* always a noun—a choice that implies more than two options)

amicable (describes circumstances or arrangements agreed to peacefully)
amiable (describes people who are friendly, kind, easygoing)

among (more than two compared or involved: *among the six of them*)
between (only two compared or involved; or when more than two things are compared, but each item or group of items is compared to one other individually: *between the two of us; between pages of the book; there were many previous contracts between the six companies involved in the merger.*)

amount (applies to mass or bulk quantities: *an amount of money*)
number (refers to separate units: *a number of orders*)

anxious (filled with anxiety, dread, worry)
eager (filled with excitement, positively looking forward to something)

apt   (suited, pertinent; inclined to; prompt to learn: *He is apt to accept the promotion.*)

ascent   (movement upward)
assent   (agreement)

assure   (to pledge or give confidence to people—use in the same way as reassure: *He assured us that he would attend.*)
ensure   (to guarantee or make certain—use in cases other than when referring to people: *This new packaging will ensure that the product arrives safely.*)
insure   (to make certain or protect against loss—use when referring to monetary payments: *This bond will insure payment up to $2,000.*)

average   (determine by adding a series of numbers and dividing by the number of quantities)
mean   (halfway between two points)
median   (middle number in a series; when the series has an even number of quantities, add the middle two numbers and divide by two)

awhile   (adverb—for a period of time: *We chatted awhile.*)
a while   (incorrect to mean "for a time")

band   (noun—a strip, an orchestra)
banned   (verb—prohibited)

bare   (without covering)
bear   (noun—an animal; verb—to carry or to hold)

board   (noun—flat piece of wood)
bored   (adjective—weary from dullness)

brake   (verb—to stop a vehicle; noun—device to stop a vehicle)
break   (verb—to shatter; noun—an interruption or stop in action)

bring	(movement toward the speaker or writer; incorrect: *Bring this to John's office when you go.*)
take	(movement away from the speaker or writer; correct: *Take this to John's office as you go.*)
can	(ability to)
may	(permission or possibility)
capital	(adjective—primary, most serious; noun—city, letter, column, accumulated possessions)
capitol	(building)
cede	(to yield; to grant)
seed	(to plant seed or sow)
choose	(present tense of to choose: *I always choose the line with the longest wait.*)
chose	(past tense of to choose: *I chose that option yesterday.*)
cite	(verb—to give a source)
sight	(noun—eyesight)
site	(noun—a location)
coarse	(rough texture)
course	(manner, class, route, part of a meal)
compare to	(focusing on similarities)
compare with	(comparing similarities and differences but focusing on differences)
complement	(verb—to make complete; noun—something that completes)
compliment	(verb—to congratulate; noun—praise)
comprise	(to include; avoid following with *of*; Tip: The whole comprises parts. *Our division comprises engineering, marketing, and accounting specialists.*)
consist of	(to be composed of)

confidant(e)	(noun—comrade, adviser, friend)
confident	(adjective—certain)
continual	(regular, but interrupted: *His temper is a continual problem.*)
continuous	(constant and uninterrupted: *There is a continuous hum in the background.*)
convince	(to appeal to logic, most often in changing beliefs, values, or "convictions")
persuade	(to appeal to logic and emotion; to cause someone to act)
council	(an assembly of people)
counsel	(noun—advice; verb—to advise)
credible	(can be reasonably believed: *a credible eyewitness*)
creditable	(deserving praise: *a creditable performance*)
credulous	(believes without reasons, gullible: *a credulous TV viewer*)
device	(noun—plan, procedure, technique, object)
devise	(verb—to plan or to design)
differentiate	(to point out differences: *We can differentiate the best applicants by their dress.*)
distinguish	(to see differences: *Susan could not distinguish opinion from fact.*)
differ from	(unlike—refers to items, ideas, or situations, not people)
differ with	(to disagree—refers to people)
disburse	(to pay out—such as money)
disperse	(to scatter—such as seeds)
discreet	(adjective—tactful, modest, trustworthy, prudent)
discrete	(individually distinct or separate)

disinterested	(impartial)
uninterested	(without interest in)
eligible	(qualified, entitled)
illegible	(undecipherable)
emigrant	(person exiting a country)
immigrant	(person entering a country)
eminent	(outstanding)
imminent	(impending; about to happen)
exercise	(to move physically; to train; to practice: *He exercised his rights in the contract.*)
exorcise	(to drive out, as with a demon)
faint	(to lose consciousness)
feint	(a pretense)
farther	(physical distance: *two miles farther*)
further	(degree that can't be precisely measured: *two ideas further apart*)
fever	(a high temperature when someone is ill)
temperature	(normal state of the body)
fewer	(use when items can be counted: *fewer letters*)
less	(use with quantities that cannot be counted: *less nitrogen*)
flaunt	(to wave; show in a gaudy manner)
flout	(to mock, insult, or jeer)
forego	(to go before)
forgo	(to give up)
foreword	(front matter in a publication)
forward	(noun—a direction; adjective—bold, aggressive)

formally	(in a formal manner)
formerly	(previously)
fort	(a strong point; a musical term meaning loudly)
forté	(incorrect to write with accent mark; never correct to pronounce *for-tay*)
forth	(out, onward)
fourth	(ordinal number for four)
freeze	(harden into ice)
frieze	(heavy wool cloth)
get, got	(colloquial for *have*; avoid in formal writing)
have	(standard usage)
guessed	(surmised)
guest	(visitor)
hanged	(refers to people: *He was hanged in the movie.*)
hung	(refers to things, not people: *We hung the picture in his office.*)
hear	(refers to sound)
here	(refers to location)
heard	(past tense of *to hear*)
herd	(a group)
hoard	(to store away)
horde	(a swarm, a wandering tribe or group)
hole	(a cavity)
whole	(complete, intact)
hours	(time)
ours	(possessive pronoun indicating ownership)

idle	(doing nothing)
idol	(image of a god)
in	(within: *The report is in the files.*)
into	(indicates motion: *He stepped into the path of the truck.*)
infers	(action of listener or reader: *I infer from her letter that she plans to leave immediately.*)
implies	(action of speaker or writer: *When he talks to each customer, he implies that he is customizing his service.*)
instance	(an example)
instants	(periods of time)
inter-	(prefix meaning between: *intercity—between cities*)
intra-	(prefix meaning within: *intracity—within one city*)
its	(possessive pronoun indicating ownership)
it's	(contraction of *it is*)
knew	(past tense of *to know*)
new	(opposite of *old*)
lay	(verb—past tense of *to lie,* meaning to recline; verb—present tense of *to lay,* meaning to place [*lay, laid, laid*])
lie	(verb—to tell a falsehood [*lie, lied, lied*]; verb—to recline [*lie, lay, lay/lain*]; noun—a falsehood)

I lie about my reasons every day.
I lied yesterday about my reasons.
I lie on the carpet and cry when he walks in.
I lay on the carpet and cried yesterday when he walked in.
I have lain here crying all week.

I lay this contract on your desk every day as a strong hint.
I laid the contract on your desk yesterday.
The unsigned contract lay on his desk for a week.

lead	(verb—to be out in front of; noun—first position in line; slang for a clue or a tip; marking substance in a pencil; a chemical element)
led	(past tense of *to lead: He led me to the source yesterday.*)
leased	(to pay money for rights)
least	(the smallest portion)
leave	(to go away)
let	(to permit)
liable	(responsible for consequences: *She is liable for the damages.*)
likely	(probable or probably: *The company will likely fold.*)
loan	(something lent or borrowed)
lone	(solitary)
loose	(adjective—unattached)
lose	(verb—to fail to win, gain, or obtain)
loss	(noun—that which is ruined, destroyed, or diminished)
mantel	(shelf over fireplace)
mantle	(a sleeveless coat)
marshal	(an official)
martial	(military)
may	(shows possibility)
might	(shows stronger uncertainty than *may*)

maze	(labyrinth)
maize	(type of corn)
might have	(correct verb phrase)
might of	(incorrect usage)
miner	(worker in a mine)
minor	(adjective—unimportant; noun—person not of legal age)
more than	(applies to a number: *He paid more than 50 dollars for the hat.*)
over	(physical condition: *The crew climbed over the fence.*)
one	(the number)
won	(past tense of *to win*)
one of the only	(illogical; prefer *one of the few that/who*)
only	(alone in its class)
pail	(bucket)
pale	(lacking color)
pain	(suffering)
pane	(section of window, door, or cabinet)
pair	(noun—couple)
pear	(noun—fruit)
pare	(verb—to reduce)
passed	(past tense of to pass: *We passed the accident site.*)
past	(period of time before the present; never a verb)
peace	(without turmoil)
piece	(a portion of)
peal	(ringing of bells)
peel	(noun—outside covering; verb—to cut away the covering)

peer	(noun—an equal; verb—to look)
pier	(dock for ships or fishing)
penultimate	(next to last)
ultimate	(last, connoting superiority)
persecute	(to oppress)
prosecute	(to bring legal charges against)
perspective	(viewpoint)
prospective	(likely to become, expected)
plain	(adjective—simple, ordinary; noun—level, treeless land)
plane	(noun—an airplane, a tool; verb—to level)
pore	(noun—tiny skin opening)
pour	(verb—to flow in a stream)
practical	(useful or workable as opposed to theoretical)
practicable	(possible, feasible)
precede	(to go before: *Chapter 2 precedes Chapter 3.*)
proceed	(to move ahead: *Let's proceed with the plan.*)
presently	(has two meanings: "in a short while" and "currently"; prefer to be precise: *The company name is currently American Universal, but it will be changed soon.*)
principal	(adjective—chief, primary; noun—one who has control)
principle	(noun—a rule or guideline)
quiet	(adjective—without noise or disturbance)
quit	(verb—to stop)
quite	(adverb—completely, positively, rather)

rapped	(knocked, as on a door)
rapt	(enthralled, enraptured)
wrapped	(covered)
real	(genuine)
reel	(verb—to stagger; noun—ring to hold tape or film; fishing equipment)
red	(color)
read	(verb—both present and past tense of *to read: I read e-mail every day. I read my e-mail yesterday.*)
regardless	(without regard for or attention to)
irregardless	(incorrect usage; not a word)
right	(correct)
rite	(noun—ceremony or ritual)
wright	(noun—person who makes)
write	(verb—to compose)
road	(pathway for travel)
rode	(verb—past tense of *to ride*)
rowed	(verb—past tense of *to row*)
rung	(noun—step of a ladder)
wrung	(verb—past tense of *to wring or to squeeze*)
rye	(a grass)
wry	(distorted)
sac	(a pouchlike part)
sack	(a bag)
scene	(view, part of a play)
seen	(past participle of *to see*)
speak to	(to tell; to greet)
speak with	(to discuss)

stationary	(immobile)
stationery	(writing material)
steal	(to take dishonestly)
steel	(iron alloyed with carbon)
straight	(direct, not curved)
strait	(narrow waterway)
teach	(to instruct)
learn	(to gain knowledge or understanding)
team	(a group working together)
teem	(to swarm)
tear	(noun—salty fluid from the eye, or a rip; verb—to pull apart)
tier	(a row)
tenant	(one who rents property)
tenet	(a rule or principle)
than	(conjunction that compares; used to link words, phrases, or clauses: *He knows more than I do.*)
then	(adverb—tells when)
their	(possessive pronoun indicating ownership)
there	(adverb telling where; an expletive: *There was a problem.*)
they're	(contraction of *they are*)
threw	(verb—past tense of *to throw*)
through	(preposition—by, because of, from beginning to end)
thru	(nonstandard spelling, meaning *through*)
tracked	(followed)
tract	(a pamphlet)

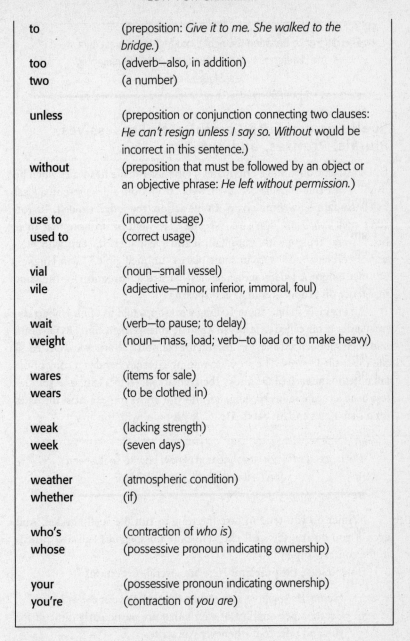

to	(preposition: *Give it to me. She walked to the bridge.*)
too	(adverb—also, in addition)
two	(a number)
unless	(preposition or conjunction connecting two clauses: *He can't resign unless I say so. Without* would be incorrect in this sentence.)
without	(preposition that must be followed by an object or an objective phrase: *He left without permission.*)
use to	(incorrect usage)
used to	(correct usage)
vial	(noun—small vessel)
vile	(adjective—minor, inferior, immoral, foul)
wait	(verb—to pause; to delay)
weight	(noun—mass, load; verb—to load or to make heavy)
wares	(items for sale)
wears	(to be clothed in)
weak	(lacking strength)
week	(seven days)
weather	(atmospheric condition)
whether	(if)
who's	(contraction of *who is*)
whose	(possessive pronoun indicating ownership)
your	(possessive pronoun indicating ownership)
you're	(contraction of *you are*)

Figure 41. Commonly Misused Words. Become aware of misused words in your own writing.

> The difference between the right word and the almost-right word is
> the difference between "lighting" and "lightning bug."
> —*Mark Twain*

Spell Correctly—Be Careful with Possessives, Plurals, Prefixes, and Suffixes

U.S. District Court Judge Sherman G. Finesilver made headlines when he threw a case out of court because lawyers from both sides presented legal briefs containing writing errors. In his action, the judge scolded, "If you can't spell *subpoena*, don't ask for one." He went on to note that their briefs were "replete with grammatical and spelling errors, and with misuse of verbiage" and were in some places "unintelligible." Lynn Hughes, another longtime federal judge, has also earned a reputation for the same insistence on proper grammar and spelling.

An engineer in one of our writing workshops told us of his embarrassment after being called to testify in a patent infringement suit. His lab notes had been subpoenaed as evidence, and the plaintiff's attorney had circled all the misspelled words. The cross-examining attorney handed a copy of the lab notes to the each of the jurors, then remarked, "If this witness is so careless or inaccurate in his spelling, how do you know you can trust the dates on his lab notes and his data?" He made his point with the jury.

> When you don't know that you don't know how to spell a word, you
> don't know to check the dictionary!

Neither do you tend to take the time to run the spell-checker. And even if you do run the spell-checker, some misspellings (misused words in the context) slip by.

How to solve the problem? Here are several suggestions:

- Memorize spellings rather than depend on your ear or logic.
- Create a personal list of words that are particularly difficult for you and refer to it whenever you write.
- Learn some mnemonic tricks to help you remember. For example, *stationery* refers to writing letters; so link the *e* in *stationery* to the *e* in letters.

- Master basic spelling rules such as those having to do with a final *e* before a suffix beginning with a consonant, changes from *y* to *i* before a suffix, and double consonants that end words.
- Study a list of commonly misspelled words and refer to the list until you memorize the spellings.

Figure 42 presents such a list. To make yourself aware of words you habitually misspell, underline the correct spellings and then check the answers in Appendix B (p. 369).

Spelling Awareness

accessible, acessible
accomodate, accommodate
accurate, acurrate
achieve, acheive
allotted, alloted
analyze, analize
antequated, antiquated
apparatus, aparratus
appearance, appearence
arguement, argument
beginning, begining
bulletin, bulliten
buoyant, bouyant
calender, calendar
category, catagory
cemetary, cemetery
changeable, changable
commitment, committment
complection, complexion
concensus, consensus
conterversy, controversy
definite, definate
dependent, dependant
describe, discribe

description, discreption
descrepancy, discrepancy
dilema, dilemma
disappoint, dissapoint
dissapate, dissipate
embarrass, embarass
ettiquete, etiquette
exceed, excede
existence, existance
exorbitant, exhorbitant
fourty, forty
grammar, grammer
guage, gauge
harrass, harass
humorous, humorus
hypocrasy, hypocrisy
imatate, imitate
inadvertent, inadvertant
independant, independent
indispensible, indispensable
inate, innate
insistent, insistant
maintenance, maintanence
mecanics, mechanics

---

mileage, milage	quandary, quandery
miniscule, minuscule	recede, receed
necessary, necessery	receive, recieve
ninety, ninty	recommend, reccomend
ocassionally, occasionally	repetition, repitetion
occurred, occured	seize, sieze
occurrence, occurence	separate, seperate
parallel, paralell	sieve, seive
perform, preform	similar, similiar
permanent, permenant	stopped, stoped
perserverance, perseverance	supercede, supersede
personnel, personel	succeed, succede
porportion, proportion	superintendent, superintendant
precede, preceed	technique, techneque
privilege, privelege	undoubtably, undoubtedly
probably, probaly	vacuum, vaccuum
procede, proceed	whether, wheather
proceedure, procedure	

Figure 42. Spelling Awareness. Identify difficult-to-spell words. When in doubt, run your spell-checker.

Now let's tackle another spelling blockade: acronyms and abbreviations.

Use Standard Acronyms and Abbreviations

- Do not use periods with acronyms (abbreviations pronounced as words).

Not: N.A.S.A.	*But:* NASA
Not: O.P.E.C.	*But:* OPEC
Not: P.I.N.	*But:* PIN
Not: Z.I.P.	*But:* ZIP

- Use either all uppercase or all lowercase letters in acronyms, depending on how the word or phrase it represents is written.

  USAR (United States Army Reserve)
  etc. (et cetera)

mph (miles per hour)
psi (pounds per square inch)

- When using both the acronym and the full designation, place the most familiar term outside the parentheses. If the terms are equally familiar, put the acronym inside the parentheses.

  URL (Uniform Resource Locator)
  IBM (International Business Machines)
  Personal Indentification Number (PIN)

- Use standard technical abbreviations.

  Not: lbs. (pounds)   *But:* lb (singular or plural)
  Not: sec. (second)   *But:* s

Capitalize Only with Reason, Not Randomly

Writers use far too many capital letters rather than not enough. There are several reasons for this habit: 1) They capitalize without thought. 2) They capitalize important words to emphasize them. 3) They capitalize specific words rather than proper nouns.

Reason 1 can take care of itself.

Let's elaborate on reason 2: If you want to emphasize important words, either **bold-print** them, *italicize* them, or put the whole word in UPPERCASE letters. Incorrectly capitalizing a word often leads to confusion.

Reason 3: To help students master the rules of capitalization, English teachers often give students a guideline for distinguishing proper nouns from common nouns: "If it's a specific city, capitalize the name of the city." Students often misinterpret that guideline and write, "If your Company approves the proposal, we can start the work within a week." They reason that *company* refers to the specific company. Wrong reasoning. Capitalization involves the issue of whether you *use* the specific name rather than a *generic reference* to a specific noun.

Here are examples:

Generic Reference: His company is filing for bankruptcy. (a specific company, but a generic reference to the company)

Proper Noun:	Allied Repair is filing for bankruptcy.
Generic Reference:	He wanted to find a job in the marketing area of our company.
Proper Noun:	Ask Marketing if the copywriter plans to supply brochures to the salespeople. (refers to a specific department or division title called by its official name)
Generic Reference:	Jorge's car needs new tires.
Proper Noun:	Jorge's Buick needs new tires.

So what difference does all this make? Capitalization aids reading. Capitalization signals the beginning of a new sentence or a "brand name" reference to something. When used carelessly, capitalization confuses readers and slows them down.

The following sentence is no joke; it comes from a joint-venture agreement between two major oil companies.

Each Company agrees that, during each Accounting Period after the Completion Date, its Company's Throughput, which constitutes Initial Facility Throughput, shall not be less than the Company's Percentage.

If you want to emphasize a key word, underline or boldface it rather than capitalize it. The standard capitalization rules follow:

- Capitalize proper nouns, the names of specific places or regions. Capitalize city, state, or federal only when used as part of the actual name.

  Colorado   Dallas   the Mediterranean   the South
  the Rocky Mountains   the city of San Antonio
  federal officials   Hill County   Mississippi River
  Vietnam   Columbus Street

- Do not capitalize directions.

  Move toward the southwestern part of the region.
  He reported that he was traveling south on I-35.

- Capitalize races and languages.

  Jewish   Caucasian   Malaysian   French

- Capitalize days of the week, months, and special days, but not seasons of the year.

  Wednesday   July   Hanukkah   winter   fall

- Capitalize historical periods and events.

  the Roaring Twenties   the Dark Ages
               the Industrial Revolution

- Capitalize trade names, company names, organizations, divisions, and agencies.

Southwestern Bell	Scotch Guard
Plexiglas	Air Traffic Control
Xerox	Tylenol
Region 7 Marketing Division	Internal Revenue Service

- Capitalize a term derived from a proper noun unless it is so familiar that it is no longer associated with the original name.

  Eschka's Mixture
  Newton's Second Law
  Parkinson's Law
  But: aspirin   hertz   ohm   volt

- Do not capitalize generic words such as the following unless they are used as part of an official name.

Not: our manufacturing group	*But:* Buford Manufacturing Inc.
Not: the engineering budget	*But:* Engineering and Quality Control
Not: to the agency	*But:* Herman Regulatory Agency
Not: forward to the company	*But:* Frito-Lay
Not: the federal government	*But:* Federal Deposit Insurance Corporation

- Capitalize the title of a position only when it precedes a name and is used as a person's title. (The only exception is titles of high government officials.) Do not capitalize the position title when it follows or replaces an individual's name. Do not capitalize a generic reference to a position or organization (unless your own corporation's style book mandates such capitalization).

  Dr. Indira Tantarri has been appointed to the task force.

  Indira Tantarri, a doctor in our local hospital, has been appointed to the task force.

  Director of Research Carlos Ortega has approved the budget.

  Carlos Ortega, director of research, has approved the budget.

  Four company officials have resigned.

  The president is not well liked here in our division.

  Our board of directors has made the decision.

  Our Board of Directors has made the decision.

- Capitalize the first word of a direct quotation, except when the quotation continues rather than begins a sentence.

  Our proposal claims, "Our staff will not initiate legal proceedings against Bilco Inc."

  "Our staff will not," he insisted, "initiate legal proceedings."

  Our proposal states that our staff will not initiate legal proceedings against the Bilco Inc.

- Capitalize the first word of an independent question within a sentence. You are also correct to use lowercase.

  The determining factor is, Will we reimburse them for the charges?

  The determining factor is, will we reimburse them for the charges?

  The determining factor is this: Will we reimburse them for the charges?

- Capitalize the first word of items in a formal list. (It is also acceptable not to capitalize items when the items are not complete sentences. It is also acceptable not to capitalize items when

the items are syntactically connected to the introducing clause
or phrase.)

The criteria include the following:

- Experience in dredging
- Equipment on site
- Budgetary provisions

The criteria are
—experience in dredging
—equipment on site
—budgetary provisions.

- Capitalize the first word and all principal words in a heading or
  title. Do not capitalize prepositions, conjunctions, or articles
  unless they are the first or last words of a title.

Fundamentals of Petroleum by Daniel T. Swenson

Follow On by Ksammoune Tempraghanh

*Quantal Release of Transmitter Is Not Associated with
Channel Opening on the Neuronal Membrane*

When hyphenation and capitalization collide, writers often grow
weary in sorting out rules. Here are three guiding principles: *Within a
sentence*, capitalize only those parts of a hyphenated word that are proper
nouns or adjectives. *At the beginning of a sentence*, capitalize the first part
of the hyphenated word but not other parts unless they are proper nouns
or adjectives. In *headings or titles*, capitalize all the parts (except articles,
short prepositions, or conjunctions, which are never capitalized in headings or titles).

Punctuate Precisely

Columnist Elizabeth Zwart, writing the *Des Moines Tribune*, once
quipped: "The older I grow, the less important the comma becomes. Let
the reader catch his own breath." I've since discovered that many business
writers use the heavy-breathing system of punctuation. When they take a
big breath, they put in a comma. But the careful business writer knows

that the comma serves a higher purpose than letting readers catch their breath.

In addition to courtesy, the purpose of punctuation is clarity. For example, consider the radically different meaning of these pairs of sentences punctuated differently.

She's against that policy however he states it. (However he interprets the policy, she doesn't like it.)

She's against that policy; however, he states it. (He's not timid; he states the policy even though she's against it.)

Here is another example:

The project team, working in Seattle, will set the launch date. (The project team will set the launch date. The team is working in Seattle.)

The project team working in Seattle will set the launch date. (The Seattle team, rather than other teams in other places, will set the launch date.)

To repeat: Punctuation often dictates meaning. Consequently, in addition to the misspellings mentioned earlier, records are rife with court cases that revolve around discussions of grammar. The vice president and general counsel of a major oil company once told me about troublesome documents written by his staff of lawyers. He said, "Frankly, I'm tired of going to court because our lawyers don't know how to use a *which* clause or where to put a comma." Commas—or their absence—cost corporations piles of money.

So, should you sprinkle commas sparingly or liberally? Either too much or too little punctuation can confuse and annoy readers. If you feel the need to write, "He broke the contract!!!!," the word choice is inadequate. Select stronger verbs to make your point. If, on the other hand, you write two or three sentences with no punctuation at all, your thoughts look scrambled.

Think of punctuation marks as road signs. They tell readers which way to go, where to stop, and when to move a head with caution (see Figure 43).

Assuming periods and exclamation points give few people problems, let's go directly to the more complicated punctuation marks.

Punctuation as Traffic Signs	
. or ?	**Come to a complete stop. Kill engine.**
!	**Come to a complete stop. Race engine.**
;	**Come to a complete stop. Keep idling.**
:	**Come to a complete stop. Keep idling. Look ahead.**
,	**Slow down.**
, words,	(commas to set off nonessential information) **Slow down and look out the window for what's between these commas.**
"quote"	(quotation marks to signal a specific comment) **Listen. (or) Look out the window to see the specific scene.**
. . .	(ellipsis dots to indicate something has been omitted) **Watch the hole in the road.**
—	(dash to highlight what's coming) **Look ahead!**
—words—	(dashes to set off and highlight what comes between them) **Look between!**
(words)	(parentheses to set off and downplay what's between) **Glance between.**
(words [words] words)	(brackets to set off words in the middle of an aside) **Glance at the chuckhole while in the valley.**

Figure 43. Punctuation as Traffic Signs. Signal your readers when to pause, stop, or move head.

Commonly Used and Abused Comma Rules

For the latest intentional twisting of words, check current political ads. And if commas can play havoc in the hands of politicians, think what they can do in the hands of technical or business writers.

A client recently gave me directions to her site with this sentence: "Once you're on the campus complex, go to the second silver crescent-shaped building for registration." I drove past the correct building twice, looking for the second crescent-shaped building—only to discover that she'd omitted a comma (the second building, which was silver crecsent-shaped).

Consider another example where commas determine meaning:

The contract doesn't cover the building where domestic hot water is our only source for dishwashing. (refers to a specific building with only one source for hot water, rather than to other buildings that have multiple sources for hot water)

The contract doesn't cover the building, where domestic hot water is our only source for dishwashing. (The point is that the contract does not cover the building. The issue about domestic hot water is simply additional information, not a defining thought.)

If you're not following this discussion about the difference the commas make, you will identify the problem by the time you're finished with this section. Commas carry clout; use them knowledgeably.

To Introduce:

Use a comma after an introductory word.

Actually, both hardware systems would serve equally well.

Use a comma after an introductory phrase.

Having completed the tests, we removed our equipment.

On the contrary, I specifically invited him to the meeting.

Use a comma after an introductory adverbial clause.

When I requested these records upon termination of the employee, I found that they had been sent to the Dallas office.

To Separate:

Use a comma between two independent clauses joined by a coordinate conjunction (*and, but, nor, or, for, so, yet*).

> We compiled the data two weeks before the due date, and then we forwarded the rough draft to this office for final interpretation and approval.

> I prefer a pre-award meeting with the vendor, but Tim Hyatt wants to begin construction immediately.

Use a comma to separate items in a series.

> The retrieval service will give summaries of the articles, current or historical market quotes, company profiles, and 10–K extracts. (The last comma is optional, but using it always aids clarity. Without a comma in such a series, the last two items may appear to be a single item.)

Use a comma to separate two or more adjectives that modify a noun separately. Here's a tip to determine when you need such a comma: Say the sentence inserting *and* between the adjectives. If the thought sounds awkward, you will have determined your intended meaning; don't use a comma.

> Stefan has had a challenging, distinguished career.

> The salespeople wore casual black shoes during the demonstration. ("casual and black shoes" sounds awkward—no need for a comma)

Use a comma to separate a contradiction from a positive statement.

> The competitors charge more than we do, not less.

Use a comma to indicate omitted words.

> The books will be shipped by truck; the chemicals, by train.

> Bob manages the Easton Region; Michelle, the Fairmont Park area.

Never insert a comma between subject and verb simply to divide or "break up" a long sentence.

Wrong: The salesperson who presented the demonstration, left hurriedly after the meeting.

Wrong: Online learning developed by our internal staff specializing in each product line, has become one of the fastest applications in our organization.

To Enclose:

Use a comma to separate nonessential (nondefining) clauses and phrases from the rest of the sentence. Do not use a comma if the clause or phrase in question is essential to the meaning of the sentence.

> The Records Committee recommends that we implement a Vital Records Protection Program for all organizational units, especially those in the New York offices, and develop a procedures manual after the pilot effort. (*Especially those in the New York offices* is nonessential, additional information.)

> This bid does not cover the Houston jobs, which were contracted for after June 15. (The bid does not cover any Houston jobs. The last clause, set off by a comma, is a nonessential explanation.)

> This bid does not cover the Houston jobs which were contracted for after June 15. (Without a comma separating the last clause, the reader knows that this essential information restricts the meaning of jobs. This bid does not cover Houston jobs under contract after June 15, but it does cover jobs under contract *before* June 15.) Generally, prefer to use *that* to link essential information and *which* to link nonessential information. But that distinction is not always made because *which* can introduce essential information if the sentence already contains a *that* clause.

> Submit your report in April, when most people have a lax period. (All of April is lax.)

> Submit your report in April when most people have a lax period. (Choose a lax time in April, not a busy time in April.)

This next, final rule about enclosing commas proves to be the most confusing. Remember this general principle: *that* introduces essential information and does not need a comma before it; *which* introduces nonessential information and therefore needs a comma before it.

The new deck that has already been fabricated and assembled includes the new mooring gear. (The *that* clause specifies which deck.)

The new deck, which has already been fabricated and assembled, will be lifted and installed next month. (The *which* phrase adds nonessential information.)

There are 28 companies actively producing the injection parts that we have considered using in our design. (The *that* clause tells which parts.)

There are 28 companies actively producing the injection parts, which we have considered using in our design. (The *which* clause expresses an afterthought.)

Use enclosing commas also with appositives. Appositives rename or explain the preceding noun or noun phrase.

My friend Oye Oguntodu will accompany me. (Tells which friend of several—restricts the meaning of friend to one person.)

My oldest daughter, Maritta, will accompany me. (The name gives additional information—the writer can have only one oldest daughter, so *Maritta* simply renames the oldest daughter and is nonessential to identify which daughter.)

In addition to enclosing clauses and phrases that give nonessential information, the abbreviations *i.e.* and *e.g.* and the abbreviations for academic degrees and titles should be set off with commas.

They considered Francine Smith, J.D., to serve on the committee.

Matt Frazier, Ph.D., presided at the meeting.

The report referred to her negligence, e.g., drunkenness, unattended toddlers, unclean food.

Punctuating a list also creates questions about whether to use commas, periods, or colons. See Figure 44, for four punctuation choices.

To introduce, separate, enclose—the comma does more than help readers catch their breath. Frequently, the neglected comma carries the total weight of clarity on its shoulder.

Questions About Question Marks

Typically, writers have only two notions about how and where to use question marks.

Use questions marks after a direct question or after a series of direct questions.

Do you know where to buy inexpensive binders?

When interviewing prospective employees, probe to discover personality traits and attitudes: Do they play sports? Have a hobby? Take regular vacations? Eat out often with friends?

The key question in selecting the best vendors is, How soon can they deliver? (The first word of the question—*how,* in this case—may be capitalized or lowercase.)

Use a period rather than a question mark when a question is intended as a softened directive.

Would you please tell him to wait until I return from lunch.

Would you send the form immediately so that I can enroll before May.

Queer Quotation Marks

Quotation marks may be set off by either commas or colons. Indirect quotations (not quoted word for word, but summarized) should never be set off by quotation marks.

Jamie said, "I distrust this vendor."

Jamie voiced her complaint openly: "I distrust this vendor."

Jamie said that she distrusted this vendor.

Long quotations (four lines or longer) may be set off in a separate paragraph. If you set them off in a separate paragraph, do not use quotation marks around the cited material.

Rules about quotation marks that fall next to commas and periods often bring resistance. Because some writers have been out of school awhile and have forgotten the rules, they depend on logic. And logic fails here:

Commas and periods *always* go *inside* quotation marks—regardless of meaning.

If these figures came from "Subsection 2," please retabulate them.

In this case, there was no "wanton conduct."

Semicolons and colons *always* go *outside* quotation marks—regardless of meaning.

These authorizations should be filed beginning with the name "Katz"; they must also be numbered consecutively.

He issued an "ultimatum": Sign or resign.

Question marks go *inside or outside* quotation marks—depending on meaning.

Who can tell me why this particular account is considered a "bomb"?

Clayton ends every discussion with "But why are we sidetracking here?"

In the preceding examples with commas and periods, reason suggests that the comma should go *after* the quotation marks (If these figures came from "Subsection 2",) because the comma sets off the entire introductory clause. But logic doesn't hold here; a rule is a rule is a rule.

Strong Semicolons
Semicolons indicate a closer relationship between ideas than a period does. Semicolons take the place of missing conjunctions (linking words).

This will be an ongoing process; it will not end when the consultant's contract is completed.

Semicolons precede connective adverbs used as conjunctions (for example: *however, consequently, moreover, therefore, hence, thus*).

The new system will not provide an income-producing program; however, the costs are significantly lower than those of conventional records storage. (Notice the comma after *however*.)

Note: The use of *however* does not require a semicolon in the following sentence because the word does not separate two independent clauses:

The costs, however, are not significantly lower. (*However* in this case is merely an interrupting word rather than a connective adverb between two complete thoughts.)

Semicolons replace commas to separate complex items in a series when the items already have internal commas.

Confusing: Your manager stopped by to deliver the following supplies: Forms 302, which have been on back order for six months, two boxes of stencils, the notebooks, minus the damaged pages, Forms 1601.

Clear: Your manager stopped by to deliver the following supplies: Forms 302, which have been on back order for six months; two boxes of stencils; the notebooks, minus the damaged pages; Forms 1601.

Uncommon Colons

Use a colon when a word, phrase, or clause amplifies or further explains the first part of the sentence. The colon stresses, or highlights, what follows.

Management's ideas are always the same: Take the risk.

Use a colon when a series follows.

Give the following tables to the graphic artist: Table 8, Table 10, Table 14, Table 17.

Four Ways to Punctuate a Formal List

1. **No End Punctuation on Separate Items**
   Use lists to:
   - Highlight major ideas in your reports or proposals
   - Break down complex information into smaller chunks
   - Overview key information quickly
   - Review key information quickly

   (Even though what precedes the colon is an incomplete sentence, the colon here is optional in a formal list. But never use a colon after a verb or preposition when the items in the series are not presented in a formally set-off list.)

2. **Colon After a Complete Sentence Used as Lead-in**
   Use lists for the following:
   - Highlighting major ideas in your reports or proposals
   - Breaking complex information into smaller chunks
   - Overviewing key information quickly
   - Reviewing key information quickly

   (The colon is required after a complete sentence serving as a lead-in.)

3. **End Punctuation on Complete Sentences as Items**
   Why use lists?
   - Major ideas can be highlighted in your reports or proposals.
   - Complex paragraphs can be broken into smaller chunks.
   - Key information can be quickly overviewed.
   - Key information can be quickly reviewed.

4. **Punctuation as One Long Sentence**
   Use lists to present
   - major ideas in your reports or proposals,
   - complex information in smaller chunks,
   - key information for quick overview,
   - key information for quick review.

   (This fourth method shows an older, more formal style of punctuation.)

Figure 44. Four Ways to Punctuate a Formal List. Items in a list should be in parallel form, but they can vary in format and punctuation.

Daring Dashes

Dashes, less formal than colons, emphasize the word, phrase, or clause set off from the rest of the sentence. (Do not confuse a dash with a hyphen.)

He cannot—and this is strictly a personal opinion—handle the job as well as Tom Bohommen did last year.

If the context calls for a dash where a comma would ordinarily be, omit the comma.

Because the figures had not been charted—the reason for this will be presented later—the report has been delayed.

If the element being set off requires a question mark or exclamation point, use it.

Smith's plan—can he have promotion on his mind?—calls for increased responsibility for that position.

Apostrophes for Possession

First, I'll the apostrophe issues that create the most confusion. Then we'll go on to the more mundane rules.

Use apostrophes to show possession with nouns. Make the noun either singular or plural first; then add an apostrophe and s. If the word already ends in an s, don't add another s unless you pronounce the extra s as a separate syllable.

the consultant's contract (one consultant); the consultants' contracts (two consultants) (Do not write an additional s on the plural form here because you do not pronounce the extra syllable.)

driver's position (one driver); drivers' positions (two drivers) (Do not write an additional s on the plural form here because you do not pronounce the extra syllable.)

operator's input (one operator); operators' input (two operators). (Do not write the extra s after the apostrophe because you don't pronounce an extra syllable.)

the boss's desk (one boss); the bosses' desks (two bosses.) (You don't write an extra s to show possession because you don't pronounce an extra syllable.)

children's instructions

women's safety regulations

Fran Potts's new office (Write the second *s* to indicate possessive; the name itself contains a final *s*. You do pronounce the extra syllable with a name.)

James's report (The name itself contains a final *s*. Write the second *s* to show possession because you do pronounce the extra syllable.)

Do not use apostrophes with possessive pronouns. These pronouns are already possessive—*his, hers, yours, theirs.*

The company agrees to hold *its* employees blameless. (Do not confuse with *it's*, a contraction, which means *it is.*)

Use apostrophes (possessive form) before gerunds.

Be aware of the *court's* construing the damage as a temporary injury. (Remember that the gerund phrase *construing the damage as a temporary injury* takes the place of a noun. Substitute the word *decision* for the gerund phrase to understand why the possessive form is necessary here.)

Be careful not to place apostrophes in the middle of a plural word or to use an apostrophe when you intend to form a simple plural noun.

Not: those employee's badges
But: those employees' badges

Not: two bulldozer's
But: two bulldozers

If a possessive normally would modify another noun, but that noun has been omitted, retain the possessive form.

The decision to cap the well was John Wiseman's.

Indicate joint ownership by adding an apostrophe and an *s* only to the last name of a pair.

Howard and Tenuta's work (one research project)
Howard's and Tenuta's work (two research projects)

Add an apostrophe and an *s* to express duration.

ten years' experience   a quarter's budget

Use an apostrophe to indicate missing letters or numbers.

best movie of the '90s   can't   I'll

Use an apostrophe to show the plural of abbreviations, acronyms, numbers, and letters used as words, if necessary for clarity.

The *c*'s in the user manual are overlapping characters.
The *126's* are out of stock.

Let clarity be your guide:

We have plans to redesign the model *234ds*. (*Note*: It is unclear if the model number is 234d or 234ds. An apostrophe would make clear that the *s* represents the plural form and is not part of the model number.)

We have plans to redesign the model *234d*'s.

Distinguish between modifiers that are intended to be descriptive and modifiers intended to indicate possession:

the operators manual (descriptive)
the operator's manual (possessive)
the client meeting (descriptive)
the client's meeting (possessive)
the competitor bid (descriptive)
the competitor's bid (possessive)
the Hewlett-Packard contract (descriptive)
Hewlett-Packard's contract (possessive)

Hyphens That Cause Hyperventilation

Why all the hype about hyphens? Once again, clarity is the issue. A geologist wrote this statement in one of his lab reports: "You'll need to use a chilled water valve." When I questioned him about the specific meaning, he took another look at the sentence and confirmed my suspicion: He had not communicated what he meant. "Chilled water valves" refers to valves that have been chilled by running cold water through them. On the other hand, "chilled-water valves" refer to a specific type valve: chilled-water valves, as opposed to hot-water valves. Both provide logical meanings for his sentence.

At the DFW airport a few years ago, before the ban on smoking in public spaces went into effect, I stood staring at a sign outside a restaurant. The sign beside the door read: NO SMOKING SECTION (with no hyphen). I couldn't decide whether the sign meant "We have no section where you can smoke" (which was confusing, because I saw people smoking inside), or if the restaurant had inadvertently omitted the hyphen and did, in fact, have a no-smoking section.

Hyphenation is not an infrequent mistake. A reporter for *The Wall Street Journal*, William E. Blundell, tells about a costly hyphen error. A supervisor at a government-run nuclear installation ordered radioactive rods cut into "10 foot lengths." He received 10 rods, each one foot long instead of the 10-foot lengths he needed. The actual dollar loss to the government remained classified.

Where do you go for the final word on hyphenation? A recently published, reputable dictionary or current software package. But to keep your sanity, please understand that words are always in a state of transition because our language is a spoken rather than a dead language. New concepts are always evolving for which we have to create language. When two words are initially used together frequently, they appear hyphenated. When they are used almost exclusively together, the hyphen is dropped and they become one word. For example: *note book* started out as two words, then became hyphenated, and now it has become a solid word, *notebook*. *Pipe line* became *pipe-line*, then *pipeline*. *Make up* became *make-up* before it hardened into *makeup*. The same evolution has produced these changes: *on line, on-line, online*; *feed back, feed-back, feedback*; life style, life-style, lifestyle. *Web site* and *e-mail* are still in transition. Currently, in major publications you'll see both terms written as two words, a solid word, and a hyphenated compound.

We have no "Board of Official Grammar" that determines whether a specific word, compound, or phrase has been in existence long enough to become a solid word, with no hyphenation. It just happens. But take heart. Other than the confusion about new concepts and new words in the world, there are additional standard rules that remove the guesswork and make your writing clear.

- Hyphenate the prefixes *ex-, quasi-, self-, all-, half-* and the suffix *-elect.*

ex-official	quasi-public	self-hypnotist
all-around	all-encompassing	alderman-elect

- In the case of almost every other prefix and suffix (*pre-, post-, over-, under-, intra-, anit-, extra-, infra-, ultra-, sub-, super-, pro, ant-, re-, un-, non-, semi-, pseudo-, supra-, co-*), write it and the root together as one word.

nonessential	reinvestigate	underestimate
extracurricular	spherelike	fourfold
subcutaneous	interracial	intravenous
presampling	contrariwise	pseudointellectual

- Use a hyphen between a prefix and a root if necessary to prevent misreading.

  re-cover (to cover again)   recover (to locate)
  anti-intelligence squad

- Hyphenate after a prefix if the root is capitalized.

  mid-September   non-Jewish

- Hyphenate two adjectives used as a modifying unit *preceding* a noun. When the adjectives *follow* a noun, do not hyphenate them unless they are in altered or inverted form.

  reduced-to-pole map   10-inch strips   four-day program

  Your employees should follow the plan step by step.
  But: Your employees should follow the step-by-step plan.

This three-phase report contains key information.
But: This report will provide information for the three phases of the project.

This bond is tax-exempt. (Add the hyphen because the structure is an altered form of *tax-exempt bond.*)

- Do not hyphenate two related adjectives used as a single unit if the two adjectives (or nouns used as adjectives) represent a single concept and are *clearly* recognizable without hyphens.

  The hydrogen peroxide solution has fully reacted.
  Your income tax statements are complete.
  The rental car agency sent a bill.
  Their high school reunion is in July.

- Do not hyphenate adverb-adjective combinations that precede a noun if the adverb ends in *ly.*

  highly publicized campaign   argely ignored plan

  But:

  well-considered alternative   less-costly approach
  much-envied team

- Use a suspended hyphen (a hyphen followed by a word space) after each prefix or word in a series that modifies the same term.

  The pre- and postgraduate work has been considered.
  The three- and four-tier platforms have been moved.

- Hyphenate compound numbers from twenty-one through ninety-nine.

  forty-four   eighty-two

- Hyphenate compound words without a noun as their base when the compound is used as a noun.

  go-between   follow-through   higher-up

Although the first few rules here have to do with spelling a single word rather than linking two different words, we have included the rules here to be complete about hyphenation.

> If you take hyphens seriously, you will surely go mad.
> —*John Benbow*

Idle Italics

Because printers now accommodate italics, italics, in lieu of underlining, now find their way into business and technical writing. Use italics in the following situations:

- Italicize words to emphasize them, but don't overuse italics. Any technique overused loses its effectiveness.

  Identifying best practices in our organization is not the best way to ensure growth; it's the *only* way.

- Italicize names or titles of books, newspapers, magazines, CDs, audios, songs, plays, movies, individual television programs and series, court decisions, and ships.

  Della's Dilemmas, written while the author sailed around the world aboard *Trojan*, received negative reviews in the *Dallas Morning News*.

- Italicize foreign words or expressions that are not considered part of the English language.

  Our *bon voyage* party seemed to draw a crowd.

  His last comment was a *non sequitur*; I had no idea how it related to our earlier discussion.

- Italicize a word or number used as itself rather than as its typical meaning. (It would also be equally correct to use quotation marks to set off such words and phrases.)

Identify all the *thank you*'s in your brochure and replace them with *we appreciate*.

The *3*'s and *8*'s on your chart seem difficult to read.

Elusive Ellipses

Ellipsis dots (three equally spaced periods) indicate omitted words in quoted comments. When the omitted words come at the end of a sentence, add a fourth period, close to the final word, to represent the end punctuation. Here are some examples: "The lawyers vehemently disagreed . . . in the Hinton case." Our policy manual states, "All employees must wear security badges. . . . "

Proofread with a Purposeful Plan

Proofreading proves difficult because, for the most part, you read what you thought you wrote. And even after letting your work "cool off," it's difficult to catch every error in a single reading. Unless you're a juggler used to fielding six or eight items in the air at once, you'll find it difficult to check for punctuation while you're reading to verify details while you're paying attention to dangling or misplaced modifiers while you're making predicates agree with their subjects.

Therefore, I suggest proofreading in layers. By that I mean to scan your document quickly several times, looking for different categories of errors with each reading. First, scan your document quickly to verify names, dates, numbers, and other data. Then scan the document again for missing or misplaced information. Then give it another reading for sentence structure and punctuation errors. Finally, read it for other grammatical errors.

Proofreading with a plan will save you pain during the process.

Grammar and clarity are inseparable. Grammatical mistakes may either muddy your message or mar your image.

15

EDIT FOR CLARITY

Measure Readability

Two factors determine how easy or how difficult your writing is to read: complexity of your words, and complexity of your sentences. Sentences should be as long or as short as necessary to serve your purpose. Both sentence length and pattern determine the reader's pace through your information.

The *average* sentence length in business and technical writing today is about 20 to 25 words. But the issue should always be clarity, not adherence to artificial restraints. Occasionally, however, technical writers will run a sentence marathon in which they try to convey every known detail and qualification about a concept in a single sentence. Consider the following example:

> By increasing the trapped-gas saturation alone, the relative permeability to water is reduced to be consistent with the relative permeability relationship measured in the lab; however, the physical system is more nearly represented by parallel flow paths for the gas and water phases so that the water-relative permeability at the increased trapped-gas saturation should be increased to the conformance fraction of the water-relative permeability at the original trapped-gas saturation. (74 words)

Technical information is complex enough for most readers without the writer making it more difficult with complicated sentence structure. The longer the sentence, the more decoding effort is required to get to the basic idea.

Consider these paraphrased clichés:

> A minuscule amount of effort to avert undesirable occurrences is the equivalent of a much greater countermeasure.

> When one comes to a point in one's life at which one experiences an overwhelming desire to pursue and achieve a specific goal, one's mental faculties, creativity, and emotional strength will overcome all obstacles standing between one and the desired goal.

Did you recognize the clichés? "An ounce of prevention is worth a pound of cure." And "Where there's a will, there's a way." In the longer versions, you have to spend so much time decoding the written symbols that the ideas themselves become obscured.

That is not to say that you should never write a long sentence. But writers who habitually use long sentences become a nuisance to readers because long sentences usually tangle ideas. Short sentences, on the other hand, add impact to the ideas they convey:

> It is most important that this section of the form be completed in its entirety because the executive research committee will be auditing our research plans in future quarters, and members are especially interested in how lab work done by employees in the E&P group relates to the plan of studies outlined for the three new chemists. Incomplete forms will be discarded.

You see how much more attention you give to the last sentence? That's because it's short. Unclear communication is more often a result of complex writing style than complex ideas.

To eliminate this unnecessary barrier, researchers have developed several methods of measuring the difficulty of written documents. Most of these formulas have to do with sentence length and pattern and word choice. These formulas also serve as the basis for software features that automatically measure complexity.

One of the most frequently used formulas is Robert Gunning's "Fog Index." When you apply Gunning's formula to a sample of writing, the resulting Fog Index represents the grade level at which you're writing. A Fog Index of 8 through 10 is ideal. According to this formula, a grade level of 8 is ideal for a well-educated business audience. You may be surprised to know that no mass-circulation magazine or newspaper in the United States is written above the twelfth-grade reading level. *The Atlantic Monthly,* a "literary" magazine, measures at the twelfth-grade reading level. Publications like *Time, Newsweek,* and *The Wall Street Journal* average 8 through 10.

Of course, these magazines are all aimed primarily at college graduates. The issue is energy. Why force readers to spend time and effort deciphering complex sentence structure when the energy can be channeled into understanding complex ideas?

Complex Sentences for Simple Ideas:

The individual appointed to the job-site field location with the responsibility for job-site procurement, and to whom the purchasing function is thereby delegated, shall have the authority and the responsibility for acting in compliance with Corporate Procedure 6001 and adherence to the requirements of this procedure. This person is authorized to make local purchase commitments without monetary limitations for materials, supplies, equipment, spare parts, and services required for job operational needs upon receipt of duly authorized requisitions within the approved job estimate. (82 words)

Why make readers read this paragraph twice to get the relatively simple message? To improve this passage, shorten the sentences and eliminate unnecessarily difficult words.

Revised:

The job-site buyer shall have the authority and responsibility outlined in Corporate Procedure 6001. With authorized requisitions, this person may buy locally all supplies, equipment, spare parts, and services within the limits of the approved job estimate. (37 words)

Do not accustom yourself to use big words for little matters.

—*Samuel Johnson*

Not only does foggy writing confuse and amuse, but long sentences often camouflage important ideas:

There is a wide variation in their chemical content, which influences their heat content, and total sulfur can be determined only by heating to 800°C a coal sample combined with Eschka's Mixture.

Did you pick up on the idea that the variation in chemical content influences heat? Here's the same thought expressed in two sentences with both ideas getting equal billing:

The wide variation in the chemical content influences the heat content. Total sulfur can be determined only by heating to 800°C a coal sample combined with Eschka's Mixture.

To avoid buried ideas and unnecessary complexity, business sentences should average no more than 15 to 20 words. Roughly, that means two to two and a half lines of print. You may have to compensate for a difficult technical vocabulary with sentences shorter than you normally write to express simple ideas and information.

An average sentence of 17.5 words will not mean writing at an elementary-school level, such as in the following letter.

Dear Mr. Jones:

The Selection Board considers all local applicants for each new position. It carefully considered all candidates qualified for this New Orleans position. You were not one of those nominated for consideration. Management is limited in the number of candidates it may nominate. Competition is often very keen.

We are most appreciative of your interest in the position. You can be sure you will continue to be considered for other vacancies.

Sincerely,

This letter averages fewer than 10 words per sentence. Revising the ideas into longer sentences still makes this letter easy reading. The following letter averages 16 words per sentence.

Dear Mr. Jones:

The Selection Board evaluates and considers all local applicants for each new position, including the New Orleans position. Because management is limited in the number of candidates it may nominate, competition is often very keen. I am sorry to say that you were not one of those nominated for consideration. We appreciate your interest in the position, and we will continue to consider you for other vacancies.

Sincerely,

Although technical writers such as scientists, doctors, and engineers are most vocal about their inability to write at readable levels, competent journalists writing for popular magazines frequently reword scientific-journal articles for easier reading. And the world's most respected philosophers, scientists, and political leaders agree about the value of simplicity in writing style:

> Most of the fundamental ideas of science are essentially simple, and may, as a rule, be expressed in language comprehensible to everyone.
>
> —Albert Einstein, *The Evolution of Physics*

> If you cannot—in the long run—tell everyone what you have been doing, your doing has been worthless.
>
> —Erwin Schrödinger, *Science and Humanism*

> Even for a physicist, the description, in plain language, will be a criterion of the degree of understanding that has been reached.
>
> —Werner Heisenber, *Physics and Philosophy*

> They who know that they are profound strive for clarity.
>
> —Friedrich Nietzsche, *The Gay Science*

> Broadly speaking, the short words are the best, and the old words best of all.
>
> —Winston Churchill

Do the most eloquent speakers and writers understand this principle about clarity? Certainly. Consider these comments from world leaders, who did not mince words, but rather chose clear, direct, straightforward, simple language:

> The news from France is bad.
>
> —Winston Churchill

> The only thing we have to fear is fear itself.
>
> —Franklin D. Roosevelt

> Ask not what your country can do for you; ask what you can do for your country.
>
> —John Fitzgerald Kennedy

> I have a dream.
>
> —Dr.Martin Luther King

> I must govern the clock, not be governed by it.
>
> —Golda Meir

When business readers consider a subject too complex, most likely the writing is at fault. Long sentences and technical jargon make readers work to decode words rather than to understand ideas.

Clear writing demands clear thinking. Clarity, rather than gobbledygook, is a true mark of intelligence. Policy manuals, instructional materials, and research reports written at appropriate reading levels, void of fog, could save businesses millions of dollars each year.

The long and short of it: Word choice and sentence length and pattern set the readers' pace as they go through your material. Aim to make your writing easy—not difficult—to read.

Position Ideas for the Proper Emphasis

Place important ideas in the spotlight. You can elevate an idea by placing it prominently, or bury it among a clutter of details (commonly known as "the fine print").

Where are the prominent spots? Consider how many advertisers pay premium prices to place their ads on the inside fronts and on the backs of magazine covers. That same placement proves paramount in attracting readers to your most important ideas.

The *body position* of most prominence is at the beginning of a document. That's why a report should begin with conclusions and recommendations rather than a history of the project, procedures, or situation. Likewise, an e-mail should begin with the message, not a warm-up drill rehashing previously discussed issues or details.

Buried Message:

Paul,

I received your e-mail in which you asked about the feasibility of coordinating our efforts on the Saudi project to be completed by our September target date. After reviewing your suggestions for coordinating our efforts, I see no limitations in proceeding as you outlined.

Revised with the Message in the Position of Emphasis:

Paul,

After reviewing the suggestions in your e-mail, *I see no limitations in coordinating our efforts in the Saudi project.*

Paragraph position of most prominence is also at the beginning. Fiction writers can shuffle topic-sentence position for variety. But in business writing, the topic sentence, if at all possible, should come first in the paragraph, immediately after any transitional thought. When you read a paragraph that begins "Actually the two procedures are similar," you know exactly what you'll find in the body of the paragraph—a discussion of similarities. With correctly placed topic sentences, busy readers can skim to find paragraphs that merit closer attention.

The *position in the sentence* of most prominence is at the end. The second strongest emphasis comes at the beginning. Clauses and phrases of least importance go in the middle. (Of course, this applies only in the placement of clauses, not words. Applied to single-clause sentences, that would mean that each word gets successively more important toward the end of the sentence, an incorrect assumption.)

Forming a sentence without attention to this natural emphasis may mislead your readers about your intended message and the implications of that message.

Currently, John Monroe and Henry Jobe are writing controls and procedures so these out-of-balances can be monitored monthly and correcting entries can be made.

In order to monitor those out-of-balances monthly and to enter necessary corrections, John Monroe and Henry Jobe are writing controls and procedures.

Either sentence sounds correct—and is, depending on the intended meaning. The first emphasizes why the controls and procedures are being written. The second emphasizes who is doing what about the problem.

It may be necessary to shorten our retention period on the magazines that we currently house in order to reduce space requirements.

In this sentence, the emphasis is on *why* ("to reduce space requirements"). But in the following sentence the emphasis is on *what to do* ("shorten our retention period").

To reduce space requirements for magazines that we currently house, it may be necessary to shorten our retention period. (least important clause buried as a connector, as it should be, in the middle of the sentence)

We have postponed the testing because the client still has economic and environmental safety concerns. (emphasizes the reason)

Because the client still has economic and environmental safety concerns, we have postponed the testing. (emphasizes the postponement)

Of course, when the "which" or "that" clause is intended as an afterthought or aside, placing it at the end of the sentence is fine. In such sentences readers understand the emphasis, no matter where the words are placed:

The board will become discolored and movies will be affected, when we use the board as a screen.

In the previous sentence, readers grab the main idea first; the last clause just hangs on, sounding weak and anticlimactic.

In a simple sentence, the most prominent positions are those of the subject, the verb, and then the object.

John kicks the ball. Mary kicks the ball. See John and Mary kick the ball.

Such are the basics of our English sentence—subject, verb, object. The subject (John, Mary) gets the most attention; when we want to know more about the subject, we read the verb.

The following sentences illustrate lackluster writing. Note that in the weak examples, the least important idea inappropriately serves as the sentence subject.

Weak:	*It appears* that only a small amount of the product is available in the reactor effluent.
Emphatic:	*Only a small amount of the product* is available in the reactor effluent. (emphasizes the small amount)
Weak:	*There was* a load of 1,950 pounds per support that was used in our analysis.
Emphatic:	*A load of 1,950 pounds per support* was used in our analysis. (emphasizes the weight)
Weak:	*It has been suggested* that the product be evaluated as a defogging component.
Emphatic:	*That the product be evaluated as a defogging component* has been suggested. (emphasizes the product as a possible defogging component)

When dealing with *two ideas* in a *simple* sentence, the most emphatic position is the subject spot. When handling two ideas in a complex sentence of two clauses, the most prominent position is the end of the sentence. In other words, climactic sentences (also called periodic or emphatic sentences) create suspense by building to a climax.

This is not to say that *all* your sentences should be emphatic or climactic. Only you know which ideas you want to emphasize, and the placement of those ideas signals your readers about their importance. Sometimes you want to slow down your readers, sustaining interest over several ideas instead of leading them quickly through peaks and valleys.

Simply be aware of the climactic technique for emphasizing key points.

You control readers' attention and what they "pick up on" by where you place an idea in the body of the document, where you place a sentence in a paragraph, where you place a clause in a sentence, and where you place an idea in a clause.

Like the well-trained ad writer, you should position the most important ideas in the high-priced spots.

Link to Indicate Proper Relationships

Analyze the logical flow of your words, phrases, or sentences, and join them properly to indicate their relationship to each other. Are both ideas equally important? Is one part of the sentence a result of the other? Is one clause a contradiction of the other? Is there a time relationship? Illogically linked clauses and phrases confuse readers. Identify the more important message in the following two sentences:

> The atomic absorption method, which we use to determine trace elements in coal, is a dry ashing-acid dissolution technique.

> The atomic absorption method, a dry ashing-acid dissolution technique, is what we used to determine trace elements.

In the first sentence the method or technique is more important because this information comes in the main clause. The linking word *which* introduces the minor clause containing the minor idea.

In the second sentence the main clause again tells the main idea— what they do with the technique, *determine trace elements*. The fact that it is a *dry ashing-acid dissolution* is subordinated in a minor phrase in the middle of the sentence—the position of least emphasis. The message in the two sentences above is quite different.

In the following examples, an improper linking *and* makes the message unclear:

> The tables are in chronological order of testing and contain the following information. (The *and* is like a plus sign—this equals that. Are both ideas joined by *and* in this sentence equal? Probably not.)

The tables, in chronological order of testing, contain the following information. (Emphasis is on the information the tables contain because *chronological order* is now only a phrase.)

The tables, containing the following information, are in chronological order of testing. (Emphasis is on the chronological order because that idea is now in the main clause rather than in an equal phrase linked by *and*.)

Nowhere is proper linking more important than in giving instructions.

Turn the lever to the right *and* depress the cylinder that opens the air chamber. (Is this one related action or two separate actions? The *and* is ambiguous.)

Turn the lever to the right *while* depressing the cylinder that opens the air chamber. (Stating the proper time relationship makes the instruction clear.)

Turn the lever to the right, *thereby* depressing the cylinder that opens the air chamber. (One action. The depressed cylinder is a result of the first action.)

The linking word *or* can also obscure meaning.

Approximately six grams of whole coal or liquefaction residue was placed in the crucible.

Is whole coal the same as liquefaction residue? Or is the writer talking about either of two elements? I had to ask the geologist who wrote this sentence, because not having an engineering background, I thought this distinction might be clear to someone in that field. No, the two items are not the same, he assured me; and no, the distinction wouldn't be clear unless an engineer specifically had experience with the liquefaction process.

To prevent misreading with the *or* link, add parentheses or use both correlative conjunctions:

Ambiguous: This stress or the stress at the outer coupling will . . . (one stress or two?)

Clear: *Either* this stress *or* the stress at the outer coupling will damage the system.

Clear: This stress (the stress at the outer coupling) will damage the system.

Study the following chart to understand the purpose of common linking words:

LINKING WORDS	FUNCTION
and, but, or, yet, either/or, neither/nor	link equal ideas
therefore, so, because, thus, hence, consequently	indicate a cause-and-effect relationship
when, as, then, while, next, later	indicate time relationships
because, although, while, where, if	express subordinate ideas

One other consideration about linking words involves hyphenation: In a nutshell, hyphenate two related words when they precede a noun but not when they follow a noun. Again, the issue is clarity. The hyphenation helps readers grasp the two related words together and consider them as a joint entity. (For an in-depth discussion of hyphenation, see pp. 225–28.)

first-rate job
two-day seminar
six-step approach
high-impact conversation
decision-making process
follow-up meeting

Only you as a writer know the exact relationship between your ideas and words; link them accordingly.

If any man wish to write in a clear style, let him be first
clear in his thoughts. . . .
—*Johann Wolfgang von Goethe*

Use Clear Transitions

Transitions guide readers through your writing and tie your ideas together. Lead readers through your thoughts; don't let them wander. That is, take care not to do a brain dump of information, sentence after unrelated sentence, leaving readers to wonder what X has to do with Y. Connect the dots.

We've already discussed punctuation marks as traffic signals; transitions provide additional directions to help readers move quickly through your document. Your transitions say "go ahead to my next point," "take a detour here for a few moments," "stay with me while I illustrate," "contrast that with what I'm going to say now," "let me qualify that with," or "look back while I remind you where we've been."

> I sometimes think that writing is like driving sheep down a road. If there is any gate to the left or right, the readers will most certainly go into it.
> —*C. S. Lewis*

Here are five techniques for steering your readers from one thought to the next:

- Line space
- New paragraph
- Transitional paragraph between sections of a document (see Figure 45)
- Intentional repetition from one sentence, paragraph, or section to another
- Transitional words or phrases (see Figure 46)

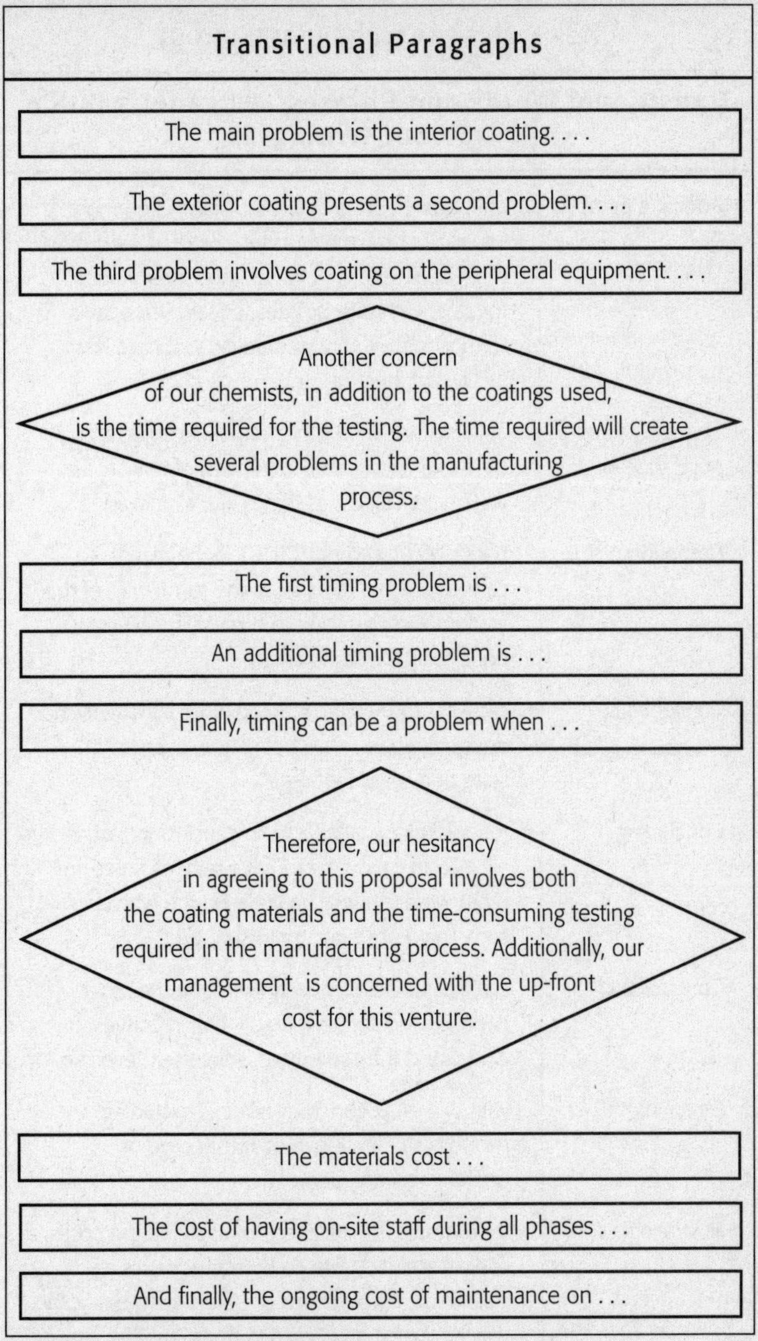

Transitional Paragraphs

The main problem is the interior coating. . . .

The exterior coating presents a second problem. . . .

The third problem involves coating on the peripheral equipment. . . .

Another concern of our chemists, in addition to the coatings used, is the time required for the testing. The time required will create several problems in the manufacturing process.

The first timing problem is . . .

An additional timing problem is . . .

Finally, timing can be a problem when . . .

Therefore, our hesitancy in agreeing to this proposal involves both the coating materials and the time-consuming testing required in the manufacturing process. Additionally, our management is concerned with the up-front cost for this venture.

The materials cost . . .

The cost of having on-site staff during all phases . . .

And finally, the ongoing cost of maintenance on . . .

Figure 45. Transitional Paragraphs. Such paragraphs bridge the gaps between major sections of the document.

Transitional Words and Phrases: A Reader's Guide to Your Writing

Adding a point	and, again, add to this, in addition, even more, especially, how much more, above all, best of all, most of all, additionally, yet more important, together with this, besides, equally important, further, furthermore, moreover, too, next, first, finally, last, here again
Changing tone or point of view	at least, for my part, in another sense, as a matter of fact, in fact, in general, of course, as the matter stands, as things are, all this aside
Comparing	parallel with, comparable to, in the same category, in like manner, in the same way, of the same nature, similarly, likewise, a similar view, equally, by the same token
Conceding	certainly, to be sure, granted, true, admittedly, no doubt, doubtless, this being true, even so, in spite of this, nonetheless
Concluding	to conclude, finally, lastly, in conclusion, last of all, in brief, in short, as I have said, as noted, in other words, in final analysis, on the whole, in summary, summing up, to sum up
Contradicting	but, yet, however, nevertheless, on the other hand, on the contrary, for all that, in contrast, by contrast, at the same time, conversely, even so
Excepting	with this exception, disregarding, excluding, regardless of, exclusive of, irrespective of, omitting this one point
Illustrating	for example, for instance, for analytical purposes, suppose, to illustrate, to demonstrate, as an illustration, for purposes of clarifying, to clarify, by way of illustration, a case in point, another case, to explain, in other words, that is to say, to elaborate

Indicating causal relationships	thereby, therefore, accordingly, consequently, thus, unfortunately so, as a result, according to, hence, because of this, such being the case, this being true, for this reason, under these circumstances, due to, on such occasions
Indicating spatial relationships	above, below, beneath, overhead, in the foreground, in the background, inside of, outside of, on the exterior, in the interior, under, over, beside, behind, in front of
Qualifying	although, although this is true, while, notwithstanding, still, furthermore, further, not forgetting, with this caveat
Returning to original point	to continue, to resume, to return, along with, as I mentioned earlier, now, again, once more, at any rate, returning to my earlier point
Showing purpose	with this in mind, so to this end, for this purpose, for this reason

Figure 46. Transitional Words and Phrases. Effective transitions carry your readers from one idea to the next.

In addition to the transitional words and phrases such as those in Figure 46, you can repeat key ideas or words to signal your readers where you're taking them next. For example:

... Their hypothesis was not motivated by nostalgia for past accomplishments, but rather by *concern* for the future. A similar *interest* turned up in the reports done ...

... Thus, the Internet had a double effect on the *research* of our designers. Their *research* revealed descriptions of ...

... These unsolved *reservations* delayed that experimenting. Nevertheless, these *reservations* served to underscore the need for ...

As you edit your work, insert transitions to guide your readers. If you don't lead, readers may hesitate or become lost along the way.

Use Clear References

Be careful using *this, that, they, it, his, her,* or *which,* when there is more than one idea or noun to which these pronouns can refer. Sometimes context makes the meaning clear; often it does not.

Unclear: Roberto has been angry with his manager for months, debating whether his policies and strategies are acceptable in today's marketplace. (Whose policies are they debating—Roberto's or his manager's?)

Unclear: Laura did further research Joan's audit findings and then altered them in her report to the full committee. (Whose report—Laura's or Joan's?)

Unclear: We are most interested in the conventions at which you've exhibited in the past twenty-four months but in no way want to limit you to that time frame in completing the application. We are also mailing you a brochure with additional information about the associated costs, housing options, and special marketing opportunities associated with the conventions in the Northwest. It (the application? the brochure?) should be received by May 10. All of these (costs? housing options? special marketing opportunities? applications?) need to be cleared with Mike McDuffy before we can take action on scheduling, which (the clearing with Mike? the scheduling?) can sometimes be difficult on short notice.

Unclear: Canister pressures were monitored closely, and head-space gas samples were taken in vacutainers whenever the pressure reached approximately 2 psi. *This* was violated during transport of the canisters. (Did they fail to monitor closely while transporting? Did they fail to take gas samples? Did the writer fail to take gas samples when the pressure was at approximately 2 psi?)

Unclear: Our campaign to interest others in the use of our intranet, causing a more rapid expansion in and of itself, may not benefit the total operation. Like many other areas in Office Services, *it* has a pressing need. (What has a pressing need—the intranet or the campaign effort?)

Unclear: Delivery of an additional vacuum pump will be required for the project, which has been postponed pending SOC approval. (What has been postponed—the delivery or the project?)

Make sure that a particular pronoun refers to only one thing, idea, place, or person.

Prefer Concrete Words and Phrases

Word meanings vary from person to person and from organization to organization. The interpretation of abstract words and phrases depends on your readers' purposes and their experience or frame of reference—not the writer's.

Rumor has it that the company's *storage facilities* are completely *inadequate*. (*Facilities:* warehouse? dock? storage tanks? filing and cabinet space? computer storage? *Inadequate:* size? location? construction? security?)

Plants in *similar* cities have proven successful. (*Similar:* size? location? lifestyle of clientele? economic strength? educational level of population?)

Such abstractions are open to multiple meanings. Use a concrete word that gives the precise meaning you intend.

Vague phrases also cause problems. For example, consider this question: "Can you get those to me *within a few days?*" When I ask workshop participants to tell me what their habitual response time would be with a request like this, their answers range from two to ten days. If the writer of such a statement has no specific deadline in mind, there's no problem. The irritation comes when the writer *does* have a definite date in mind, cloaked behind *within a few days*, and readers respond on their own timetable, a later one.

Granted, you may be able to tell from the context what a phrase like *within a few days, inadequate, similar, unsuitable conditions,* or *unavoidable delay* means. But often you cannot.

It takes no more time to be specific and clear than it does to be general and vague. When you want action, if you don't take the time to find out the specifics to be persuasive, your chances for a favorable response decrease drastically. When you're considering the time required, think of the total time involved in getting results. If you're unclear and vague the first time, chances are you'll be corresponding about the situation several times before it's resolved. Consider these versions to identify which will get the quickest action:

General, vague, ineffective:

The accounting people need to do something about the paper-work they're sending us because most of it is redundant and time-consuming to complete. Can you contact somebody over there to complain?

Specific, clear, strong:

Art Jones in Audit sent me a Form 3126, asking me to list minor-ity vendors that we deal with. The form took me twenty minutes to complete, and the requested information is already available on Form 4511. Could you call Rosita Gonzales (or another man-ager) over there to make her aware of the duplication?

When pointing out imprecise words to writers (such as those in Figure 47), frequently we hear the response, "But wouldn't the meaning be clear in context?" The answer is almost always no. Avoid vague gener-alities such as the following that will require a lawsuit to enforce or defend:

The product will be designed to the satisfaction of the project engineer.
The contact will be considered complete when the project is acceptable to the client.
Chemical impurities may be cause for rejection.
Testing procedures may be waived at the discretion of the inspector.
Additional trips to the site may be required.
Aerial photos may be required.

Unless you have something to hide, why be vague when you can be specific?

DON'T WRITE . . .	WHEN YOU COULD BE SPECIFIC . . .
major-incident response unit	ambulance, police car, fire truck
technical exposures	error in the software
limited resources	limited staff, expertise, money
educational venture	public seminar, online course
several factors	cost, staff, safety
bad weather	hurricane
transportation systems	pipelines
storage facility	warehouse, hard-drive space
environmentally controlled	chemical-free
nurturing unit	parent, grandparent

Hedging: Qualifiers, Intensifiers, and Vague Abstractions

QUALIFIERS

to some degree	rather	primarily
to some extent	tolerable	largely
reasonably	generally	may possibly
considerable	commonly	perhaps
appears	seems	apparently
more or less	significantly	should be

INTENSIFIERS

very	purely	well under
absolutely	especially	well over
so	genuinely	completely
quite	extremely	simply

VAGUE ABSTRACTIONS

various factors (scheduling? personnel? money?)
several approaches (to an airport runway?)
similar types (similar in cost? in materials? in design?)
facilities (warehouses? hotels? toilets?)
units (pencils? lots? buildings?)
in this manner
in this mode
in this fashion
has various capabilities to
quite a few
a number of
a small amount
a significant amount

Figure 47. Qualifiers, Intensifiers, and Vague Abstractions. Be
straightforward and confident in your writing. Hedging and vague qualifiers
overshadow key ideas.

Some writers use less precise words because someone may have
advised them, "Don't keep repeating the same word over and over—
choose a synonym." A teacher may admonish students to switch from
house to *cottage* to *dwelling* to *residence.* That's understandable advice
when you consider that a teacher's objective is often to help students
build a large vocabulary. But the primary goal of business or technical
writers is to be clear.

Once you have chosen the most precise word, stay with it. If, however,
you can use alternate words without losing precision and creating confusion,
by all means do so. But repeating key words or phrases is preferable to using
imprecise alternatives that distort what you intend to say.

Additionally, to be precise means to understand both the denotation
and the connotation of the words and phrases you choose (Figure 48). For
example, airline companies have begun to call their red-eye flights "moon-
light specials." They know the power of words to control thought.

Denotation and Connotation		
NEUTRAL	**POSITIVE**	**NEGATIVE**
employees	associates/partners/team	support function
temporary	alternate	makeshift
strong	tenacious	obstinate
initial	pioneering	primitive
odorous	fragrant	foul-smelling
inherent	essential	ingrained
shelter	safeguard	conceal
change	stimulate	agitate
imitation	substitute	fake
altered	improved	replaced
firm	confident	opinionated
residence	home	hovel
satisfactory	ample	adequate
end	finish/conclude	abandon/terminate
cost	inexpensive	cheap

Figure 48. Denotation and Connotation. Be aware of unintended shades of meanings in the word you use.

Some words can be interpreted either positively or negatively—and will be, according to the experience and background of the readers. Consider this series of near synonyms: *surprising, interesting, novel, amusing,* and *revealing.* Such word choices often leave translation open to readers, usually a dangerous thing to do.

To summarize: Simple, concrete words and phrases lead to precise writing and clear action.

Know When to Use and to Avoid Jargon

Vague phrases such as the ones previously mentioned may have carelessness or courtesy at their source. But vagueness resulting from unnecessary jargon irritates readers. Why do writers lapse into jargon when a simple, clear statement would communicate the message just as well? Some use jargon to impress; others use it out of ignorance, unaware that others don't know what they mean; some use it to hedge or cover up for having nothing to say.

The following paragraph is part of a note from a client:

On page 9 of Section I of your report, you commented that RWW has not charged the venture for any amounts related to the "cost of money for facilities capital." John Duke of RWW has asked me to request that you clarify the meaning of the above-mentioned "cost of money for facilities capital" and additionally that you review the concept for the Far East operation.

Clarify, indeed. I agree. Why didn't the writer of the original report just say *interest on the real estate loan for the new learning center* rather than the vague *cost of money for facilities capital*?

Of course, you need to use the jargon of your profession on occasion. Words such as *turnkey* contract, or *footage* contract, or *daywork* contract may substitute for more than a sentence or two of explanation. Chemists, physicians, accountants, lawyers, teachers, gymnasts, plumbers—all have vocational jargon useful for expressing complicated ideas to their colleagues. But the key to jargon usage is in my last phrase—*to their colleagues.*

I'm perturbed rather than impressed when I go to my doctor with an infection and hear her utter every medical term she has at her disposal to describe my condition and cure. When she writes a referral letter to another specialist, she can use all the medical jargon she chooses, but I expect to be informed in terms understandable to the layperson.

People from other departments of your organization, managers removed from the specific workings of your division, and clients expect the same from most writers—simple, clear words. If you don't say what you mean, don't be surprised or angry that you don't get what you want.

Jargon is like rhetoric. It always describes what the other guy does.
We argue; he indulges in specious rhetoric. We make ourselves
clear; he speaks jargon.
—Richard Lanham

Avoid Unnecessary Foreign Expressions

The trend in both business and technical writing is to avoid foreign words and phrases. Use them only if there is no good English equivalent.

Technical-writing workshop participants frequently ask us to clarify the difference between *e.g. (for example)* and *i.e.(that is)*. If so many technical professionals misunderstand the difference between the two, why use them? Why not write *for example* or *that is*?

Et cetera, meaning "and others of the same kind," is another frequently misused term.

Unclear: In the meeting with the client you will need to bring your laptop, lab notes, etc.

What's the *et cetera*? A goat? Maybe a pail of water? This sentence establishes no clear pattern with which to identify what is to follow. Rather, the use of the term shows lazy thinking.

Clear: Table 6 clearly shows that the displacement values have increased in direct proportion to the addition of our Theyal mixture: 3 percent, 6 percent, 9 percent, 12 percent, etc. (A clear pattern is indicated.)

Et al. (period always included) is another frequently confused phrase, meaning "and other people." It does not refer to things. Correct use: "The project push came from the Rhode Island group, Rochelle Lemmons *et al.*"

If your goal is to be clear to all readers, use foreign words and phrases only when there is no English equivalent.

Eliminate Gaps in Logic

Each idea should build logically on the preceding ideas. Readers shouldn't be left with a "So what does that have to do with what you just said?" feeling. Readers frequently have that feeling about hurriedly prepared e-mail. Suppose you are watching a TV movie. Your attention is totally absorbed by the action. Then the screen goes black and the sound becomes muffled with static. When the picture and dialogue resume, it's apparent you have missed something.

Readers often have the same frustrated feeling about ideas strung together without an apparent connection. In such cases, they are inclined to respond, "So what? I don't get your point." Consider the following examples:

> Margaret makes an enormous salary, *and* she drives an older model Ford. (So what's the point or connection?)

> Margaret makes an enormous salary, *but* she drives an older model Ford. (Probably the point is that even though she could afford any model she wanted, she doesn't have much interest in prestigious cars.)

> Nuha is divorcing Adele, *and* he took her to lunch. (So what's the point or connection?)

> Even though Nuha is divorcing Adele, he took her to lunch. (Probably the point is that they are still associating with each other.)

Such gaps in logic are much easier to detect in someone else's writing than in our own because we as writers are familiar with our subject matter. In any piece of writing, the ideas and the logic behind them probably seemed clear to the writer, or he or she wouldn't have expressed them in such a way. Compare the following two passages:

> The testing equipment mentioned in the specifications will cost $10,480. A Bithurg Labs representative has proposed to reevaluate the test results on our first samples. (So what's the point, the connection?)

But rewritten, the connection is evident:

> The testing equipment mentioned in the specifications will cost $10,480; *therefore*, we may decide to wait before purchasing that new equipment. A Bithurg Labs representative has proposed to reevaluate the test results on our first samples *to determine if the old equipment itself was the cause for the discrepancies in our results.*

Some writers struggle so long with a sentence that once they get the prepositional phrases and the adverbial clauses tucked into some out-of-the-way place, they fail to consider the logic of the sentence in its entirety. Comparisons can frequently be the culprit in illogical sentences.

Incomplete Comparison:

Our site readings varied more than your analyst.

Complete Comparison:

Our site readings varied more than those taken by your analyst.

Incomplete Comparison:

The workflow in Diagram 6 is more complex than Diagram 7.

Complete Comparison:

The workflow in Diagram 6 is more complex than that shown in Diagram 7.

Imprecise words represent convoluted thinking. Consider these classics I've collected over the years:

We are going to preboard the plane. (How can you board an airplane before you board it?)

I want to take a day out of your time to discuss this. (Not if I can help it! A day out of my schedule, maybe.)

The appreciation of a host-controlled environment will become not only the best way but the only way to implement complexity of a distributed network. (Is the appreciation a way? Why would they want to implement complexity—job security?)

The question may no longer be valid for all brick walls—changes in construction materials and methods jeopardize its truthfulness. (How can brick walls be truthful? Does the writer mean integrity or stability?)

A clear understanding of the conversion that will take place is illustrated by the diagrams that follow. (The understanding is illustrated? There is a diagram of brain waves?)

The following list of security coordinators has authority to write policy statements. (The list is going to write the statements? Does that mean the coordinators themselves can go home?)

Fuzzy thinking produces fuzzy writing. Think about the logic of the entire sentence and make sure the words linked together state exactly what you mean. Leave no cracks between ideas for your reader to fall through and lose your line of reasoning.

> The "of" strings are the worst of all. They look like a child pulling a gob of bubble gum out into a long string.
> —*Richard Lanham,* Revising Prose

Maintain a Consistent Viewpoint and Voice

"First person" point of view means using *I* or *we;* the writer talks about himself or herself. In "second person" point of view the writer talks directly to readers: "You cannot transfer these records." The *you* may be understood, as in this sentence: "Do not transfer these records." In "third person" point of view the writer talks *about* someone or something other than himself or the readers: "The company has paid the claim." "Service has been interrupted."

Notice the inconsistency in the point of view in the following excerpt:

Requisitions should be approved by department heads or their designated representatives. Have all Forms 200 filled in and submit them to Accounting for processing.

The first sentence is third person; the second sentence is second person—"you" do something. Therefore, whose responsibility is it to send the requisitions to Accounting for processing? Heads of the departments mentioned in the first sentence? Or the "you" addressed in the second sentence?

Revised: Fill out Form 200, have it approved by a department head or his or her designated representative, and then submit it to Accounting for processing.

Many writers, however, even when they are consistent about using third person, write passive-voice sentences, dropping out all the people.

Passive: It was found to be a viable alternative to sell the
             compressors because the storage area has been unused.
             (Who found? Who didn't use the storage area?)

Active: We discovered that selling the compressors was a viable
             alternative because the Snowden branch no longer uses the
             storage area.

Passive voice often creates a clarity problem because the "doer" in the sentence sometimes hangs on awkwardly and begs to be lopped off the end.

Passive: Arrangements to have these signed forms in my office by
             Friday, February 12, should be announced immediately by
             each supervisor.

The "by each supervisor" sounds awkward, so the tendency is to omit this information. And therein lies the problem:

Passive: Arrangements to have these signed forms in my office by
             Friday, February 12, should be announced immediately.
             (still passive and also unclear about who is to make the
             announcement)

In business writing, who does what is usually an essential part of the message. Instructions that mention no person can be deadly—literally. At the very least, such instructions will be ignored or may be misconstrued.

A case in point: A passive-voice sentence without the people ended up before the state Supreme Court in New Jersey a few years ago. The questionable lease stated: "Water shall be provided." Whether by the lessee or the lessor became the unresolved issue that cost litigants and tax-payers considerable time and money.

Name a person and be consistent from sentence to sentence about who does what.

Editing your own writing for clarity is difficult; nothing sounds unclear to you because you know what you mean. But when readers question a phrase or detail, when recipients of your documents phone or e-mail you to ask for explanation you thought you had already provided, or when people don't follow your instructions, interpret these questions and reactions as warnings about unclear writing.

Arrange to have a colleague edit your important documents before they go out, and then listen to the questions raised or the suggestions made. If you do the same editing for your friend, the time spent will be a trade-off.

In summary, when editing for clarity: Consider readability. Place key ideas in the spotlight. Link to show relationships. Use clear transitions. Use clear references. Place modifiers as close as possible to the noun or pronoun they describe. Prefer specific words and phrases rather than vague ones. Use a consistent viewpoint and voice.

Remember: Your documents are always clear to you, or you wouldn't have written them as you did. The primary test: Are they clear to others?

16

EDIT FOR CONCISENESS

The most frequent complaint I hear from reading executives concerns document length. Writers take five screens to say what they could say more concisely in two. To cut length saves both writing time and reading time—both translate into money.

Another benefit is that brevity adds punch. Consider these clichés: "Familiarity breeds contempt." "Pride goes before a fall." "Haste makes waste." "Forewarned is forearmed." These have become clichés because they are strong, precise, concise.

The more words you pour into a sentence, the weaker the message. In a long document, the main ideas often are buried in a mound of details. Good writers know the value of getting to the point.

> The most valuable of all talents is that of never using
> two words when one will do.
> —*Thomas Jefferson*

Prefer Active-Voice Verbs

"Voice" refers to the relationship of a verb to its subject. "Active voice" means that the subject of the sentence *does the action* of the sentence. "Passive voice" means that the subject of the sentence *receives the action*.

Passive:	The study *was completed* by our investigators.
Active:	Our investigators *completed* the study.
Passive:	The package *is being shipped* overnight.
Active:	Bill *is shipping* the package overnight.

Passive:	The terms *can be negotiated* at a later date.
Active:	Hilaire *can negotiate* terms at a later date.

Passive:	The gauges *will be revamped* next week.
Active:	We *will revamp* the gauges next week.

Passive:	Metallurgical analyses *are being performed* by Brighton, Inc.
Active:	Brighton, Inc. *is performing* metallurgical analyses.

Passive:	It *is expected* that the meeting won't last longer than half an hour.
Active:	The marketing manager *expects* the meeting to last no longer than half an hour.

Passive:	The design of those systems *was simplified* by the use of hydraulics.
Active:	The use of hydraulics *simplified* the design of those systems.

Passive:	The significance of the makeup and test procedure on the connectors *is evaluated* by a tool that extends the size range from 7 inches to 16 inches.
Active:	A tool that extends the size range from 7 inches to 16 inches *evaluates* the significance of the makeup and test procedure on the connectors.

Passive:	Your business *is* sincerely *appreciated.*
Active:	We sincerely *appreciate* your business.

Passive voice creates a flat, lackluster, stilted, impersonal tone; thus, the term "passive." Active voice, on the other hand, sounds alive, personal, immediate; thus, the term "active." A side effect of this passive construction, as mentioned earlier in the Edit for Grammar section, is the dangling verbal phrase.

Then, in Edit for Clarity, I said that passive voice often omits people, and that who does what in business writing is usually important. Passive voice comes under attack again because, on average, it lengthens sentences by 15 to 50 percent.

Passive:	Separate requisitions should be prepared by each buyer. (8 words)
Active:	Each buyer should prepare separate requisitions. (6 words)

Passive:	The investigation has been concluded by our client, and the paperwork has been signed. (14 words)
Active:	Our client has concluded the investigation and signed the paperwork. (10 words)
Passive:	Variations in canister pressure and air temperature were accounted for in the calculations by our investigators. (16 words)
Active:	Our investigators accounted for variations in canister pressure and air temperature in their calculations. (14 words)
Passive:	Your prompt attention to this matter will be appreciated. (9 words)
Active:	Please attend to this matter promptly. (6 words)
Passive:	The system was developed by our staff. (7 words)
Active:	Our staff developed the system. (5 words)
Passive:	The tension was maintained by mechanical locks and anchors. (9 words)
Active:	Mechanical locks and anchors maintained the tension. (7 words)

What's the big concern if your sentence has 16 words rather than 8? Nothing—if you write only one sentence. But if you habitually write in passive voice, you unnecessarily turn a five-paragraph e-mail into a ten-paragraph one.

Some writers, however, may prefer passive voice because "it sounds more intellectual," or "it sounds more objective," or "business writing has always been done that way." But none of this is true. Note the personal references and active-voice verbs in the excerpt from Louis Pasteur on fermentation. I could have chosen excerpts from any number of other intellectuals from Francis Bacon to Thomas Paine—excerpts written in active voice with personal pronouns.

Louis Pasteur on Fermentation:

The following experiments were undertaken to solve this double problem: We took a double-necked flask, of three litres (five pints) capacity, one of the tubes being curved and forming an escape for the gas; the other one, on the right side (Fig. 1), being furnished with a glass tap. *We* filled this flask with pure yeast water, sweetened with 5 percent of sugar candy, the flask being so full that there was not the least trace of air remaining above the tap or in the escape tube; this artificial wort had, however, been itself aerated. The curved tube was plunged in a porcelain vessel full of mercury, resting on a firm support. In the small cylindrical funnel above the tap, the capacity of which was from 10 cc. to 15 cc. (about half a fluid ounce) *we* caused to ferment, at a temperature of 20°C or 25°C (about 75°F), five or six cubic centimetres of the saccharine liquid, by means of a trace of yeast, which multiplied rapidly, causing fermentation, and forming a slight deposit of yeast at the bottom of the funnel above the tap. *We* then opened the tap, and some of the liquid in the funnel entered the flask, carrying with it the small deposit of yeast, which was sufficient to impregnate the saccharine liquid contained in the flask. In this manner it is possible to introduce as small a quantity of yeast as *we* wish, a quantity the weight of which, *we* may say, is hardly appreciable.

(Reprinted with permission of the Harvard Classics, Grolier Enterprises Corp.)

Neither does leaving people out of your writing make it more objective. Haven't you read "third person" passive-voice newspaper or magazine articles that were, without doubt, politically or morally biased? Such articles show biases by which details the journalists choose to include and which they omit, by which sources they quote and which they ignore. Passive voice does not ensure objectivity, only length.

Finally, just because reports, policy manuals, or procedures in your organization "have always been done that way" doesn't mean that the practice should continue. Aren't new ideas and methods the reasons for promotions? Few will argue against clarity and efficiency.

So how do you convert passive voice to active voice? Add the "actor" before the verb. That "actor" may be a person, an object, or an idea. Determine who or what is doing something in the sentence, and then place that actor at the beginning of the sentence. Go back to the previous examples of passive and active voice and note placement of the actor at the beginning of each active-voice sentence.

Can passive voice be all bad? Of course not. Continual use of active-voice verbs would be monotonous and at times pompous. Passive-voice sentences can be useful on occasion.

Passive Verbs Add Variety

We preinsulated the injection string with calcium silicate. Then we insulated a concentric injection string that had been in use earlier. Finally, the production casing *was prestressed* in all wells. (The last passive-verb sentence changes the pace.)

Passive Verbs Soften Commands

The procedures *should be revised*. ("Revise the procedures" is a strong command to deliver to a client or peer.)

The operation of the plotter *should be* carefully *explained* to all users before the program *is initiated*. (Active voice: "You should carefully explain the operation of the plotter to all users before you begin the program." Although this active-voice sentence is certainly clearer and more direct, it may sound more demanding or authoritarian than you intend.)

Passive Verbs Sound More Courteous and Less Accusatory

A mistake *was made*. (Such a statement doesn't sound overbearing or accusatory to a client.)

Several deficiencies *have been revealed* by an audit. (This comment downplays the idea of people checking on people.)

The format commands *were programmed* incorrectly. (This is less threatening than "You programmed the commands incorrectly.")

Passive Verbs Emphasize Results When the Doer Is Unimportant or Unknown

Eighteen websites *have been investigated* for fraudulent claims. (Who encountered them is unimportant.)

All employees *were evacuated* before the explosion. (by whom or what is unimportant)

Passive Verbs Allow Writers to Be Evasive or Obscure

It *has been decided* that incentive awards will no longer be given. (Who has decided?)

The accident *was* never *investigated*. (Who failed to investigate? No one is to blame.)

A quality and location differential of the crude oil *will be established* to force the buyer to proceed with the acquisition. (This verb choice downplays the issue of who will force the buyer.)

Passive Verbs Slow the Pace

The development of the ROV has not been continuous. Several years elapsed before we recognized and exploited the potential of the original model. This hiatus *was* profitably *filled* by diving contractors, who began testing equipment and techniques to improve human endurance in progressively deeper waters.

Unless you have one of these specific reasons for using the passive voice, prefer active voice to make your writing direct, clear, and concise.

I made this letter longer than usual because I lack the
time to make it short.
—*Blaise Pascal*

Dig Buried Verbs Out of Noun Phrases

To shorten some sentences, all you need do is locate the legitimate verbs hiding in nouns. Words ending in *-ion, -tion, -ing, -ment, -ent, -ance, -ence, -age, -ancy, -ency, -tian,* and *-ology* signal that you've found a noun. Take away that ending and use the remaining verb in another of its purer forms:

They *will perform an analysis of* the work done. (9 words)
change to:
They *will analyze* the work done. (6 words)

I still have available details from the administrative meeting and will identify specific data for your use in *arrangement* and *solicitation* of proposals. (23 words)

change to:

I still have available details from the administrative meeting and will identify specific data to *arrange* and *solicit* proposals. (18 words)

This plan will provide for the *elimination* of the time for *review* and *comparison* of bids. (16 words)

change to:

This plan will *eliminate* time for *reviewing* and *comparing* bids. (10 words)

They *experienced a reduction* in construction time by the *initiation of slip-dredging operations.* (13 words)

change to:

They *reduced* construction time by *slip dredging.* (7 words)

We have designed the operational auditing course for *the training of* auditors *in conducting an independent review and evaluation of* policies. (21 words)

change to:

We have designed the operational auditing course *to train* auditors *to review and evaluate* policies. (15 words)

The organization has decided *to make recommendations for* ways to correct the problem rather than *filing a lawsuit* against them. (20 words)

change to:

The organization has decided *to recommend* ways to correct the problem rather than *to sue* them. (15 words)

Digging out buried verbs shortens sentences and adds impact.

Avoid Adjective and Adverb Clutter

"Familiarity breeds contempt." These are words of fact, or at least they sound like fact. Nouns and verbs bear the weight of your message. "Too much familiarity often breeds unwanted contempt." These adjectives and adverbs are words of opinion. For most purposes, business writing should sound factual, not opinionated.

You will *probably* gain the background you need. (*Probably* is opinion; it weakens the impact.)

When all proposals are received, they can be *leisurely* evaluated on *a truly* comparative basis.

When all proposals are received, they can be evaluated on a comparative basis. (no opinion words; sounds factual)

These *important* goals provide *clear* direction for *your budgeting* efforts. (Stronger: These goals provide direction for your budget.)

Granted, adjectives and adverbs can add emphasis or provide a trap-door: "This report is *completely* worthless." The adverb here adds emphasis. "This new machine will *probably* be more expensive to operate." The adverb hedges, providing an outlet that an outright claim would not.

Unless you have a specific purpose in mind for such words, develop the habit of writing with nouns and verbs, omitting adjectives and adverbs where possible.

> As to the adjective, when in doubt, strike it out.
> —*Mark Twain*

Eliminate Redundant Words, Phrases, Clauses, and Ideas

Besides being filled with adjective and adverb clutter, business and technical writing reeks with fat. Trimming clichés, redundancies, little-word padding, and weak-verb padding will make your writing emphatic and crisp. But finding the fat in your own work can be exacting. If you feel the phrase "roll off your tongue" "with little or no effort" (as the last two phrases just rolled off mine), that's a clue that you're using a cliché.

Sentences that incorporate redundant words and ideas are harder to recognize: for instance, *continue on*. To continue means to go on; when you add the *on*, you're stuttering. "If you're not sure how to spell *accommodations* run the spell-checker to verify it." The entire last idea is redundant: "If you're not sure how to spell *accommodations*, run the spell-checker."

Little-word padding also clutters and dilutes messages.

This proves true only *in the case* in which more than three tests were performed.
This proves true only when more than three tests were performed.

Our experience in handling large-scale programs is particularly suited for this *type of* project.
Our experience in handling large-scale programs is particularly suited for this project.

The number of shifts worked could be attributed to *various factors such as* market size, labor problems, and management philosophy.
The number of shifts worked could be attributed to market size, labor problems, and management philosophy.

The following symbols are used *in all portions of* this report.
The following symbols are used *throughout* this report.

The attached form is for *your use in* developing the necessary data.
The attached form is for developing the necessary data.

They talked *in terms of* time and money.
They talked about time and money.

They committed acts *of a* hostile *nature.*
They committed hostile acts.

The manager spoke *in a* belligerent *manner.*
The manager spoke belligerently.

Attached is *a copy of* the form *that must be* completed *in advance* before *they will give us the* service.
Attached is a copy of the form to be completed before service.

Jack *is a man who* dislikes waste and irresponsibility.
Jack dislikes waste and irresponsibility.

The company *is one of those that* takes illegal shortcuts.
The company takes illegal shortcuts.

Despite the fact that he called, we have decided to boycott the trade show.
Despite his call, we have decided to boycott the trade show.

A sentence should contain no unnecessary words,
a paragraph no unnecessary sentences, for the same reason
that a drawing should have no unnecessary lines and a
machine no unnecessary parts.
—*William Strunk*

Examine the following chart (Figure 49) for your own redundancies. Recognition is half the solution in stripping them from your writing.

PAIRED NOUNS AND ADJECTIVES EXPRESSING THE SAME IDEA

subject matter	facts and figures
goals and objectives	few in number
in this day and age	costs the sum of $222
period of time	during the month of August
point in time	during the years 1998–2006 inclusive
brown in color	summer months
small in size	the reason is because
cylindrical in shape	the reason is why
a distance of 220 miles	first and foremost
the time of day	separate and distinct
200 words in length	ways and means

VERB ADD-ONS

continue on	finish up
refer back to	open up
consolidated together	cancel out
grouped together	circulate around
joined together	first began
connect together	distribute out
combined together	send out
attach together	continue to remain
add together	still remain
add up	still continue
try out	still persist
plan ahead	start out
repeat again	balance against each other

ADVERB AND PREPOSITION PADDING

in the amount of (for)

for the purpose of (for)

in reference to (about)

with reference to (about)

in connection with (about)

with regard to (about)

pertaining to (about)

to be in a position to (to)

in order to (to)

in order that (to)

with a view toward (to)

for the express purpose of (to)

in the event that (if)

if it should turn out that (if)

if it is assumed that (if)

inasmuch as (as)

in spite of the fact that (although)

with the result that (so)

by the same token (similarly)

on a regular basis (regularly)

in most cases (usually)

in all cases (always, all)

at all times (always)

not infrequently (often)

until such time as (until, when)

during the time that (while)

a large number of (many)

on two separate occasions (twice)

on account of the fact that (since, because)

for the reason that (since, because)

to say nothing of (and)

in view of the foregoing circumstances (because)

it is apparent therefore that (so)

along the lines of (like, as)

in the nature of (like)

by means of (by)

until such time as you (when)

with the exception of (except)

the question as to whether (whether)

in conjunction with (with)

if at all possible (if possible)

in all other cases (otherwise)

a sufficient number of (enough)

in the vicinity of (near)

it would seem that (it seems)

it would thus appear that (apparently, probably)

it may well be that (perhaps, maybe)

in a satisfactory manner (satisfactorily)

after this has been done (then)

at this precise moment in time (now)

at the present time (now)

at this point in time (now)

at an early date (soon)

at a later date (later)

whether or not (whether)

of a confidential nature (confidentially)

in the very near future (soon)

REDUNDANT IDEAS	
alternate choices	conclusive proof
desirable benefits	true facts
basic fundamentals	honest truth
important essentials	consensus of opinion
basic essentials	final completion
main essentials	advance warning
serious crisis	adequate enough
necessary requisite	disappear from sight
close together	following after
end result	equally as effective as
current status	foreign imports
few and far between	any and all
final outcome	as a general rule
future plans	in actual fact
free gift	equally as well
past experience	in two equal halves
past history	symptoms indicative of
early beginnings	completely surrounded
new breakthrough	as you may or may not know
separate entities	on pages 20–30 inclusive
different varieties	this particular instance
empty space	regular weekly meetings
close proximity	exactly alike
surrounding circumstances	precisely correct
joint partnership	group meeting

Figure 49. Redundant Combinations. Redundancy indicates careless thinking and weakens the impact of your ideas.

Redundancy in a document is like stuttering in a speech: both detract from the ideas you are presenting. That is not to say all repetition is bad; some writers repeat key phrases and ideas to serve as transitions between parts of a document and to reemphasize major points. But redundancy is *needless* repetition, which has no place in effective writing.

He can compress the most words into the smallest idea
of any man I ever met.
—*Abraham Lincoln*

In short, prefer active-voice verbs, dig buried verbs from noun phrases, avoid adjective and adverb clutter, and eliminate redundancies. Writing long sentences is like adding water to tea; the more words, the weaker the message.

EDIT FOR STYLE

The trend in today's e-commerce falls between the two extremes: "stuffed shirt" writing and T-shirt writing. Like our work clothes today, the preferred writing style has become business casual. And just as the business-casual dress code has some people stumped, so has the business-casual writing style.

Style reflects individuality; it is your personal logo. Some people write with a warm, personal, flowing style; others have a formal, impersonal, stilted way with words.

So how do you select a writing style to reflect a pleasing personality on paper or screen? Just as a company's logo consists of artwork, colors, and their arrangement, your writing style is reflected in three ways:

- The structure of your ideas
- The illustrations you select to make your ideas clear and memorable
- The language you use

Because other chapters of this book have dealt with the first two points, this chapter will focus on use of language.

The trend in today's e-commerce falls between the two extremes: stuffed-shirt writing and T-shirt writing. Like our work clothes, the preferred writing style has become business casual. And just as the business-casual dress code has some people stumped, so has the business-casual writing style.

Strive for a Style Somewhere Between Stuffed-Shirt Writing and T-Shirt Writing

Although stuffed-shirt writing may be difficult to define, it's easy to recognize. Those who write in a stuffy style bury the meat of their ideas in passive verbs. They select weak sentence subjects. They bury key actions. They add unnecessary qualifiers and intensifiers to vague abstractions. Finally, they drape their ideas in trite, verbose statements.

At the other extreme are writers who send e-mail that could pass for a T-shirt slogan. They choose aggressive words, without tact. They make up words when they can't think of the correct words. They ramble on and on, without sorting the main ideas and details from the irrelevant. They misspell, omit punctuation, and write incomplete thoughts, leaving clarity as the reader's problem.

Stuffed-Shirt Style:

> It can easily be seen that when large volumes of gas are metered and when variations in the gas temperatures become commonplace, the resulting circumstance is going to be a loss of revenue if corrective action is not taken.

Simple, Direct Style:

> As large volumes of gas are metered, gas-temperature variation will result in lost revenues unless we take corrective action.

T-Shirt Style:

> Large volumes of METERED gas—big problem in about two months we're gonna lose our shirt unless somebody gets off their duff and okays something.

Stuffed-Shirt Style:

> Provided herewith is a report on the remainder of the findings with regard to our market research. The contents should be consistent with your present requirements, but if further clarification is required, please advise Mike Finch.

Simple, Direct Style:

I've attached the report on our market research. If you have questions, please call Mike Finch.

T-Shirt Style:

Info pulled together. Questions? BTW, if you get hung up, give Mike Finch a holler.

The first step in striking a happy medium between overly formal and overly informal writing is the appropriate word choice. Use simple words (see Figure 50), not pompous ones or inappropriate slang.

Dignity, closely aligned with simplicity, means a writing style appropriate to subject matter and void of colloquialisms and grammatical errors. Pomposity, on the other hand, means excessively ornate or exhibiting self-importance. (In selecting jewelry you know that the most ornate is not always the most expensive or the most elegant.) This is not to say that you should avoid complex words altogether—especially if the complex word states exactly what you mean. But don't overlook the simple word in an effort to sound dignified, formal, "official." A writer who continually uses pompous words and phrases when simple ones will do is an amusement to readers. Likewise, an e-mail full of slang may cause a colleague or customer to doubt your competence or interpret your informal word choice as a reflection of a don't-care attitude or a sloppy product or service.

When the simple word has the same meaning, always prefer the simple word to the complex or the slang.

I never write *metropolis* for seven cents when I can get
the same price for *city.* I never write *policeman* when I can
get the same money for *cop.*
—*Mark Twain*

COMPLEX WORDS	SIMPLE WORDS
abbreviate	condense
aggregate	sum, total, whole
anomalous	unusual
antithesis	opposite
cessation	stop, end
cognizant	aware
commencement	beginning
concept	idea
conjecture	guess
demonstrate	show
disengage	free
duplicate	copy
elucidate	clarify
enumerate	number, list
facilitate	help
homogeneous	like, similar
impairment	harm, damage
implement, implementation	put into use, use
incision	cut
incombustible	fireproof
initiate	begin
methodology	methods, procedure
minuscule	tiny
modify, modification	change
opine	think
optimum	best
subsequent	next
sufficient	enough
terminate	end
utilize	use
verification	check, proof

Figure 50. Bland, Complex Writing Versus Strong, Simple Writing. The key to strong, lucid prose is simplicity.

Prefer a Personal, Conversational, Professional Tone

E-mail emulates conversation more closely than writing on paper. That can be both good and bad. Good, because our words can sound warm, personal, honest, sincere. Bad, when our words sound angry, sarcastic, aggressive, or flippant. To grasp a clear understanding of tone in writing, consider the following passage written in different styles:

Inappropriately Informal:

> I'm gonna need more proof to take this up with my boss. Where did you get it? Are you sure from our website? How do we know you didn't break it when you opened it, or maybe they damaged it in shipment?

Informal:

> I'll need some form of documentation to send you a refund in this case. Where did you order it? Did you notice if it was damaged in shipment?

Formal:

> I'll need your order confirmation number from our website to issue you a refund. When you opened the package, did you notice any apparent damage that took place during shipment?

Pompous:

> As you may be aware, customers frequently attempt to return merchandise not purchased through our website but rather through other distribution channels such as local dealerships, discount warehouses, or mail-order organizations. As no mention was made of a confirmation number, a refund cannot be issued without proper documentation that the purchase was indeed made online through the website. Damage can also be done to the merchandise when opened by buyers. If any further information regarding such damage can be supplied, that will need to be provided with the above-mentioned confirmation notice.

Inappropriately Informal:

This product stinks. Obviously, the marketing mavens don't have a clue. Stomp it and let's start from ground zero.

Informal:

This product doesn't work. Neither does Marketing have the right idea about how to describe it. I suggest we start over.

Formal:

The Titan product doesn't work as we have described it in our marketing literature. I suggest we reexamine the overall design and rebuild it, if necessary, to fit our original objectives.

Pompous:

The Titan product specifications have not been followed; consequently, the product does not work as initially envisioned. It is my understanding that the marketing literature regarding this product line conveys the product features and specifications in such a manner as could be misconstrued by customers, thereby creating culpability and subjecting the company to potential liability should litigation arise out of such discrepancies. It is my advised opinion that an overall redesign and redeployment should be considered.

Take another look at the differences in the following messages:

Inappropriately Informal:

You've already been told this once. We gotta cut the cost of gas. It's gonna be up to you guys to put it to your people about how they drive their company cars. Evidently some people don't have a clue about how much we're spending on their racing around town on company wheels. If those gasoline bills don't come down, somebody's gonna be kicking butt.

Informal:

You all are pretty much aware that one of the main themes for division managers will be overseeing and controlling gasoline usage by your employees. This theme will be hammered at hard and heavy throughout the year and, I am sure, in the years to come. It will be up to you to set stringent guidelines to help your people better plan their schedules and to see that they operate company cars efficiently. I'm convinced that a number of our people do not give the same attention to the company cars as they would to their own family cars when they have to buy gasoline out of their own pockets.

Formal:

As you are aware, one of the main objectives for division managers will be supervising and regulating gasoline usage by our employees. The company will repeatedly emphasize automobile economy throughout the years to come. Managers must set firm guidelines to help employees better plan their schedules and use company cars efficiently. Such objectives should encourage employees to give company cars the same careful attention as they give their personal cars.

Pompous:

As all management is cognizant, one of the principal objectives for division managers will be the supervision and regulation of gasoline usage by personnel. Economic and efficient usage of automobiles will be a recurring concern in the years to come, and it is incumbent that stringent objectives be established for all personnel with due respect to efficient juxtapositions of appointments within the same geographical region and to the prudent utilization of company vehicles. These objectives should incorporate incentives for personnel to render company transportation the same meticulous attention as would be afforded personal vehicles.

No style is good that is not fit to be spoken or read aloud with effect.
—*William Hazlitt*

In general, to choose the appropriate style for a document, consider how you would express your ideas in conversations with the same reader or readers. Show concern, be sincere, be direct. But be careful to omit repetitious details, choppy sentences, and grammatical errors that may creep in as you speak.

Consider three issues in determining the formality or informality of your document:

- Your relationship to the reader
- The subject of your document
- The purpose of your document

For example, if you're writing to reprimand an employee, your tone should be firm and objective. On the other hand, if you're wishing your staff a nice holiday, you'll probably want to use a light, folksy style. Finally, the purpose of your document may dictate either a formal or informal tone. Although you may be writing to someone you know well, the recipient of your e-mail or letter may intend to pass it along to the board of directors as supporting evidence of a newly proposed idea. In that situation, of course, you might decide to change your usually informal chitchat to a more formal approach, without colloquialisms or intentional sentence fragments. Your relationship to the reader, the subject, and the purpose—all three will determine the appropriate style.

Also, consider the following tips to make your writing friendly, honest, and authentic.

Use a person's name and spell it correctly. A missing or misspelled name tells readers they aren't too important to you. An online search or a phone call will typically produce the correct names and titles. And if you would do so in conversation, address a person by his or her first name. A good clue about reader preferences is to pay attention to how they introduce themselves on the phone or in their voice-mail greeting.

Use proper titles. If you don't know whether "Jody" is male or female, don't guess. Call to verify or use both the first and last name in your greeting: "Dear Jody Smith." Or, for form correspondence going to both genders, you may prefer to use a position title rather than names: "To Committee Members," or "Hello, Project Team," or "Dear Board Members."

Select appropriate salutations and closings. Make the opening and closing of your e-mail, memo, or letter match the subject matter and your relationship with the reader. The following list indicates the variety of choice, from most formal to informal. With very informal e-mail or memos, you may have no salutation or closing at all.

Dear Mr. Williams:
Yours truly,

Dear Gary:
Sincerely,

Dear Gary, (comma)
Sincerely,

Dear Gary,
Cordially,

Gary,
Regards,

Gary, I finally have an answer about the game. It's at 2.
—Susan

Prefer active voice. Put people in your writing. State who does what: "The client will identify the last group of users on Tuesday" rather than "The last group of users can't be identified until Tuesday."

Use personal pronouns. Say *I* when you refer to yourself, and *you* when you refer to the readers. "I appreciate your work on the project. Let me know if you need extra time or help."

Use contractions. Contractions such as *I'll, wouldn't, they've* sound conversational and natural, not formal and stilted.

Direct questions to the reader. Write, "Do you think the idea will be acceptable to the client?" rather than "Should this idea, in your opinion, not be acceptable to the client, please let me know."

Include pleasantries. When in order, mention upcoming holidays, refer to past conversations, or express congratulations or praise. But be sincere; overstatement sounds sarcastic and artificial.

Watch "fight" words. Mistaken, failed, overlooked, misled, and *ignored* trigger an adverse gut reaction. If you're writing to request corrective action, such words will thwart your purpose.

Focus on the positive. Tell people what you can do, not what you can't do. *Not:* "We can't complete the project without further documentation from you," *but:* "We can complete the project as soon as we receive further documentation from you." *Not:* "Your insurance doesn't cover damage from flooding," *but:* "Your insurance covers damage from natural calamities, except for flooding." *Not:* "We can't have the paperwork ready until Friday," *but:* "We can have the paperwork ready Friday."

Use humor and wit, but remember that humor is subjective. Use humor to grab attention and make your message memorable. But be aware that what you say tongue in cheek (even with emoticons) may not meet an appreciative reader. Humor comes from interpretation, not intention.

Never tell someone what he or she thinks or feels. Humorists know better than to tell someone, "The funniest thing happened. . . . " The listener is set up for disappointment. Likewise, a statement such as, "We all know you will enjoy making this trip to the East Coast" may bring the reaction, "Oh, yeah?"

Don't be too arbitrary. When possible, give sufficient reason for actions or requests. People with a reason tend to cooperate better—even when they don't agree.

Don't be too patronizing. Do not give unnecessary explanations or talk down to your reader. *Examples:* "You obviously are unaware of the problem about . . .'"; "For our less informed visitors . . . "; "I know you're upset, but if you calm down and provide me with the appropriate information, I'll research the issue."

Answer all questions specifically and promptly; avoid indifference or carelessness. Avoid choosing details you think readers need while omitting others as privileged information. Nothing garners the ire of customers today like visiting a website, being invited to e-mail the organization with questions, and, after doing so, receiving an auto-responder that disregards the specific question asked or the information requested.

Certainly, auto-response e-mails and form letters have a place in the business world. But when you want to influence your readers favorably, give careful thought to original phrasing and take time to address the readers' special concerns in a personal way.

Use original wording rather than clichés. They not only add length, as mentioned earlier, but also mark you as a lazy thinker. For example:

If I can provide further information, please do not hesitate to call.
If you have questions, please feel free to call me.

If you will be kind enough to . . .
Pursuant to our meeting . . .
We take pleasure in . . .
After due consideration . . .
Attached herewith please find . . .
In reference to the matter of . . .
As per your e-mail . . .
Thanking you in advance . . .

Adam was the only man who, when he said a good thing, knew that
nobody had said it before him.
—*Mark Twain*

Such clichés make your writing sound like an auto-responder, as if someone merely touched the Print button. If something is worth saying, phrase it with original wording.

Close with a reminder of the action. If you're puzzled about a warm, non-clichéd closing to your e-mail or letter, an effective closing thought is a reminder of the next action: "I'll be in touch again on Friday"; "If you'd like to talk further, I'll be available after the trade show"; "I'll look forward to your signed contract"; "We'll see you at the meeting to put final touches on the strategy"; "Thanks for agreeing to participate in this project"; "As soon as I get your go-ahead, I'll begin collecting bids."

Prefer Directness and Brevity with Tact

Yes, e-mail has taught otherwise verbose people to be concise. But brevity can be interpreted as brusqueness. Particularly, that's the case when the message or information provided is in any way negative. Consider the difference in the tone of these three e-mails:

Brief but Brusque:

We've returned the tapes of your briefing.

Direct, with Tact:

Brady, we're returning the tapes of your briefing. Thank you for lending them to us on such short notice.

Brief but Brusque:

> No.

Direct, with Tact:

> No, I'm not attending the meeting. I'll be out of town.

Brief but Brusque:

> I don't agree.

Direct, with Tact:

> I don't agree with the decision. Here's why . . .

> Writing, when properly managed, is but a different
> name for conversation.
> —*Laurence Sterne*

Vary Sentence Pattern and Length

Variety in sentence pattern is to writing what voice inflection is to speech. A steady diet of any one construction makes for boring reading:

Monotonous: Note the attached charts, and please submit to me a written report explaining irregularities. Obviously, corrective actions were ineffective, and I cannot accept this situation. You will need to give me a written report of all past financial procedures, and also you will need to delineate new ones to establish and maintain effective controls. I will review your corrective proposals personally, and I would like for you to be conversant with the appropriate publications. These proposals should be in my office no later than October 21, and our conference will follow within the next few days. (sentence patterns: compound, compound, compound, compound, compound)

A page of this pitter-pat, pitter-pat, pitter-pat would put a reader to sleep. The writer has joined every other independent clause with *and*. Note the difference in the following revision:

Revised: Note the attached charts, and please submit to me a written report explaining irregularities. Obviously corrective actions were ineffective. Because I cannot accept this situation, you will need to give me a written report of all past financial procedures and delineate new ones to establish and maintain effective controls. When I review your corrective proposals personally, I would like for you to be conversant with the appropriate publications. These proposals should be in my office no later than October 21, and our conference will follow within the next few days. (sentence patterns: compound, simple, complex, compound)

A little editing for variety's sake goes a long way.

In addition to creating variety in pattern, vary length. Follow a 30-word sentence with a 5-word sentence. The jolt will make your reader sit up and pay attention.

Revise Weak Verbs

Spice bland writing with potent verbs. Some writers make a timid attempt to jump into their subjects with weak verb constructions such as *there is, there are, it is,* or *it was.*

Weak: There are problems in remaining static.
Strong: Remaining static presents problems.

Weak: There were some objections voiced during the meeting.
Strong: Some voiced objections during the meeting.

Weak: It has been firmly established by previous research that this machine will improve the operation.
Strong: Previous research firmly establishes that this machine will improve the operation.

Weak:	It is difficult to maintain movable equipment.
Strong:	Maintaining movable equipment is difficult.

Weak:	This is a product line that will excite our customers.
Strong:	This product line will excite our customers.

Of course, not all such weak verb constructions can be revised; alternatives may sound awkward. But prefer a strong verb to command the readers' attention.

Spice bland writing with potent verbs.

Action Verbs:

McNamara popped a fly to center field. Ted Brown plucked the ball out of the air and hurled it toward home plate, but not in time to catch Bill Frosh sliding in for the score. In the meantime, Jorge Salinas raced toward second, plowing into Lenny Davis and bloodying his nose. In the shuffle, Max Silverton sprinted toward third, edging Frank Mahoney out of the running for most stolen bases of the season.

Okay, so sportswriters sometimes get carried away, but they have the right idea.

In summary, when editing for style, prefer the simple word when the simple word will do. Prefer a conversational, personal, but professional tone. Be direct and concise, yet tactful. Vary sentence patterns and length. Revise weak verbs to strong ones. The result will be an engaging style that represents your product or service well and reflects the professionalism of you and your organization.

However great a man's natural talent may be, the art of writing
cannot be learned all at once.
—*Jean-Jacques Rousseau*

PART 5

LET'S GET TECHNICAL

18

GUIDELINES FOR DOCUMENT VARIATIONS ON THE MADE FORMAT™

Words fly, writings remain.
—*Latin proverb*

The MADE Format™ will be the primary structure for 90 percent of the documents you'll write in the workplace. But for the other 10 percent, you'll need some additional guidelines and formats.

Why? Step 2. If you recall, Step 2 involves anticipating special reader reactions to various situations and messages: skepticism, low priority, loss of face, deadlines, resistance to change or extra work, budget considerations, and so forth. Those special reactions necessitate special attention to detail selection and arrangement and wording of the message and action.

What follows are those specific guidelines and structures that tailor the MADE Format™ to accommodate these special situations, interests, and biases.

Directives

The format for directives varies slightly from the MADE Format™ in that the message *is* the action; these two segments become a single item. Generally, a directive should begin with a reason. Walk into a meeting in the middle of the afternoon and announce that attendees need to evacuate the building immediately. "Why?" is almost an automatic response. On the other hand, walk in and announce that because there's been a bomb threat, attendees need to evacuate immediately. They'll beat you through the doorway.

If you're going to ask employees to go through the trouble of filling out new insurance forms, explain that you are changing insurance companies because past claims have not been paid promptly and that you want your employees to be reimbursed fully for their expenses as soon as possible. A plausible reason makes almost any directive less arbitrary.

Consider the following disorganized directive:

To: All Company Employees
Subject: Copy Machine Use

A list of civic organizations for which the management has approved use of the company copy machines is posted in Room 202. It has long been company policy to extend our services cordially to such activities and organizations. However, in the past months there has been a rash of nonbusiness use of our copiers, which has overextended our budget allocations for copying. It is important that we watch future expenses closely. It is the responsibility of everyone to utilize stationery supplies and copiers for company or especially approved businesses.

When employees read this e-mail, they have to wade through the first three sentences (two-thirds of the document) to get to anything that interests them. The author has violated the first rule of writing: Consider the interests of the reader. While reading the first few sentences, employees are wondering, So what? What does this have to do with me? Then when they get to the point—that you want to restrict personal use of the copiers—they still don't know to what extent. Does the "especially approved businesses" at the end of the e-mail refer to the already approved civic uses mentioned earlier? Or can these employees ask you to "especially approve" other copying for them when the need arises? In the writer's mind, he has probably connected those two details, but other readers will not necessarily go back and make that same connection.

If you write such a disorganized directive, you'll find yourself doing several follow-ups to get the point across—as the writer of the e-mail admitted he had had to do.

Compare the preceding disorganized document to the following one arranged in the basic directive format:

To: All Company Employees
Subject: Guidelines for Personal Use of the Copiers

To stay within our budget allocations for copying, I am asking that all employees limit nonbusiness copying to approved civic activities. If you are in doubt about which activities are approved, please check the attached list, also posted on the bulletin board, Room 202.

Notice that this version is shorter but leaves no doubt about what action (or inaction, in this case) the writer intends. Organization always improves clarity.

Transmittals

Another slight variation to the MADE Format™ is the transmittal document. By its very nature, the message is "Here it is." The opening message statement appropriately refers to the attachments or enclosures and gives a brief summary of the information you're sending. For example, the summary statement for an attached sales report might be, "I'm enclosing our Region 7 sales figures for March. You'll notice that we have exceeded quota by 22 percent this quarter; increases were especially significant in Boston." The summary for a transmittal accompanying a sales proposal to a client, however, might be three or four paragraphs overviewing the product/service you propose, along with benefits and cost.

Second, you will state what action the readers should take with the information you're sending: Do you want readers to process the information? Verify it and return the document to you? Distribute the information to others? Let you know if they agree or disagree with it? Buy something? See your product demonstrated?

Next, in the detail section, you may need to elaborate on directions to take the required action. Or you may need to anticipate and answer special questions your reader will have about the information.

If you're not sending all the readers expect, explain why and state when you will be sending the remainder.

Figures 51–53 provide transmittal models.

Model: Transmittal

Dear Mr. Harrison:

Enclosed are three copies each of the following documents necessary for executing the contract between your company and ours for the purchase, delivery, and installation of subscriber carrier equipment:

RHP Form 994, page 6 (proposal page)
RHP Form 994C, page 13 (contractor's bond)
RHP Form 334, page 16 (listing of all maps)

Please note that **all three copies** of these documents **must be signed by either the president or a vice president** of your company.

Additionally, the bond (RHP Form 994C) must be furnished by a surety or sureties **listed by the United States Treasury Department** as acceptable.

Upon execution of the enclosed documents, please return them to our office. Because we handle only the processing of these contracts, if you have specific questions about the contracts or maps themselves, we suggest that you contact engineer Bill Jones directly at 234-5678.

Sincerely,

Figure 51. Model—Transmittal. In a transmittal, the message states what's attached and summarizes the attachment.

Model: Transmittal for Audit Report

Subject: Audit of Eastern Division, Australia

We have completed our review of Eastern Division, Australia, for the current year. Our full report is attached.

Our audit revealed weaknesses in the following areas:

- **Cash Disbursements Untracked:** The Blodgett plant does not cancel vendor invoices to prevent possible duplicate payments.
- **Lack of Inventory Control:** There are no written instructions on how supplies are counted, documented, summarized, or used either by employees or contractors.
- **Payroll Charges Misapplied:** Numerous employees' wages have been charged to the incorrect accounts. These errors appear across all functional areas.

We think our detailed recommendations in the enclosed report require serious and immediate attention. Please reply to us by March 15 about the action taken on these recommendations and planned procedures for future use.

Jill Johnson provided valuable help during our audit process, and we sincerely appreciate your making her available to our auditors during the past few weeks.

Figure 52. Model—Transmittal for Audit Report. Summarize the key conclusions and recommendations from the full report.

Model: Transmittal for Sales Proposal

Dear Mr. Thevalingam:

We are pleased to submit the accompanying proposed plan for a high- and low-voltage monitor to use on a single-phase 120v electrical outlet. After thoroughly studying the project, we think our proposed design offers both a practical and marketable monitor. Simplicity will be the key to user acceptance of this product.

The accompanying preliminary schedule of the work provides ample time to complete the various tasks by May 1, and we are confident that we can adhere to this schedule despite the possible delays you mentioned in our initial meeting.

Project engineer Richard Schwalm will call you on August 16 to see if you are ready for us to begin this project. We're looking forward to designing this attractive and practical new product for you.

Sincerely,

Figure 53. Model—Transmittal for Proposal. When submitting a proposal, use the transmittal letter to summarize the executive overview of the proposal and ask for the order.

Requests for Voluntary Action

When responses are voluntary, readers may find it easy to take no action at all. You may be creating extra work for them, giving them a short deadline, or asking them to do something they consider a low priority. Therefore, when requesting voluntary action, you need to motivate readers and make things easy.

- As with a directive, briefly pave the way for your request.
- Center on one action you want readers to take. Don't make your request a by-the-way item in the final paragraph.
- Give your readers any necessary details to take the action.
- Supply an incentive if possible—promise goodwill or recall other values for readers.

Figure 54 provides a model document requesting such action that will likely meet a responsive audience.

Model: Request for Voluntary Action

Dear Ms. Ojukwu:

The recent closing of your account is of special concern to us. We are interested in the reason behind your decision and would like your suggestions as to how we might improve our services.

Would you please help us by answering a few questions on the survey below? Any additional comments you may have would be very much welcomed. Do not feel that you must sign identify yourself in the survey form. You may generate your own e-mail response to us (Degnes@International.com), print out the survey form and fax it to us at 334–399–5587, or mail it to the address at the bottom of the form. If you prefer speaking to one of our representatives about the difficulty you experienced, please phone us at 800-444-5353.

It is always a pleasure serving you, and we only hope to serve you better on future orders. Again, thank you for any help you may give us in completing the survey.

Sincerely,

Figure 54. Model—Request for Voluntary Action. Pave the way, focus on the action, and make things easy. If the tone is pleasant, even angry customers may give you their attention again.

What makes this request effective, even to an angry client who has closed her account? First, the opening paragraph sounds as if the writer has the reader's interest in mind. And, of course, anyone likes to have someone ask for his or her opinion or advice.

Second, the desired action is central to the message, not a by-the-way matter in the closing paragraph. The writer also has made it easy for the reader to give her opinion. You'll note also that the writer doesn't assume the reader will respond; the last statement says, "Again, thank you for any help you *may* give us in completing the survey."

Finally, the writer offers incentive—improved service to the customer should she ever reconsider doing business with the company again.

Figure 55 presents another such request to an internal reader—a manager who can help the writer meet his career goals.

Model: Request for Voluntary Action

Brad:

I share our company's commitment to provide our customers with quality technical support for the equipment we provide them. And I know there is a requirement for more systems engineers in our office. Would you help me meet this need?

Specifically, will you consider arranging an internship for me as a systems engineer? Although I have not had extensive experience to date, this internship will provide me with the hands-on, day-to-day opportunities necessary to develop strong technical skills.

A brief résumé of my academic background, training, experience, and accomplishments here at Fredco-Morris (including a list of my current accounts) is attached. Please feel free to forward it to any of your colleagues who may need someone with similar skills.

I'm eager to develop the skills that will benefit both your systems-engineering unit and the Detroit branch office. Thank you for any help you can give with the internship.

Steve Maxwell

Figure 55. Model—Request for Voluntary Action. Motivate the reader, center on the action, and make things easy for the reader to take up your cause.

The e-mail focuses on the specific request, gives all the information necessary to take the action, and closes with a goodwill statement of benefit to both writer and reader.

Negative Responses

The structure for a negative response varies more drastically from the MADE Format™ than any other we've mentioned. In fact, most negative or "bad news" responses should be arranged in the ascending, not the descending, format. Why? With a "no" message directly up front in the document, the message sounds doubly hard-hitting. In fact, the reader may not even finish the document to learn your reasons for the "no" or to understand the issues or criteria involved in your decision. On the other hand, if you first present the issues, reasons, or criteria for your decision, the reader slowly becomes aware of the apparent message before he or she actually gets to that "no" statement. As a result, the message sounds softer and less arbitrary.

Nevertheless, with a negative response, the reader will typically be disappointed or even angry. Therefore, when stating a tactful yet firm "no," make sure your tone conveys caring. If possible, help the reader save face by letting him or her have the final say on any other options involved in the situation.

The following guidelines will help:

- Begin on either a neutral or positive note. You may simply wish to state the topic of your document.
- Give your reasons or explain your criteria for the negative decision.
- State the negative firmly, yet as positively as possible. (Physical position is important. Place the negative in the internal part of the paragraph.)
- Suggest an alternative when possible.
- End with a goodwill statement unrelated to the negative decision.

Figure 56 provides a "no, thank you" note that leaves a pleasant taste in the reader's mouth.

Model: Negative or "Bad News" Response

Dear Carlita,

We received your announcement of the seminar "Managing Your Inventory"; this subject is of particular interest to many in the industry. However, our purchasing is handled by each supervisor at the project site because needs differ from one facility to another. Therefore, our staff here will be unable to take advantage of your presentation.

Please contact us again about other presentations; we would be particularly interested in a workshop that considered some of the same topics as your executive seminar of May 15.

Best wishes for your continued success.

Cordially,

Figure 56. Model—Negative or "Bad News" Response. Reverse the MADE Format™. Start with the reasons, issues, or criteria; then state the "no" message positively.

The writer begins with a compliment that the seminar presenter has chosen an interesting topic to many in the industry, then follows with a specific reason his staff will be unable to "take advantage" of the presentation. By the time the reader gets to the last sentence of the first paragraph, she already knows she's going to get a "no" but doesn't feel a personal put-down. And the closing statement is not only positive but also flattering. Who doesn't like to be considered a success?

Figure 57 also contains a "no" document that allows the reader to save face. First, the writer opens with a positive statement, provides a logical reason for the turn-down, suggests an alternative to meet the reader's need, then leaves the final decision with the reader.

A negative response doesn't have to sound blunt, vindictive, or even disappointing. To keep a relationship intact and make your negative response acceptable, use the ascending arrangement, give specific reasons for the decision, show a concerned tone, and offer an alternative.

Model: Negative Response or "Bad News" Message

Scott,

The additional features you proposed in your August 5 e-mail would greatly enhance our JBEN program. I appreciate your offer to do the additional work at home.

Because sales of our laptops are currently very high, we have a large backlog of customer orders. Therefore, we don't have an extra company-owned laptop available to offer you at the present time.

But I have talked with Harriet Snowden, a supervisor in Building 3, which is near your home. She has a laptop that circulates among her three traveling reps on an "as needed" basis and is willing to lend it to you if you can give her some advance notice and if the laptop is not in use.

If this alternative is acceptable to you, please let me know and I will make the necessary arrangements. Thank you for your willingness to do this additional work to improve our product.

Regards,

Figure 57. Model—Negative Response or "Bad News" Message. Reverse the MADE Format™. Start with the reasons, issues, or criteria; then state the "no" message. If possible, suggest alternatives and let your reader be the final decision maker.

Complaints

Some people consider a complaint the easiest document to write, especially when the error or problem has nothing to do with their own ineptness and when they share no portion of the blame. A complaint, however, is probably the most difficult document to compose when the objective is to get a problem corrected and to leave a good relationship intact.

What's the special problem here? Readers of complaints will generally be defensive, even if they didn't create the problem. To compound the situation, often the person assigned to respond to your complaint has not been previously involved in the situation, so he or she may be confused about what has happened to date and what action is necessary to correct the situation.

With these special problems in mind, consider the following guidelines for making your complaint effective:

- Give a brief overview of the problem or error.
- State exactly what you are asking the reader to do.
- Be confident in tone, not sarcastic or aggressive.

If you were Mr. Yamamoto, which document would you be more likely to respond to—the one in Figure 58 or the one in Figure 59?

Ineffective Complaint

Mr. Yamamoto:

On November 13, I ordered five perma-stamp items from your website. The requirements were explicitly detailed in my e-mail (copy attached) and in your order confirmation (copy attached).

On January 11, I received four of the required stamps—eight weeks after the order. Of these four, three were specified to be deluxe mount; all four were furnished as spring mount! We were advised that the fifth stamp was back-ordered, even though this particular stamp was one of your *stock* stamps, No. ST-844. Today, ten weeks from our order date, we have received this stock stamp. And this stamp as supplied is *not* in accordance with your catalog or website illustration.

Mr. Yamamoto, we are extremely disappointed over Zurich's performance in this matter. You have ignored our specifications and shipping orders and ignored your own catalog and website descriptions! Since this is not the first time we have experienced problems with the manner in which our requirements are serviced, we have to question seriously the desirability of continuing to purchase your product. In view of this, I thought I ought to call your attention to these facts.

Max Davis

Figure 58. Ineffective Complaint. State the corrective action you expect, without an aggressive or sarcastic tone.

Model: Complaint

Dear Mr. Yamamoto,

On November 13, I ordered five perma-stamp items from your website (copies of my e-mail and your confirmation are attached). This order has not been filled to our satisfaction.

On January 11 (eight weeks after our order), I received four of the five stamps. Three of these four stamps were spring mount rather than the deluxe mount, as specified in our order.

We were told at that time that the fifth stamp was back-ordered, even though this is one of your stock stamps, No. ST-844. The fifth stamp finally arrived today (ten weeks after our order date), and it does not match your catalog or website illustration.

Therefore, I am returning the three spring-mount stamps and keeping the one deluxe-mount stamp that we can use. Do not send the other three deluxe-mount stamps as previously ordered, because we have had to purchase those locally for immediate use. I am also returning the fifth back-ordered stamp, No. ST-844, because we specifically need the features pictured in your catalog and on the website.

Please refund to my credit card the total amount for all items but the one deluxe-mount stamp, also allowing reimbursement for our shipping charges in returning the incorrectly sent merchandise.

Thank you for your prompt attention in correcting this order.

Sincerely,

Figure 59. Model—Complaint. Summarize the problem; state the action you expect; be confident in tone.

If you would more likely respond to the second e-mail complaint, I'm with you. The major weakness in the first one is that Mr. Yamamoto has no idea how the customer expects the problem to be corrected: Does the customer want to keep the substituted stamp? Should the company send on the delayed deluxe-mount stamps? Does he want a refund on everything?

The second weakness, of course, in the first complaint is the tone. Words and phrases like *explicitly detailed, extremely disappointed,* and *ignored* make the reader feel like an incompetent person. (He may well be, but you'll likely not motivate him to be competent with such phrases.) And did you hear the writer shouting with the italicized words and the strong punctuation marks? The threat toward the end of the e-mail leaves the reader ready to call the bluff, and either way the cards fall, he'll probably not be too disappointed.

So what to do if this level-headed approach doesn't resolve the problem? Escalate your next action. The next e-mail or letter should again state the action you want, and then state *your* next action if the reader doesn't resolve the issue. In such situations, you have no other choice but to continue to escalate the action—all the way to court, if necessary. A key caution: Make sure you never threaten anything you won't or can't carry out.

Again, writing a complaint simply to "let off steam" or "clear the air" is one matter; but when you're writing to get corrective action, be specific about the problem and the solution and show a positive, confident attitude that your reader will see things as you do.

Apologies

As a general rule, you can expect readers of apologies to be disappointed or angry over a situation. In her research for *Medicine and Culture,* author Lynn Payer reports that physicians are sued more often for their bedside manner than for their medical mistakes. Your job as writer is to restore an upset customer's or coworker's goodwill, both by corrective action and a concerned "bedside manner."

Follow these guidelines to accomplish your purpose with angry readers:

- Focus immediately on positive action taken to correct the situation rather than recall the details of the issue or problem.
- Briefly, in a positive way, explain how the mistake happened.(An explanation shows concern for the reader's understanding and adds credibility to your investigation and command of the situation.)
- Show concern; apologize with an empathetic statement.
- Assure the reader that you will take precautions against future errors, but never state that there will be no further problems. Remember Murphy's Law.

- Make the reader feel that you value his or her goodwill or business.
- Be sincere.

Figure 60 contains a letter responding to an upset insurance client who had filed a theft claim and found her coverage inadequate to allow her to replace the stolen items. In her complaint she blames the insurance company for not talking with her about adding coverage with past renewals of her policy.

Model: Apology

Dear Ms. Knarr:

We have enclosed the new appraisal schedule for jewelry to be covered in your renewal policy. If the increased coverage outlined in the attachment is satisfactory, please sign and return the appraisal to our office.

Although we often depend on clients themselves to make us aware of the need for increased coverage on new purchases, we also should share in that responsibility. I'm sorry that your new representative did not bring the need for reappraisal to your attention earlier. Although he is working feverishly to get to know each of our clients' needs thoroughly, he should have been more attentive to the reappraisal issue in your case. He has made client familiarity a number-one priority for the next six months.

If you have other items that may need to be reappraised, such as cameras, china, silver, furs, coins, or fine art, we'd be happy to come to your home again and work with you in providing adequate coverage on these items.

We're making a note in your file to review your appraisals annually so that you will be fully protected in case of future loss.

Thank you for the opportunity to provide this coverage.

Sincerely,

Figure 60. Model—Apology. Focus on the corrective action; explain briefly how the mistake happened; and show concern with an empathetic statement.

The writer sounds apologetic and concerned, even though he is not entirely to blame for the customer's lack of coverage. He has apologized with action (the attached reappraisal schedule and an offer of another visit) and a reason for the oversight. Notice that he says he will take precautions against future losses, but wisely he does not state that the client never will be underinsured again. Claims of future perfection convince few people and disappoint many. Customers often forgive the biblical seventy times seven when you throw yourself on their mercy, but expectations run high for saints.

If you bow at all, bow low.
—Chinese proverb

The apology in Figure 61 particularly soothes an upset reader because the writer immediately discusses solutions to the problem. Also, note that the most frequently used cliché in apologies—"I'm sorry for any inconvenience this may have caused you"—is, fortunately, omitted here. Why does this clichéd statement irritate customers? Consider the comment carefully. The phrases *any inconvenience* and *may have caused* imply that the writer is unaware of any specific problem. The word *inconvenience* often represents a drastic understatement. What the writer considers an inconvenience may be a major issue with the customer; such a comment minimizes the situation. Instead, the writer lets the reader know specifically that he or she understands the problem caused by the malfunctioning elevators.

Model: Apology

Miguel:

We have taken the following steps to reduce the possibility of the parking garage elevators' malfunctioning as they did on July 24.

The original control valves for these elevators are "Southeastern" valves. A Maxon valve, the most technologically advanced valve, is being installed on elevator #3. If this valve proves to be successful, then the other two elevators will be fitted with Maxon valves.

Each of the three elevators has been given a total preventative maintenance check. Also, the guard orders for Surco personnel have been rewritten to emphasize the importance of responding to the elevator alarms promptly.

We apologize for the frustration and the delays the malfunctioning elevators caused your employees, particularly during the early-morning and late-afternoon hours. Please know that we will strive to keep such situations to a minimum.

Sincerely,

Figure 61. Model—Apology. Apologize with action, concern, and sincerity.

Let the reader know you understand the problem caused. Apologize with concern. Be specific and sincere.

Global, generic statements of apology only make already upset customers angrier.

The great enemy of clear language is insincerity.
—*George Orwell*

Accomplishment or Status Reports

Status reports should link past and present work to the future. These reports have two main purposes: 1) to keep management informed about your work; and 2) to aid in your own final report preparation. Status reports do not necessarily have to present positive results or give conclusions.

A status report describes the progress being made on research, on a design, or on a process. Progress is measured against predetermined project objectives, specifications, schedules, and budgets.

Why prepare status reports? Some researchers dread the preparation of such reports because they consider them an unnecessary nuisance. (And some are, particularly when requests come too frequently.) But to lessen the irritation, consider status reports as *part of your work* rather than an interruption of it. And remember that the organization has invested stockholder resources in your project and is, therefore, duty-bound to keep track of it.

The primary purpose of status reports is to keep others informed—to report on budgets and schedules that may need to be adjusted or to report trends that may be cause for changing the direction of your work or abandoning a project altogether. But a secondary benefit, one of the chief benefits to you as the writer, is that these periodic reports will help you in completing the final project report. Not incidentally, regular informative status reports will make your boss's job easier and will enable you to summarize your contributions at performance-review time.

These reports seem particularly difficult for writers involved in long, ongoing projects, because they often think that: 1) they haven't accomplished "enough" to report; 2) they have only negative results to report; or 3) their reports are repetitious.

Another question that often stumps writers: So what is progress? Or what is an accomplishment?

Keep in mind that these reports are simply steps to a final project outcome. Therefore, progress does not necessarily mean *completion* of any one phase. Consider preparatory work as progress: development of sampling or testing procedures, the ordering of equipment, negotiations with suppliers, a demo done for a key customer who can potentially place a large order.

There's even progress in failure. When you run into a blind alley, say so. When you have tentative results or conclusions, say so. All these interim phases, obstacles, or problems are part of moving toward the final results, conclusions, and recommendations.

Also remember that some repetition is inevitable—and even desirable—in status reports. That is, most readers need a reminder of the purpose of your work and what had happened since the last time you reported. Your periodic report should *briefly* bring them up to date on the *why* and *what* of your past work, focus on the present interim period, and then *briefly* outline future work.

Management will usually have these key questions in mind when reading your status or accomplishment reports:

- What have you accomplished on the current project or in the reporting time frame?
- Are you ahead of, behind, or on schedule with completion dates?
- Are you ahead of, behind, or on target with cost or revenue projections?
- Have you discovered anything that will materially change the objectives, course, cost, or chance of success of the project? If so, what is it, and what are its effects?
- What is the significance of your accomplishment? How does this work contribute to the overall project, the organization's mission, or, in the case of routine (versus project-specific) reports, your own expertise and therefore value to the organization?

The following examples illustrate both incomplete and complete overview statements:

Status Report with "Holes":

Accomplishment Report for May

The equipment recovery group developed and implemented a plan for getting all old pickup orders processed by March 31. Once the cleanup is complete, ERG will attempt to dispatch all orders and get the equipment picked up within five days of the order's appearing on the ERG user group.

Strong Status Report:

Accomplishment Report for May

Based on performance during the first two months of operation, new equipment pickup supplier Bird USA has reduced time frames for picking up de-installed subscriber equipment from more than 30 days to 8 days. Bird retrieves equipment from customer locations within 3 days of dispatch, significantly improving service to subscribers. Bird returns the equipment to our warehouse within 5 additional days, increasing our equipment redeployment opportunities.

Status Report with "Holes":

- Attended a Bynum Structure Chart class
- Finished assembling interview packets
- Met with Sue White and Belinda Tombs about the security issues
- Reconciled all bank balances

Strong Status Report:

- *Completed a Bynum Structure Chart class.* I learned skills that will decrease our time to prepare internal geological maps by at least 50 percent, so I recommend that all employees in our division take this training.
- *Finished assembling 200 interview packets for May recruitment fairs.* Interview packets now include a general-information brochure with complete contact information.
- *Met with Sue White and Belinda Tombs about the security issues.* We have decided that dealers should go directly to Reception in the applicable building rather than stopping at the guard house.
- *Reconciled all four bank balances to zero.* This is the first such reconciliation since the system has been in operation over the last six months.

Figure 62 presents a diagram of the structure for a typical status or accomplishment report. Figure 63 provides a model accomplishment report.

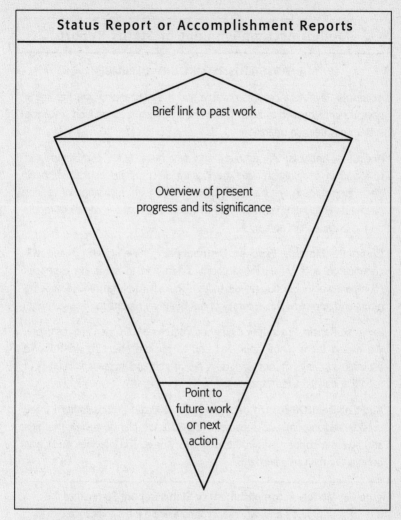

Figure 62. Status or Accomplishment Report. Status reports link past, present, and future, but primarily focus on the present.

Model: Accomplishment or Status Report

SUBJECT: STATUS REPORT, JULY–DECEMBER

Accounts Payable: Accounts payable and the outstanding voucher listing have been reconciled to zero. This is the first such reconciliation since the system has been in operation.

Accounts Analysis: All account analyses have been completed and reviewed in conjunction with the closing of corporate books. We have discovered three major problems having to do with duplication of vendor payments amounting to more than $14,000. I'll provide a complete report on those issues by February 1.

Corporate Monthly Expense Distribution: I have approved and will continue to approve all the account distribution to corporate expenses (comparing actual to budget expenses). This approval has reduced coding errors and improved the accuracy of our quarterly reports to management.

Expense-Report Procedures: New procedures are 90 percent complete. We expect them to be approved and to go into effect by April 1. We estimate a savings of four work days per month and increased accuracy in reporting travel-related expenses.

Audit of Field Offices: To date, we have collected proposals from three outside auditing firms, all for under $30,000. We plan to review the bids and award a contract within the next two weeks. The previous audit was done more than six years ago.

Figure 63. Model—Accomplishment or Status Report. Summarize the status of your projects and, when appropriate, state the significance of the contribution, step, or progress.

One special difficulty in organizing status reports is finding an appropriate format when simultaneously reporting on several major, ongoing projects. We suggest the multi-project format shown in Figure 64.

Format for Multi-Project Status Reports

Executive Summary

Use informative subheadings and/or bullets to give a one- or two-sentence overview of progress for each project.

Project #1 Major Heading
Brief Link to Past Work
Overview of Present Status
Significance of Work
Next Step

These sections are expansions of the brief overview given in the executive summary. All points may be covered in a single sentence or paragraph.

Project #2 Major Heading
Brief Link to Past
Overview of Present Status
Significance of Work
Next Step

Project #3 Major Heading
Brief Link to Past
Overview of Present Status
Significance of Work
Next step

Attachments

Any data sheets for optional reading

Figure 64. Format for Multi-Project Status Report. This special status report format allows readers to skim quickly for highlights regarding several projects.

19

MEETING MINUTES

Meeting minutes serve several purposes: To overview results for others not in attendance. To confirm to attendees the key conclusions and any follow-up actions. To document for the files key decisions and opinions. Meeting minutes should *not* be meeting transcriptions (a verbatim record of all that was said).

The format for meeting minutes closely follows the MADE Format™ (Figure 65).

The MADE Format™ for Minutes of Meetings	
Message	Summarize key conclusions. In the case of multiple issues, summarize conclusions on each agenda item.
Action	State key recommendations or any follow-up actions agreed upon.
Detail	Elaborate on key details (generally how and why). Summarize briefly important "pro" and "con" discussion leading to a key conclusion or recommendation.
Evidence	Mention any attachments (such as reports or data provided by meeting attendees) central to understanding conclusions or recommendations.

Figure 65. MADE Format™ for Minutes of Meetings. Make your meeting minutes matter by focusing on conclusions and follow-up actions.

These guidelines will help with other issues about layout and details:

- If you have a formal agenda, arrange topics to follow the agenda order.
- If you have no formal agenda, arrange topics in most-to-least-significant format.

- Use headings to help readers skim to agenda items of specific interest (see Figure 66). On occasion, you may want to use your discussion topics as headings and then record your conclusions and decisions in tabular format, as shown in Figure 67. (My earlier book, *Communicate with Confidence*, suggested setting up a meeting agenda in four columns; you can use this same format to record the minutes.)
- Remember that space given to recording a topic discussion suggests its importance; don't get carried away with minutiae. (Avoid the once-upon-a-time detail that typically surrounds each discussion topic and focus on the major problems identified or solved, the major questions raised or answered, and results and/or related follow-up action.)
- Include any specific follow-up assignments with each item—who should do what by when.
- Include names of attendees last.

Record carefully. Your minutes may be the only document standing between the meeting attendees and total confusion about conclusions reached and next steps of action.

Model: Meeting Minutes

The third safety meeting, held December 8, focused on establishing a new Accident Investigation Committee, companywide publicity efforts, and verbal accident reporting:

Accident Investigation Committees Formed: By January 15, management will appoint 12 employees from each site as an "accident investigation pool." When an accident occurs, the district manager will notify three people from this pool to investigate the report as follows:

- They will contact any injured employees, any witnesses to the accident, and the supervisor at the job site to gather information on causes, responsibility, and prevention.
- They will make a written report of their findings to the district manager within three working days after the accident.
- The district manager will forward this report and any recommendations for disciplinary action or preventative action to the appropriate senior vice president within ten working days.

Publicity Focus: We agreed that the primary focus of all publicity should be to make supervisors realize their responsibility for safety for all employees in their departments.

- Accident-free days will be posted on the intranet.
- Flo Mayahen suggested and will take responsibility to see that large safety banners are posted in all field sites.

New Requirements for Verbal Reporting of Accidents: Any employee involved in an accident, along with his or her team leader, will be required to meet with the safety division at its next scheduled session to present the circumstances of the accident, to report on lost time, and to recommend preventative measures.

Miscellaneous Items:

- We agreed to change the safety-meeting format on occasion to allow for field-related topic presentations by team members.
- We discussed videotaping "staged" accidents as the basis for future safety training. No conclusion was reached.

Follow-up Assignments:

Dusty Miller—Notify managers by December 15 about their appointing a 12-member "accident investigation pool" at each site by January 1.

Phuong Lam—Draft the discussed procedures for distribution to the "accident investigation pools." Have draft ready for committee approval by March 6 meeting.

Flo Mayahen—Investigate costs and design of safety banners and bring a recommendation for the next meeting, March 6.

Attending:

Flo Mayahen	Henry Armory
Dusty Miller	Kate Hendrix
Phuong Lam	Roberto Sanchez

Figure 66. Model—Meeting Minutes. Summarize key conclusions and recommendations; record follow-up actions, including who is responsible and any deadlines; and arrange the minutes in an easy-to-skim format. Choose the narrative format when many of the agenda items are merely reports or informative discussions rather than decision-making items.

Model: Meeting Minutes in Tabular Format

AGENDA ITEM	FORMAT: PERSON REPORTING OR LEADING	CONCLUSIONS/RECOMMENDATIONS	FOLLOW-UP ACTIONS, PERSON RESPONSIBLE, DUE DATE
Do we need accident teams at each site?	Kate: Open discussion	By January 15, management will appoint 12 employees from each site as an "accident investigation pool." When an accident occurs, the district manager will notify three people from this pool to investigate the report: —They will contact any injured employees, any witnesses of the accident, and the supervisor at the job site to gather information on causes, responsibility, and prevention. —They will make a written report to the district manager within three working days after the accident. —The district manager will forward this report for disciplinary or preventative action to the appropriate vice president within ten working days.	Dusty Miller—Notify managers by December 15 about their appointing a 12-member "accident investigation pool" at each site by January 1.

AGENDA ITEM	FORMAT: PERSON REPORTING OR LEADING	CONCLUSIONS/RECOMMENDATIONS	FOLLOW-UP ACTIONS, PERSON RESPONSIBLE, DUE DATE
What should be the focus of our publicity around the safety issue?	Flo Mayahen: Report on past efforts, followed by discussion	The primary focus of all publicity should be to make supervisors realize their responsibility for safety for all employees in their departments.	Phuong Lam—Will post accident-free days each month on the intranet. Flo Mayahen—Will make sure that safety banners are posted in all field sites by March 1.
What are the new requirements for accident reporting?	Henry Armory: report	Any employee involved in an accident, along with his or her team leader, will be required to meet with the safety division at its next scheduled session to present the circumstances of the accident, to report on lost time, and to recommend preventative measures.	
Should we change safety meeting format?	Open	We agreed to change format on occasion to allow for field-related topic presentations by team members.	

AGENDA ITEM	FORMAT: PERSON REPORTING OR LEADING	CONCLUSIONS/RECOMMENDATIONS	FOLLOW-UP ACTIONS, PERSON RESPONSIBLE, DUE DATE
Videotaping for future safety training?	Open	We discussed videotaping "staged" accidents for future safety training. No conclusion was reached.	

Figure 67. Meeting Minutes in Tabular Format. This agenda format suggested in my earlier book, *Communicate with Confidence*, can be completed during the meeting by attendees and easily e-mailed to non-attendees in the same agenda format they typically receive.

20

SERVICE AND INSPECTION REPORTS

The biggest temptation (and flaw) in writing service and inspection reports is to begin at the beginning and present the details in chronological order. Writers err, too, in telling readers all about the trouble involved in performing the test or putting the system, equipment, or site back in operation.

Service and inspection reports may focus on an activity, a failure, a malfunction, or an accident and its cause. The condition of the equipment, site, or system after the reported activity or problem is always a consideration. Finally, recommendations about preventive maintenance and other issues are of major interest to decision-makers.

The primary task in such a report is to analyze the reasons for any problem or deficiency. If the causes cannot be determined, say so directly; don't avoid addressing the cause altogether.

Include your opinion on whether this is a one-time, infrequent, or recurring problem. Such information will possibly suggest more extensive preventative maintenance, replacement of equipment, or revised operating procedures or service.

Finally, calculate, if appropriate, any time and dollar loss due to the failure so that management can assess alternatives for prevention. (See the model in Figure 68.)

Model: Service and Inspection Report

To:

From:

Subject:

The top bearing combination on the Spindle Bottom 600 failed for the second time in a month. The motor was installed with a top bearing combination of 9320 UPDT/7320 PDT with a 40° angle of contact. This bearing combination is designed for large down-thrust loads, and it is receiving only about half its design load. Therefore, the inner ring of the bearing in contact with the shaft tends to slide across the ball bearings instead of rotating them. This condition causes extreme heat buildup and premature bearing failure.

We have two options to correct the problem; I recommend the first.

Option 1: Reduce the contact angle to 29° to allow more down-thrust bearing contact.

Option 2: Remove the balls from the 7320 bearing. This action will put the total downward thrust on the 9320 bearing and cause the balls in this bearing to rotate.

WRC normally does not stock bearings with a 29° angle, and there is a 28-week wait on delivery. If you decide to approve Option 1, we need to order as soon as possible to keep downtime to the minimum. Total cost will be approximately $1,200 for Option 1, or $400 for Option 2. The recommended solution should keep the machine in excellent working condition for at least two years.

The attached drawing illustrates both modifications with the proper 29° angle.

Figure 68. Model—Service and Inspection Report. Service and Inspection reports should focus on what happened—with what results, and why. Recommendations and supporting details should follow.

21

PROCEDURES

Just for fun, I decided to present guidelines for writing procedures as a model procedure. Be my guest.

Updating a manual is like changing tires on a moving car.
—Edmund Weiss

Overview of Procedure: This procedure will tell you how to conceptualize procedures, arrange the steps in an easy-to-skim format, word each instruction clearly, distinguish steps from explanations or examples, and illustrate key steps with appropriate visuals.

Step 1: Conceptualize the best approach for providing procedures for your specific process.

1.1 Analyze your audience.

Ask yourself these questions to select the best way to convey your procedures: Who will use this procedure? How will they use this procedure? When will they need this procedure? Where, physically, will they use this procedure?

1.2 Anticipate special reactions.

If you anticipate inexperienced users who will become frustrated quickly if problems develop, give special attention to a format that looks easy to skim and a text that looks easy to read. Avoid unnecessary jargon and technical terms. Prefer simplicity above thoroughness. Be careful also about assumptions about their basic knowledge to begin the procedure.

1.3 Determine whether the procedure can best be conveyed through written words, pictures alone, or a combination of both graphics and text.

Examples of Various Procedure Formats:

- Graphic schematic
- Pictorial steps
- Job aid (online, posted on location, printed card)
- Reference manual (online or hard copy)

Figure A. *Use graphics liberally.*

Step 2: Begin all procedures and operating instructions with an overview statement about the complete task.

Before starting through a process, people generally like to know what they'll be able to accomplish with the procedure and exactly what's involved: how simple or complex the procedure is. Focus on major steps of the process rather than simply repeating all the steps.

Example: This procedure will convert numeric values to string values. This function differs from STR$ because it does not really change the bytes of the data—just the way BASIC interprets those bytes.

Step 3: Create an appropriate instructional format and page layout to guide the reader quickly from step to step.

If you follow the guidelines in this chapter, you will have designed a functional format. The reader should be able to skim, quickly separating actions from explanations and examples. Use bold print, italics, various fonts, headings, indentation, and adequate blank space to guide the reader's eye.

Step 4. Determine if there are any necessary safety precautions. If so, plan to place those safety precautions *before* the step to which they apply.

> *Example:* CAUTION: Prior to performing any tests on a point-to-point or multi-point private line, have a transmission circuit layout (TCL) card available. This card will allow you to identify the 4–wire facility before proceeding to the next step.

Step 5. List all steps in the procedure.

5.1 List first all the primary steps for the complete procedure.

5.2 List substeps under each primary step.

5.3 Add explanations under each step or substep, where necessary.

5.4 Provide examples for complex steps. Place each example as close to the related text as possible.

Step 6. Separate action steps from explanations.

6.1 Number all steps.

6.2 Use color, icons, art, or other graphical effects to distinguish actions from explanations.

> Notice how easy it is to distinguish each step from each example or explanation throughout this chapter. The reader should not have to wade through paragraphs of text to find action items.

> Numbers suggest a chronological order to a procedure. To number explanations, examples, or any other items confuses readers about whether some specific order is involved. Therefore, reserve numbers for sequential actions.

Caution: Do not proceed to Step 7 until you are sure you have included all steps in the correct order. Otherwise, you will waste time in editing what you may eventually have to delete.

Step 7. Edit the language in each step and substep.

7.1 Put each action in a separate sentence.

7.2   Revise any passive-voice sentences to active voice.

Active voice means that the subject of the sentence does the action. In passive-voice sentences, the subject of the sentence receives the action of the verb. In general, active-voice sentences are clearer, shorter, and more direct than passive-voice sentences.

Example (passive voice): The scan lines are numbered beginning with 0 at the top of the character position by the F2 command.

Example (active voice): Use the F2 command to number the scan lines beginning with 0 at the top of the character position.

Example (passive voice): The disk should be inserted in Drive A.

Example (active voice): Insert the data disk in Drive A. Insert the utility disk in any other available drive.

7.3   Link ideas clearly.

Use time links *(as, then, next, first)* to show time relationships. Use cause-and-effect links *(so, then, as, because)* to indicate that one action or situation happens as a result of the other.

Example (unclear): Set the transmit amplifier control to the full counterclockwise position and deactivate the detector. (Are these two separate actions? Do you do them simultaneously? Is this a cause-and-effect relationship?)

Example (clear): Set the transmit amplifier control to the full counterclockwise position *as* you deactivate the detector.

Example (clear): Set the transmit amplifier control to the full counterclockwise position, *thus* deactivating the detector.

Example (clear): Set the transmit amplifier control to the full counterclockwise position. *Then* deactivate the detector.

7.4   Revise all backward "then . . . if" statements.

Example (backward statement): Press Return to continue printing if the KP message appears.

Example (improved): If the KP message appears, press Return to continue printing.

Step 8.   Add illustrations liberally.

Use pictures to displace long text passages when possible. Pictures help skimming readers to grasp ideas quickly.

8.1 Add an informative title and caption to each illustration.

8.2 Number all illustrations consecutively.

8.3 Group illustrations at the end of logical sections if brief text passages would "get lost" scattered among many charts and graphics.

Step 9.   Cross-reference steps and procedures where necessary, but avoid loops and go-to directions, even if you must be repetitious.

Readers do not like to be given the runaround with procedures any more than callers or visitors to your office do. Don't refer them back and forth from section to section to find steps or explanations that appear elsewhere (*"Turn to section XX* and *proceed as directed there"*). Procedure writers sometimes fear being repetitious and wasting space by repeating directions. However, wasted user time and errors resulting from confusion are far more expensive than duplicated information in a procedure.

Step 10. Test your instructions.

Have someone with little or no knowledge of the task or equipment work through the procedure. If he or she has difficulty, revise the instructions. Do not assume that the real end user will have a better technical background and understanding than your "person on the street."

The ease of use of a product is inversely proportional to the length of its instruction manual.
—*William Horton, from* Horton's Laws

22

FORMAL TECHNICAL REPORTS

Title and Title Page

The purpose of a title page is not to be a cover sheet; a blank white page would do nicely for that. To serve its appropriate function, a title page should look balanced and uncrowded and include the vital information:

- Title of report
- Code, contract, or project number, if any
- Author(s) of report and affiliation
- Where presented or to whom submitted
- Date of submission or presentation
- Security, copyright, or confidentiality notice, if any

All of these pieces of information belonging on a title page are as easy to prepare as hitting keys on a keyboard—except the title.

Creation of an effective title may take hours of thought. Publishers routinely go through agony over book and article titles to be splashed on front covers. An effective title can sell a mediocre book, and a poor title can hide a potential best-seller. To authors and publishers, effective titles translate into big bucks.

But you as a technical writer have much more at stake than dollars. Your research may be lost to the business or scientific world altogether if your title is so ineffective that it gets no attention or if it is too vague to be appropriately abstracted for further research. Such is the case in company archives as well as professional abstracting services. Much research is duplicated simply because titles and abstracts are so poorly written that no one can retrieve the information hidden within them. Report or article titles should be descriptive enough to allow accurate abstracting for other researchers.

Can you imagine how an abstracting service listed the reports carrying the following titles? Can you imagine how many Internet searches would turn up these articles with such broad titles—and how unrelated they might be to specific search objectives?

Web Design for Market Research

Diet and Cancer

Artificial Chromosomes

Laboratory Antarctica: Research Contributions to Global Issues

So how do you write an effective title?

The title should distinguish your report from all others. What about your study makes it unique? Whatever it is, you should somehow include it in your title. Generally, the more specific your investigation has been, the more words it will take to describe it clearly.

The Effect of Internet Research on Relationships Between Cardiologists and Patients

Dry-Coupled Ultrasonic Elasticity Measurements of Sintered Ceramics and Their Green States

Quantitative Flaw Characterization with Scanning Laser Acoustic Microscopy

Potassium/Lime Drilling-Fluid System in Navarin Basin Drilling

Fatal Thrombotic Disorder Associated with an Acquired Inhibitor of Protein C

Filtration Method Characterizes Dispersive Properties of Shales

Evidence for Divergent Plate-Boundary Characteristics and Crustal Spreading on Venus

Flow Distribution in a Roller Jet Bit Determined from Hot-Wire Anemometry Measurements

Because you need so many precise, descriptive words to set your research apart, you should eliminate all deadwood (the obvious, the unnecessary, the general):

A History of . . .
The Use of . . .
A Study of . . .
A Report on . . .
An Investigation into . . .
Various Aspects of . . .
Several Approaches to . . .
Various Techniques of . . .
An Analysis of the Performance of . . .

Finally, consider your title and abstract as a unit. Rarely will readers see one without the other. Therefore, try not to repeat the title verbatim in your opening abstract statement.

Table of Contents

The table of contents is the key to the functionality of reports and proposals; it is not window dressing. The table of contents serves the following functions:

- Directs senior executives to the most important information
- Directs other skimming readers to specific technical sections
- Overviews the scope and contents of the report
- Highlights key ideas
- Helps readers relocate information

Therefore, items in the table of contents should be as informative as possible. Don't settle for unimaginative listings such as *Introduction, Scope of Project, Conclusions, Recommendations,* and *Testing Procedures.*

If you *do* use these general categories, then provide more specific subheadings. In addition to supplying a generic heading such as *Advantages,* give a capsule phrase of each advantage:

Advantages
Increased Accuracy in Reporting
Higher Pain Threshold
Subdued Melting

In addition to supplying a generic heading such as *Recommendations,* give a capsule phrase of what you propose:

Recommendations
Telecommunications for Cyber Processing
Telecommunications for Remote Users
Interface to Manufacturing Process Control
Network Monitoring
Replacement of SXT/377

Put yourself in the reader's place and consider which of the tables of contents shown in Figure 69 makes the information more accessible.

Uninformative Table of Contents
Purpose and Scope
Environment
Specifications
Report Examples
Programs
Utilities

Figure 69. Uninformative Table of Contents. Prefer to use specific headings rather than vague general categories.

Informative Table of Contents

Purpose of the Proposed System
    To Input Monthly Safety Summaries at the Refineries
    To Calculate Statistics
    To Print Reports at Headquarters

Environment
    MXC Computing Center
    User Restrictions by Law

Specifications
    Database
    Screen

Programs
    Identifying Obsolete Equipment
    Modifying New Parts
    Securing Approvals and Authorizations
    Notifying All Users about Changes
    Initiating and Canceling Orders within Seconds

Report Examples
    Monthly Summaries
    Statistical Summaries at the Refineries

Programs
    Menu
    Input

Utilities
    Database
    Input

Figure 70. Informative Table of Contents. A table of contents must be specific and informative to serve both the reader's and writer's purposes.

A table of contents should not include entries for pages that precede it, such as a title page or a transmittal document. But everything else in the report should be listed.

Finally, list the full titles of all tables and figures separately because readers will most frequently refer to these again and again.

Let accessibility be your guide. The table of contents, as a reading tool, should be functional: specific, informative, and easily accessible.

Other Front Matter: Preface, Foreword, and Acknowledgments

The preface, foreword, and acknowledgments should not repeat the bibliographic or other introductory sections of your report. Rather, they should contain only highlights. Many readers will not read the front matter at all.

The preface or foreword is an introduction, usually written by the author, that explains such things as the scope, the purpose, and the background of the document. A preface or foreword may also acknowledge those who helped in your work: your technical research team; those with whom you discussed your findings, conclusions, and recommendations; those whose published works you have drawn from in your own research; and finally, those who helped in manuscript preparation. Modesty wears well.

If other parts of your paper present your purpose, scope, and background, forgo having a preface or foreword and cite those who helped in a section entitled Acknowledgments.

Abstract

A key question we ask of a prospective client in order to customize a technical-writing workshop is: Do your professionals write abstracts or executive summaries?

The client often gives us a puzzled look. "Well . . . I don't know. I think it's probably a combination of the two, or something in between. Give me your definitions, and I'll see if what we do fits."

Our point is that there is much confusion about the terms "abstracts" and "executive summaries." In general, you provide executive summaries for proposals, reports, feasibility studies, projections, and strategy plans. Abstracts typically accompany research projects reported to other technical professionals either through internal publications or external scholarly journal articles or white papers.

Some technical writers use the terms interchangeably; others outline differences. To clarify what you need to write for your job or for publication, we'll take our stand by defining them differently and presenting examples of each. Then you can decide which are required for your own projects.

Executive Summaries

- provide information for decision-makers or nontechnical audiences.
- give more attention to conclusions and recommendations than to procedure.
- establish the framework for understanding the details and significance of the full report.
- may or may not follow the order of the report.
- run much longer than an abstract—sometimes several pages.

Abstracts

- provide information for technical audiences.
- summarize new contributions to a field.
- provide key words for electronic searches.
- follow the exact order of the full report.
- devote the same emphasis to each section that the full report does.
- usually run no more than 250 words.

A title and an abstract fit together as a unit; therefore, the title should not be repeated verbatim in the abstract. An abstract fulfills a vital function within a report. It:

Abstracts come in two varieties: "descriptive" (sometimes called "indicative") and "informative."

Descriptive Abstracts: A descriptive abstract reads much like a table of contents in paragraph form. It focuses on the development of the report rather than on the key pieces of information. In other words, a descriptive abstract promises to tell you something informative—later, when you read the entire report. For example:

> This report will review an argument between John and Mary. It will explain how the argument began and the possible repercussions of that argument, should it not be settled at some later date. The attitudes of both Mary and John will be discussed, and their decision to go their separate ways and pursue other interests will be analyzed. Recommendations about further relationships with other interested parties will be presented.

The readers of such abstracts always have questions. For example: What was the argument about? What was John's attitude? What was Mary's attitude? Why did they decide to go their separate ways? What are their "other interests" and "other relationships"?

So when do you use such promising, but uninformative, abstracts? In two situations: 1) when the results, conclusions, or recommendations are so numerous that they cannot be presented in brief abstract form; and 2) when you are presenting a paper orally and you don't want your audience to read your abstract, learn your secrets, and then skip your session. (*Note:* This situation works only if the paper was not published before the meeting.)

To develop a descriptive abstract, simply review your table of contents and turn your topics into sentences. However, never write a descriptive abstract when you can provide an informative one.

Informative Abstracts. An informative abstract informs; it is the telegram version of the entire report (and can include quantitative information). For example:

> John and Mary had a major disagreement about how to spend the $8 million they'd won in a state lottery. John wanted to spend it on a condominium in Cancun, a private jet, and a trip to the Orient. Mary wanted to save the $8 million for retirement at the age of fifty. John secretly withdrew his half of the money, bought his jet, and landed on Ruth's rice paddy in the Orient. He forgot about Cancun. Angry at the deception, Mary withdrew her $4 million, hired a lawyer, and sued John for half his rice cakes. She and her lawyer retired to Cancun while waiting for the appeal to be heard by the Supreme Court.

Always prefer an informative abstract over a descriptive one. An informative abstract is clear and specific. It presents an accurate picture of the report itself.

To develop an effective, informative abstract, review your headings and opening overview sentences under each heading. Select the most important points from each section, and prune away the less significant ones. Tell what was done, why it was done, and how it was done. Always include key findings and conclusions.

Because an informative abstract presents all the key information of a report or article, some readers can find all they need there and may never have to read the entire report. Even readers who want more detailed information can ascertain from such an informative abstract precisely what details they will find in the complete document.

In a nutshell, abstracts summarize new contributions to a field, provide key words for computer searches, establish a framework for the significance of an entire report, allow meeting attendees to select sessions to attend, and remind attendees or readers of what they've heard or read. Informative abstracts provide stand-alone summaries of key report information. Descriptive abstracts merely tell readers the general nature of the information they'll find in the full report. Always prefer an informative abstract to a descriptive one.

Executive Summary

An executive summary is a report in miniature and therefore should present all key information. It is, however, generally addressed to nontechnical audiences. Executive summaries give more attention to conclusions and recommendations than to procedure, may or may not follow the order of the report, and run longer than abstracts—sometimes several pages. A report may include both an abstract and an executive summary.

Whether to use an abstract or an executive summary or both depends primarily on your audience and the purpose of your document. Many writers and readers become confused about the differences between an informative abstract and an executive summary (see the preceding section).

Write an executive summary if your readers are nontechnical and if your readers are more interested in your conclusions and recommendations than in your procedures.

Write an abstract if your readers have the same technical background as you do and are just as interested in your procedures and findings as in your conclusions and recommendations, or more so.

Write both an abstract and an executive summary if you have a large audience with varied backgrounds and interests.

Because the executive summary is intended for those in management, emphasis should be placed on your project's big-picture implications for the organization. The summary stresses the purpose of your research and your conclusions and recommendations rather than your methods.

Various ratios suggest the appropriate length of a summary (for example, a 1-page summary for a 20-page report, or a 1-page summary for a 50-page report), but only you can be the final judge of what key points must appear in your summary.

Like abstracts (discussed in the preceding section), executive summaries should be informative and not merely descriptive of what readers will find later in the report. Compare the following two summaries.

Uninformative Executive Summary:

The Hudson B Sand Unit is located in Harris County in southeastern Colorado. Searson International's working interest in the unit, covering 1,900 gross acres, is 0.7565. The Hudson B sand reservoir has been producing for the last ten years, and the current unit well status is shown on the attached map. This report represents the culmination of a study in which the profitability and potential of the Hudson B were investigated.

Many questions still remain: What is the current unit well status? What is the profitability and the potential of Hudson B?

Informative Executive Summary:

Our recent study of the Hudson B Sand Unit (located in Harris County in southeastern Colorado) reveals that current operating conditions and oil prices make the field uneconomical. The monthly operating loss is $3,056 and the net year-to-date loss is $26,044. (The net gain for last year was $223,353.) Remaining reserves in the field are only 30,000 bbl, and average water cut is

92 percent. Current labor and transportation costs make tertiary recovery uneconomical, even if the current oil price doubles. We therefore recommend that Searson International sell the field.

Consider a longer example. Notice that such a summary may accompany a 50-page report.

Informative Executive Summary:

The Curtailment Statistical System (BT378) is designed to retain and report data for Universal's new Barbann Sales Division. The system will enhance present facilities and do much that is currently done manually. With this system, we estimate a savings of four work days per month in collecting operational data and preparing sales reports.

This new system design will:
- Convert the user's curtailment file
- Maintain the curtailment data through online inquiry and update utilities
- Compute and store the database with the customers' daily allocations
- Generate reports that compare supplies with projected sales

The system will interface with the measurement system for daily and historical actual volumes and with the sales information system for key verification and customer/key-meter static information.

Data-Med recommends that the system be installed at all locations during the fourth quarter. We also recommend that principal users at each site run the system in a parallel/testing mode for the first three months.

The executive summary is not a promise; it does not just mention information that can only be found somewhere else in the report. Rather, the executive summary informs. If executives stop reading your report after its summary, will they be adequately informed about your work? If not, be more specific in your summary.

> Those who write clearly have readers; those who write obscurely
> have commentators.
> —*Albert Camus*

Body

Reports should be organized in a descending format—from the big-picture message to supporting details. Many writers, however, cut their teeth on essay writing in English Composition 101. Therefore, they learned to begin with once-upon-a-time details and then proceed to the they-lived-happily-ever-after final paragraphs. This format is appropriate for essayists and novelists; however, the ascending, chronological arrangement is a serious flaw in technical or business-report writing.

Readers do not understand details or the significance of details until they have the main message and a mental pegboard on which to hang those details as they read. Compare the ascending and descending arrangements presented in Figure 71. Always prefer a descending arrangement to give readers the big-picture message, which will be the basis for understanding and appropriating the rest of the report.

	Ascending and Descending Arrangements for Technical or Business Reports		
	ASCENDING	DESCENDING	
Audience Interest			Audience Interest
Some readers	**Introduction**	**Conclusions & Recommendations**	*All readers*
A few readers	**Discussion** • Procedures • Test results • Qualifications • Unresolved Issues	**Discussion** • Background information • Procedures • Test results • Qualifications • Unresolved Issues	*Some readers*
All readers	**Conclusions & Recommendations**		
A few readers	**Attachments/ Exhibits**	**Attachments/ Exhibits**	*A few readers*

Figure 71. Ascending and Descending Arrangements for Technical or Business Reports. Use the descending format for research reports.

The Introduction

The introductory section should establish the writer's purpose and create a context for understanding the significant conclusions and recommendations.

Don't limit your thinking here to traditional background information. The "this is the problem and this is what has been done until now" approach is well worn and usually contains information that readers either already know or don't care to know. Unless your report will be important as an archival document, leave commonly known information out of your introduction.

Instead, try a fresh approach. Begin with a statement of a problem, a striking quote, an apt analogy, a statement of universal need, a provocative question, or any other attention-getter. Then lead into the purpose of the report and a definition of the project goal, explaining why the work was done at the present time or how it contributes to what has already been done on the subject. Also mention limitations of your report.

Provide only background that is essential to understanding conclusions. Much of the traditional background information included in reports fits best in the discussion section. And many "background" details should be omitted altogether.

The Conclusions

Although many readers prefer numbered or bulleted statements, the conclusions may be in paragraph form. Conclusions must always answer questions raised by the stated purposes in the report. The conclusions, in other words, present the results of the research findings.

Your conclusion should do the following:

- Summarize key facts or results
- Restate cautions or qualifications
- Mention alternate explanations or approaches
- Emphasize implications

Unless your reader will immediately understand the implications, you should avoid simply stating data or measurements. For example:

The temperature inside the controller box ranged from 46° to 62°C during the test.

This may be fine as a conclusion if your purpose was to determine the temperature variations inside the controller. However, if your purpose was to evaluate the accuracy of the controller under fluctuating temperatures, then the following would be a much better conclusion:

The controller maintained a ±0.3 percent accuracy over a temperature range of 46°C–62°C.

The Recommendations

The recommendation section takes the conclusions one step further for the decision-maker: You may recommend further areas of study, the abandonment of research on a subject, changes in current policies or procedures, or actions that management may take to capitalize on the research results—actions such as developing a new product or a new service.

The recommendation section is the most important section in many reports. It is here that you attempt to change human behavior or organizatonal goals—no small task. Unfortunately, many reports fail miserably in this section. Why? Because it's so easy to make high-sounding recommendations without addressing the problems involved in accomplishing them. For example, you conclude that overtorquing caused a component failure.

Your recommendation is: Control the applied torque to within a range of 2,500–2,700 ft lb. The recommendation, if followed, may solve the problem. But what if the available torque-measuring equipment is accurate only to ±500 ft lb and new equipment is prohibitively expensive? If you ignore these facts, the recommendation becomes meaningless. It may get you off the hook with respect to the project, but your report does not ultimately change things for the better.

In short, make sure your report recommendations are viable.

The Discussion: Procedures, Test Results, Qualifications

The discussion section contains the supporting detail for all that has gone before in the summary, conclusions, and recommendations. You may include:

- experimental or preliminary research
- descriptions of testing apparatus
- testing procedures
- testing or sampling errors and their significance
- test results
- interpretations of findings
- explanations of alternate interpretations
- qualifications
- cautions

Keep in mind that few decision-makers will read the discussion section in detail. So why write it? For one thing, you need it to support your conclusions. For another, you need the details for the files and for later reference. Finally, secondary audiences may find the discussion details of interest.

Primarily, readers of this section will be other technical specialists interested in how and why you did what you did. They may build on your work, refute it, or further analyze or interpret it. But unless they are acting as secondary experts who are to advise management, they are reading primarily to be informed about your research, not to take managerial action.

The discussion is a necessary, but little-read, section of most reports.

Appendix

The appendix contains supporting documentation (data presented in spreadsheets, charts, tables, graphs, drawings, maps) that will be of interest only to a few secondary readers. A summary of the significant information from the tables or graphics should be included in the text of the report. A reader should not have to turn back and forth from text to appendix to read and understand the report.

Think of an appendix as one large footnote that is of interest mostly to secondary readers, not to decision-makers. Appendixes provide a way to present raw data and calculation methods to secondary readers without inundating your main audience, which has no interest in such detail. Never hide key information there without summarizing it in the main report text itself.

If primary readers need to see the information presented in an illustration or chart as they read your text, place the graphic in the text (not in the appendix) as close to the text reference as possible. Readers do not like to have to shuffle back and forth from text to appendix to read and understand the report itself. If you can summarize the data, put the summary in the text and the myriad other details in the appendix.

Number the appendixes in capital Roman numerals and title each one. Skimming readers will love you if you're accurate; they'll be infuriated if they run into a reference to Appendix D in the text and find no such attachment at the end of the report.

Because an appendix can go on forever, you can still appear to be a succinct, clear-thinking writer with a brief report containing only the significant details. But don't destroy that image by throwing into the appendix everything you learned in graduate school.

Glossary

A glossary provides definitions of terms or explanations of symbols and abbreviations used in the text of the report. It's virtually impossible for anyone to know all the standard symbols and abbreviations for every discipline. And even if that were possible, there is much duplication from one field of study to the next.

Therefore, analyze your audience to decide whether your report needs a glossary. Continually stopping to define or explain interrupts the flow of the report and becomes a nuisance to those readers with the same technical background as yours. But you have a responsibility to less technical readers and those from other disciplines who may also make up your audience. You must provide them with the necessary definitions in a glossary, placed either at the beginning or at the end of the report.

Remember, too, that the benefit of a glossary is partially lost if its component information is difficult to find; therefore, make sure entries are in alphabetical order.

Technical writing is a form of brain damage, caused by an over-development of the *corpus callosum*—a sort of cerebral cross-wiring. It manifests itself as a compulsion to explain complex things so that mere mortals can understand them.

—*William Horton*

23

PROPOSALS

Use the Proposal as a Sales Tool

To be used as a sales tool, a proposal must incorporate a strategy, address the reader's needs, and then persuasively present the proposer's solution and capabilities.

"We write proposals but we don't want them to *look* like proposals—we want them to sound like informational, technical reports," a client told us. Although I didn't go into a philosophical discussion with him, I filed the remark away as a basic misconception about proposals.

Selling an idea or solution needn't be akin to selling used cars on local TV. Nevertheless, a proposal must be attractive. It must be everything a good e-mail or sales letter is—but much more specific. A proposal presents a problem or need and persuasively outlines a project, service, or product that the proposer can oversee or provide to solve the problem or meet the need.

You may find yourself offering a proposal in one of two situations: 1) You send an unsolicited proposal to persuade the reader he or she needs your product or service; or 2) The reader is aware of a need, but you must persuade him or her that you are the best source for the product or service to meet the need.

Your proposal may, in fact, take the form of a single-page sales letter, a formal 2,000-page document, or an e-mail with only price quotations and specifications.

It's usually not the form of a proposal but its substance that brings rejection. However, a sloppy proposal does leave a lasting negative impression about the quality of your service or product.

Avoid Common Proposal Mistakes

No Strategy

The most important feature of your proposal should be your theme or strategy, which is repeated and developed throughout the document. Why should the bidder select *your* organization over all the rest? Do you have the best design? Do you have the most thoroughly trained technicians? Do you have the most up-to-date equipment or information? Can you do the project most inexpensively? Can you do it more quickly than the competition? Give your reader one or two basic overriding themes to capsule your capabilities. Avoid saying simply, "Well, so can we!"

Carelessness About Apples-to-Oranges Comparisons

Help your reader remember the key points when comparing your offer to the offers of your competitors. Clearly identify the important issues and then point out how you can address each. Force the reader to evaluate the competition with regard to *your* issues.

Failure to Show Adequate Understanding of the Problem

Some proposers have all the answers before they hear the questions. A necessary part of your job is to communicate to the reader a full understanding of the problem or objective so that he or she will be convinced your solution is the appropriate one.

Answers to the Wrong Problems

Study the client's request for proposal (RFP). Propose to do what the prospective buyer wants. Notice that we didn't say you should necessarily propose to do what the buyer *says* he or she wants—make sure you investigate those stated needs or wants. What an RFP says and what can be gleaned from a discussion with the buyer may be vastly different.

Many, including us, have learned this truth the hard way. A few years back, we received a request to propose a training program; the request already included within it a detailed course outline. Because there were several places where we thought improvements could be made to the outline, we called the prospective client and asked if the topics were firmly set. "Oh, yes. That's exactly what we want. All our VPs and technical experts have signed off on that course outline."

Therefore, we developed our proposal along those lines, only to have the proposal rejected. The client's explanation: "The winning proposer completely scrapped our course outline. What his company presented makes a lot more sense, and we're really excited about the changes."

You will perhaps discover the differences between stated needs and criteria and the real needs only by flushing out and investigating discrepancies. Give clients what they need, but be sure to find out what the *real* needs are. Trying to discover the real needs is especially important if you are providing products or services that the prospective client may not understand as fully as you do.

Vagueness

Proposal writers often fear that they will give away too much information in outlining their approaches and solutions to problems. There is, of course, always the danger of having a prospective buyer read your proposal and attempt to implement your solution without your help. But the bigger fear should be of giving so little detail that the reader doesn't think you know how to do the job.

One often vague section in proposals is the list of references. Name contacts and provide addresses and phone numbers.

Closely related to vagueness about references is evasiveness about the background and experience of the proposed project staff: "have graduate degrees in related areas"; "has had ten years' experience in the industry"; "has handled similar projects both nationally and internationally." Readers often interpret such comments thus: "Nothing to brag about, huh?"

Extravagant Claims

Readers raise eyebrows when organizations claim to have expertise in everything but the treatment of ingrown toenails of rabbits. Be wary of hyperbolic language—phrases such as "the most extensive," "the most authoritative," "unequaled," or "the undisputed leader." Tone claims down to the point at which you can support them with facts. Instead of using high-flown language, include published articles, survey results, test data, testimonial letters, or sample products—whatever supports your claims. Overstatement begs the reader to be skeptical.

Failure to Provide Memory Aids

By the time a buyer reviews five or six lengthy proposals, disorientation sets in. Which proposal writer claims to be able to do what, why, where, when, how, and at what cost? Don't assume that your reader will be as eager to work at understanding and remembering your key points as you are. Instead, provide help by way of overview statements in each section, summary blurbs beside lengthy text, informative headings, and high-impact graphics with full captions.

Include the Nine Essentials of a Formal Proposal

A proposal must 1) analyze the buyer's need or problem, 2) present the technical solution to the problem, 3) discuss the management and business issues, and 4) persuade the buyer that the proposing organization is the best suited to do the work. A formal proposal can accomplish these objectives with a variety of organizational formats and informative headings.

There are at least as many ways to organize a proposal as there are industries. Your specific project will determine, for example, if you need a section entitled "Deliverables" or "Testing Procedures." Most proposals, however, should follow the general structure of a formal report, with an executive overview and the remainder of the document in descending format (see the previous section on formal reports).

But whatever arrangement and specific divisions you select, a proposal should do the following:

- Present a thorough analysis of the buyer's needs or problems
- Propose technical solutions
- Discuss the management and business considerations of the project
- Persuade the buyer that the proposing organization is the best suited to do the work

Following are descriptions of the nine parts that should be included in most proposals.

Title Page
The title page should contain the following:

- A title indicative of what you are proposing
- The name of the recipient
- The date of submission
- Any RFP, contract, or project number
- Any statement of security or confidentiality

Table of Contents

For proposals of more than 10 to 12 pages, there should be a table of contents that lists informative subheadings to provide another review of benefits and other key issues.

List of Exhibits

The exhibits should have informative titles (for example, not "Cost Analysis" but "Cost Comparison of Software Development").

Matrix Response Sheet

The matrix response sheet is a two-column chart listing the stated evaluation criteria and the pages that respond to each point.

Executive Summary

An executive summary should state the following:

- Who you are
- What the problem is
- How you propose to solve the problem
- What the key benefits will be
- How you will manage and evaluate the project
- How long you will take to complete the project
- How much the project will cost (unless costs are required in a separate document, or unless you expect to be the high-price vendor)

Analysis of the Problem, Need, or Situation

This analysis should include the following:

- A discussion of the proposal problem, mission, and goals *in terms of results*
- The specifications established by the buyer
- The assumptions and qualifications imposed on the research
- A search of past work done
- Client-provided data as support
- The proposed solution
- The advantages of the solution
- The feasibility of the solution
- A plan for performance testing and measurement of the solution
- Alternatives and pros and cons of each

Approach to the Solution or Proposed Project

This part of the proposal should include the following:

- Plans for various phases, experiments, and tasks (a flowchart is helpful here)
- Management and staff requirements
- A description of equipment and site preparation
- Contingency plans
- Scheduling and procedures
- Deliverables (quantitative and qualitative data)
- Control and quality-assurance plans
- Evaluations
- Certifications
- A schedule of meetings or other interactions and checkpoints with the buyer
- Progress reports and final reports
- Costs, methods, and terms of payment
- Guarantees

Credentials

The credentials provided should include:

- Those of the proposing organization (specific company references, along with names, addresses, and phone numbers of contact persons; past achievements and awards; facilities; equipment; staff)
- Those of the assigned staff (patents, achievements, awards, publications; years of experience in what positions with what organizations; involvement in relevant projects; education)

Miscellaneous Exhibits

Among such exhibits might be:

- Brochures
- Testimonials
- Certifications
- Patents
- Published white papers, articles, and books
- A list of similar jobs completed (with references) and other evidence

Use Strategic, Well-Developed Analogies and Slogans for High Impact

"My daughter has a pimple on her chin, and she's unhappy. She's eighteen. I have a pimple on my chin, and I'm happy. I'm fifty-two. It's called perspective." So goes the opening paragraph of a memo by George Ball, former CEO of Prudential-Bache Securities. His subject? Deep cuts in the big brokerage firm's investment-banking department. His audience? Wall Street. His purpose: to make a key point memorable.

A director of information technology once wrote to the committee holding the purse strings on his new budget: "Trying to do what's needed with the equipment we have is like trying to cut your lawn with a pair of scissors." His audience? The executive decision-makers. His purpose: to help them grasp the enormity of the problem.

Example is the best precept.
—*Aesop*

Buyers of products, services, or even ideas have short memories. It's always appropriate to add creative analogies to your technical information to make it more understandable. Slogans, strategically placed throughout your proposal, have the same effect as headlines on the front page of a newspaper. They summarize, highlight, and make memorable your key points. Where would advertisers be without slogans? Out of business. Just make sure any analogies and slogans mesh with the overall tone (formal or informal) and purpose of your entire proposal.

Know the Difference Between Persuading and Informing

People are fed up with hyperbole-laced writing. Such language has become more than annoying; it drives customers to competitors. Websites that simply have an online brochure or ad will never snag today's buyers. Technical writers and readers particularly live by the principle: "Just the facts, ma'am." Interpreted facts, yes. Nevertheless, facts and reasons rather than hype.

Yes, most business writers must at times be persuasive. Even though your job may not involve selling a product or service, you must sell your ideas and your credibility. But in an age of political spin and Internet banner ads, hype has given persuasion a bad name. To many writers, persuasion has become synonymous with exaggeration, braggadocio, and superlatives. Consider the following example, which is filled with high-flown language:

> Our system has been *widely tested* in its *exceptional* capabilities to provide the most *up-to-date* search capacity, the *most thorough* cross-referencing capabilities, and *unsurpassed* workmanship on terminal design.

"As a matter of fact" precedes many a statement that isn't.
—Mark Twain

The essence of persuasion is knowing exactly what your reader values, wants, or needs, then presenting your information to meet those needs or support those values. If your reader values accuracy, you will document the precision of your testing tools. If your reader values production speed, you will emphasize how your solution quickly converts raw material into a finished product.

Persuasive writing also means emphasizing benefits rather than specifications or features. How will you solve the reader's problems? Why is this the best solution?

In proposals, persuasive writing requires sound logic and thorough research and interpretation. You add credibility to your work when you cite alternatives for solving a problem or designing a model and then give reasons for your choice. Credibility also increases when you are careful to define what your process or design can and cannot do. In other words:

- Don't ignore opposing views or options.
- Be straightforward.
- Prefer understatement to overstatement; let the reader develop his or her own enthusiasm for what you have to say.

Because an erroneous idea of what persuasive documents involve may weaken rather than strengthen your writing, let's focus more specifically on what persuasive writing is *not*.

Hyperbole. Overstatement used for emphasis generally calls attention to the exaggeration rather than to the key point.

> Stripping this field without the expertise of our chemists who've had decades of experience will be as impossible as your internal staff's earning a medical degree in a month.

Often such hyperbole angers a thoughtful reader or one who is biased against your position.

Understatement, deliberate downplaying of the possibilities of your idea, can be much more effective in motivating a reader to champion your cause.

Mysterious Sources. Common lead-ins to unsupported generalizations include such statements as these: "As leading experts will agree . . . "; "A search of the literature reveals . . . "; "Long known to industry experts . . . "; "A leading representative of the field . . . "; "Several professors at major universities . . . "; If you have a renowned source, identify that source. Hidden authorities, as in the following passage, invite readers to ignore, or at least be skeptical of, your idea.

> Some advanced compounds *are said* to have broken the processing-time barrier: One-minute cycle times are already possible, *with some producers* estimating 45-second part-to-part times in the near future. In addition, many of these materials *are said* to provide surface qualities better than those of other polymers and even steels. *Many believe* that these products offer a number of inherently better qualities than KPR casings molded by today's technology. However, *some of the most ambitious predictions by the auto makers* for usage through the earlier part of the next decade have been modified. Costs have not come down to expectations, *according to some users*, while *many observers* feel that these materials are simply too new to inspire needed confidence of *the auto makers. (italic emphases added)*

Vague Qualifiers and Hedging. Many writers fear someone will take their words out of context. Therefore, they add qualifiers and hedgers in every sentence nook and cranny. The overall result is diluted writing. That is not to say that you should make absolute statements that are unsupportable. But do watch for unnecessarily vague weasel words and hedgers.

For example, note the wishy-washy effect of the following statements (hedgers and qualifiers are in italics):

The paint *should* resist dust and *should* reduce maintenance costs *significantly*.

It should be *strongly* emphasized that the *probability* of a *worst-case situation* occurring is *apparently very low*.

Listed below are *suggested possible* courses of action that *appear* to warrant *further consideration*.

On most occasions, the regulator meets the criteria established by our research team; however, *possible deviations may suggest* that NRC reevaluate the decision to modify our *current needs*.

Name-calling. Calling the competitor's research, product, or service "insignificant," "intolerable," or "primitive" doesn't make it so. Refuting option A does not necessarily lead the reader to embrace option B, which you favor. In fact, criticism of another's work can set your own work up for closer scrutiny than you desire. It is better simply to offer your work to your readers and let it speak for itself.

Oversimplification. Simple answers to complex problems are tools of politicians. This fact no doubt explains their shoddy record at actually solving problems. No, we don't mean that readers dislike simple solutions; but oversimplification invites skepticism and makes the knowledgeable reader doubt the writer's understanding of the situation.

Calling something simple doesn't make it so. You need as much evidence and explanation to support a simple answer as you do for a complex one—maybe more.

Facts Presented as Reasons. Don't confuse facts with reasons. To be persuasive, facts need interpretation.

Why should we offer the lab-supply business a sole-source contract? 1) Vendor A will give us a 15 percent discount as our sole-source contractor; 2) Vendor B has had difficulty filling our chemical orders from the Lafayette lab; 3) Vendor C has been doing business with our competitors for the past eight years.

None of the above facts by itself is a reason for awarding the sole-source contract to Vendor A. We can't evaluate the 15 percent discount until we compare it to the prices of Vendor B and Vendor C. Vendor B's difficulty in filling orders has nothing to do with Vendor A's or Vendor C's ability to fill orders. And Vendor C may or may not have a conflict of interest in dealing with us and our competitors.

One of the biggest weaknesses in persuasive writing is the tendency to present facts without interpreting them in light of the question at hand. Facts are not reasons.

For example, let's say Rachel's company is considering getting into the pen or pencil business, and the president has asked her to evaluate the potential of the two kinds of products and determine which would be the most profitable to manufacture and sell. Rachel's key points might be these:

- Inks come in a variety of colors.
- Pens are good for signing legal documents.
- Pens are cylindrical and lightweight.

Rachel concludes that her organization should manufacture and sell pens.

But why? The listed statements do not support the conclusion. Perhaps the argument is in the writer's head, but it's not on the page. Yes, pen ink comes in many colors, but so does pencil lead. And what does a variety of colors have to do with bottom-line profits? Is the writer saying that the variety of colors will attract more buyers? But readers might also conclude that the inventory and start-up costs would have to be greater with a variety of ink colors.

And concerning the usefulness in signing legal documents, what if only one out of every 1,000 documents written by the customer is a legal document? That "benefit" is really of little value.

Finally, what does their cylindrical shape and weight have to do with their manufacturing and marketing? Should Rachel's company improve on that design? Retain the customary shape and weight? Or make a heavier, square pen instead?

Many technical writers assume that "the facts speak for themselves." Rarely is that the case. Facts and evidence need interpretation. When that interpretation is not evident on the page, the reader stumbles over the gaps in logic.

Begging the Question. Begging the question involves talking around the issue without addressing it. Technical writers often beg the question, stating the obvious:

I suggest users perform these tests quarterly because the results will give them further information. (Obviously. Do results ever give *less* information?)

The consultants determined that we should reinforce the structure because this was the wisest preventive solution. (Right. Do they otherwise advise the dumbest preventive solution?)

More testing may be useful because it may shed more light on the subject. (Will more testing ever shed *less* light?)

Persuasive language involves a logical presentation of facts and information, not a fanfare of fancy, overblown pronouncements that are trivially true.

24

WEBSITES

Businesses are becoming increasingly alarmed by the potential for risks of liability for a variety of claims: copyright and trademark infringement, defamation, and technology failures. Although such liability can cost big bucks, the biggest costs are a result of lost business due to weak website writing and poor design.

Because website design deserves its own book, the following guidelines focus only on the words and the layout of the screens.

Create a "Summary" on Your Home Page

Just as with the MADE Format™ for other documents, visitors to your site need an overview of your business and your uniqueness. That summary may be provided in a few headlines, by the labels in the menu, or in a graphical representation. However you do it, the home page should answer these questions: What do you do, and how do you do it? What's your brand? If you doubt the importance of that summary, ask yourself how many websites you've visited, after a colleague's referral, where you couldn't figure out what the business or organization was all about. The overall purpose of your site (internal information only, external information only, online sales, interactivity to generate traffic, and so forth) will determine what your summary should convey.

Focus on Visitor Benefits Rather Than on Information About Your Own Organization

As usual, the first step in writing anything is to consider your audience: Why should they care about what you have to say? How will they be better off after having visited your site? Talk about problems they have in terms of the help you can provide. In short, as with all other writing, tailor your content to the audience. Be relevant.

Help Visitors Stay Focused; Avoid Clutter

Just as you do not want to add irrelevant details to an e-mail, avoid distracting bells and whistles, banners and bulletins on a web page. Irrelevance has the same effect on-screen as it has on paper: confusion. Consider this analogy: If you walk into a room that has only one picture on the wall, chances are great that you'll notice that picture. If you walk into the same room, where there are 100 pictures on the wall, chances are great that you'll not notice any single picture. The same is true of cluttered websites.

Position Ideas in Order of Importance in Each Window of Text

Use the descending arrangement, put your key message up front. The first sentence of each paragraph or section should tell the story. Details should follow. Users scroll only after they're thoroughly engaged.

Chunk Information so People Can Remember It

Seven is the magic number. Our brains can comprehend only seven or fewer menu items: tasks, subtasks, or bullet points. Anything longer overwhelms us and forces us to reread, if—and that's a big if—we take the time to linger.

Provide Answers to Typical Questions

Most visitors are goal-driven; they are looking for specific information and answers. What will visitors need to know before they can make the decision you want them to make? Give any dates, deadlines, costs, guarantees, credentials, track record, and helpful how-to's.

Tell Visitors How They Can Communicate with You

A survey sponsored by Brightware, a Novato, California, maker of customer-response software, revealed that many Fortune 100 companies (half of those 100 companies surveyed) didn't have an obvious e-mail link on their websites, and 10 companies had no e-mail link at all. When the same survey was conducted last year, only 15 percent of the companies contacted responded to an e-mail that asked: What is your corporate headquarters address? The response times were even more exasperating. A host of companies did not respond within a month!

Use Specific Words

Many customer complaints center on this one issue: The visitor buyer or inquirer interpreted a vague word or phrase to mean something quite different from what the writer intended. With vague, general words, you are setting up your visitor for disappointment.

Forget the Technobabble

Translate, translate, translate. Write error messages in plain language. Give usable feedback.

Make Response Easy

Remember that response is voluntary. Website visitors measure their trouble by number of clicks, quantity of clutter, and seconds spent in confusion.

Make Copy Easy to Skim

Studies show that we read more slowly online than we read print. So help visitors along. Put your message in informative headlines. Provide complex or detailed information in list format or in short paragraphs. Add color to highlight key points. And above all, be consistent. That is, express equally important ideas in the same color with the same typeface and size. At a glance, the layout should convey the correct relationship between ideas. In short, give visitors control of what they want to read in what order.

Don't Create Elements That Resemble Ads

Visitors are trained to ignore ads. We have cut our teeth on magazine and newspaper ads, skipping them whenever possible. Hence, the "advertorial" copy in magazines that advertisers design to look like editorial content. Be careful that design elements don't scream to visitors, "Skip this ad!"

Group Like Items Together, Based on Their Function and Frequency of Use

Consider your website layout like pegs for your garden tools hanging on the garage wall or like mug trees for your coffee cups. Readers must understand the structure of the pegs (pages, bullets, buttons, categories) so they can hang information on them.

Keep Visual Metaphors Consistent

If your site design uses physical health and fitness as a metaphor for organizational fitness, keep that same analogy throughout the site. Whether we're talking about horses or horoscopes, don't mix metaphors midstream—written or visual.

List Menus in Logical Order

The same advice holds true for websites as it does for written reports. Analyze and plan; then write—not the reverse.

Label Menus, Buttons, Symbols, and Graphics

Conventional wisdom claims a picture is worth a thousand words. That's true—if people understand the picture. Use descriptive rather than general labels. Test your graphical design to find out where visitors become confused. The test need not be complex or expensive; simply observe.

Don't Trick People

Be honest about what you offer. Think about how you feel when you read all the way to the end of a five-page direct-mail piece only to discover the writer is asking you to send in "only $39.95" for a widget. Tricked. And angry. That's the same feeling visitors to your website experience when a headline on a form seems to promise them something for free, and only after spending five minutes filling out the online form do they discover they'll be charged for hitting the Submit button.

Make the Copy Readable

Prefer sans serif typefaces (without lines, curls, or angles at the top or bottom of letters) for headlines, and serif typefaces for body text. As with e-mail, avoid using "artsy" typefaces that are difficult to read. Make sure the lettering contrasts properly with the background. White lettering on a dark background slows down reading time.

Use Exclamation Points and Uppercase Sparingly

As mentioned earlier, uppercase represents shouting. Exclamation points also express strong emotion. Prefer to let the visitors to your site decide how excited they are rather than telling them how excited they should be.

Take Care with Humor

Aim for personality and pizzazz, of course, to engage visitors. But keep in mind that witticisms, puns, and other forms of humor must work for international visitors.

Words on your website must both communicate your message and trigger emotion or action in your reader. Information can sprawl for pages and pages for only pennies; space is cheap. Time is not. Make each word count.

A FINAL NOTE TO THE READER

After reading this book, you may be wondering: Should I try to write e-mail, letters, proposals, procedures, or reports at all? That question should not be taken lightly. Before you sit down at the computer, consider the following reasons for putting your message in writing: Is the person too difficult to reach by phone? Will your reader need to keep the written document for later reference and reminder? If you're writing to several readers, do they all *really* need this information? Do you need a permanent record of this communication for legal reasons?

Much business and technical writing does not and cannot stand on its own; writers must interpret their message in person or by phone and then send a confirming e-mail, letter, proposal, or report.

But when you must write and when your writing must work, review and practice the five steps detailed here for effective communication.

I love being a writer. What I can't stand is the paperwork.
—*Peter de Vries*

BIBLIOGRAPHY

Booher, Dianna. *2001 Business Letters* (software, CD-ROM, and web versions). Model Office: Austin, Texas, 1997.

———.*2001 Sales & Marketing Letters* (software, CD-ROM, and web versions). Model Office: Austin, Texas, 1997.

———.*Clean Up Your Act!* New York: Warner Books, 1992.

———.*Communicate with Confidence.* New York: McGraw-Hill, 1994.

———.*Cutting Paperwork in the Corporate Culture.* New York: Facts On File, 1986.

———.*The Executive's Portfolio of Model Speeches.* New York: Prentice-Hall, 1991.

———.*Good Grief, Good Grammar.* New York: Facts On File, 1988; and Ballantine Books, 1989.

———.*Great Personal Letters for Busy People.* New York: McGraw-Hill, 1997.

———.*To the Letter: A Handbook of Model Letters for the Busy Executive.* New York: Jossey-Bass, 1989.

———.*The Letterwriter's Almanac: Letters for Personal, Social, and Business Occasions.* Englewood Cliffs, NJ: Prentice-Hall, 1991.

———.*Winning Sales Letters: Time-Saving and Ready-to-Use Sales and Marketing Letters to Help You Get Customers and Keep Them.* New York: Jossey-Bass, 1990.

———.*Would You Put That in Writing?* New York: Facts On File, 1992.

———. and Tom Hill. *Writing for Technical Professionals.* New York: John Wiley and Sons, 1989.

Brockman, John R., and William Horton. *The Writer's Pocket Almanack.* Santa Monica, CA: InfoBooks, 1988.

Grossman, John. *The Chicago Manual of Style,* fourteenth ed. Chicago: University of Chicago Press, 1993.

Gunning, Robert. *The Technique of Clear Writing.* New York: McGraw-Hill, 1968.

Locke, Christopher, Rick Levine, Doc Searls, and David Weinberger. *The Cluetrain Manifesto: The End of Business as Usual.* New York: Perseus Books, 2000.

Sabin, William A. *The Gregg Reference Manual,* ninth ed. New York: McGraw-Hill, 2000.

Strunk, William, Jr., and E. B.White. *The Elements of Style,* fourth ed. New York: Allyn & Bacon, 1999.

GRAMMAR GLOSSARY

absolute	a group of words grammatically unrelated to the rest of the sentence; begins with a noun or pronoun; differs from a clause in that it does not have a complete verb (*The reports finished,* we left early.)
acronym	abbreviations that are pronounced as words (ZIP, AIDS, PIN, NASA)
adjective	describes, points out, limits, or numbers a noun or a pronoun
Descriptive	*black, difficult, provocative*
Limiting	*a, an, the, this, that*
Numbering	*two, many, several*
adverb	tells how, when, where, why, how much, or to what extent about a verb, adjective, or another adverb (*much, excessively, cautiously, later*)
antecedent	a word to which a later word refers (The *plan, which* is highly workable, can be initiated immediately. *John* told the group that *he* was working on a new plan.)
appositive	an inserted explanation; can be a word, phrase, or clause; usually follows the noun or pronoun it explains or equals (The fact *that we left early* can't be argued.) (The target area, *the Saudi job site,* can . . .)

clause	a group of words containing a subject and a predicate
independent	a clause that expresses a complete thought (After the job estimate came in, *he proceeded on schedule.*)
dependent	does not express a complete thought and must depend on the independent clause for full meaning (*After the job estimate came in,* he proceeded on schedule.)
restrictive	restricts the meaning of the main clause; essential to the meaning (Replace only the tubes *that have been damaged.*) (tells which tubes)
nonrestrictive	adds nonessential information to the sentence meaning (You must replace all the tubes, *which will be rather costly.*)
complement	follows a linking verb (is, are, was, were, become, looks, seems) and completes the meaning of the verb
subjective	renames or describes the subject of the sentence (Mr. Smith is president.) (Mr. Smith became angry.)
objective	tells about the direct object (He considered the project *a failure.*)
conjunction	a word that joins other words or groups of words
coordinate	joins elements of equal rank (and, or, nor, for, but, yet, so)
subordinate	joins elements of unequal rank (since, if, although, because, as)
correlative	conjunctions used in pairs (either-or, neither-nor, whether-or not, both-and, not-but, though-yet)
expletive	a word having nothing grammatically to do with the rest of the sentence; often introduces the subject (*There* is nothing more we can do.) (*It* is difficult to do these tests.)

fragment	an incomplete sentence; usually incomplete because the group of words contains no verb (All procedures outlined in the first ten pages of the report describing the absorption processes)
interjection	a word expressing strong or sudden feeling; grammatically unrelated to the rest of the sentence; a separate entity. (Oh! Cheers! No!)
modifier	a word or group of words that describes, points out, or limits another word (*difficult* task) (plan *that was inadequate*)

mood

indicative	verb form that states a fact (My e-mail confirms the opinion.)
subjunctive	verb form that states idea, event, or condition contrary to fact; expresses a strong wish or resolve (If he would let me, I'd resign.)
imperative	verb form that states a command (Sign this form.)

noun	the name of a person, place, thing, or idea (Mr. Brown, warehouse, schedule, freedom, Canada, the Statue of Liberty)
noun of address	the person to whom the rest of the sentence is addressed (*Mr. Smith*, I can't thank you enough.)
number	refers to noun, pronoun, or verb; indicates whether one or more is meant (building, buildings; indicates, indicate; mine, ours)
object	a noun or a pronoun that follows a complete (transitive) verb
direct	a word that receives the action of the verb (Brown injected the *solution* into the samples.)
indirect	the receiver of the direct object (We gave *the job* our best efforts.)

prepositional	a noun or a pronoun that follows the preposition and is linked to some other word by the preposition (He monitored the valve *throughout the day.*) (He went *into the warehouse* unescorted.)
parallelism	sentence elements in like structure (He looked *in the closet, on the shelf,* and *in the desk.*) (all prepositional phrases) (The manager demanded the following: *reduction in labor charges; change in shipping procedures; improvement in delivery service.*) (all nouns followed by prepositional phrases)
parenthetical element	a word, phrase, clause, or sentence that has no grammatical relationship to the rest of the sentence; may be set off by commas, dashes, or parentheses (I believe—*and this is strictly a personal opinion*—that he should be fired.) (We have two choices, *to postpone the survey or cancel it,* and neither one is satisfactory.)
phrase	a group of words not having a subject or a predicate (*in the beginning; old, faulty repair; having finished early*)
predicate	that which tells something about the subject The engineers *have been satisfied with the results of the tests.*)
preposition	a word that shows the relationship between its object and some other word in the sentence (in, at, about, as, between, during, except, of, on; *in* the box, *between* the men)
pronoun	a word substituted for a noun
personal	indicates a person (I, you, they)
demonstrative	points out (this, that, these, those)
relative	relates an adjective clause to its antecedent (who, whom, whose, what, that)
interrogative	asks a question (who, what, which)

indefinite	does not stand for a definite person, place, thing, or idea (someone, few, some, none, all, both)
reflexive	refers to the subject (myself, himself, themselves)
nominative	used as the subject of a clause or sentence (we, they, it, I, you, he, she)
objective	used as objects of verbs, objects of prepositions, and subjects of infinitives (him, her, you, us, them)
possessive	indicates ownership (his, her, hers, your, yours, their, theirs, my, mine, ours)

run-on sentence   two or more sentences incorrectly written as one (He could not quote the salary, therefore, all the applicants felt they had wasted their time. The first comma should be replaced by a semicolon or a period to end the sentence.)

sentence   a group of related words expressing a complete thought and containing a subject and a predicate

   simple   contains one subject and one predicate; either or both may be compound
   (Two inspectors and surveyors left and returned twice during the day.)

   compound   contains two or more independent clauses
   (The representative called on the company, but he could not sell our services.)

   complex   contains one independent clause and at least one dependent clause
   (When the pressure falls, cut off the machine immediately.)

   compound-complex   contains two or more independent clauses and one or more dependent clauses
   (Show me the reports when they come in, but don't forward them until I've checked with his supervisor.)

subject   part of the sentence that names what is talked about
   (*The tubing in the front* is worn out.)

tense   property of verbs that indicates time of the action
   present   *investigate* today

past	*investigated* yesterday
future	*will investigate* tomorrow
present perfect	*has investigated* several times
past perfect	*had investigated* before you called
future perfect	*will have investigated* by this time next week

verb   a word that shows action or state of being
(stops, fills, aids, concludes, pressurizes, is, seems, becomes, struck, was)

verbal   verbs used as other parts of speech

gerund   verb + *-ing*, used as a noun
(*Testing* is going slowly.)

participle   verb + *-ing* or *-ed*, used as an adjective
(*Testing the pipes,* he could not turn his back to the meter.)

infinitive   *to* + verb, used as a noun, adjective, or adverb
(*To test* the pipes requires three hours.)
(Caps *to stop* the leakage are hard to find.)
(He rearranged the charts *to show* the results in optimum light.)

voice   a form of the verb that indicates who or what does the action or receives the action

active   when the subject is the actor in the sentence
(The tests *reveal* pollution.)

passive   when the subject receives the action in the sentence
(Pollution *was revealed* by the tests.)

APPENDIX B

ANSWERS TO SPELLING AWARENESS EXERCISE

accessible, acessible

accomodate, accommodate

accurate, acurrate

achieve, acheive

allotted, alloted

analyze, analize

antequated, antiquated

apparatus, aparratus

appearance, appeerence

arguement, argument

beginning, begining

bulletin, bulliten

buoyant, bouyant

calender, calendar

category, catagory

cemetary, cemetery

changeable, changable

commitment, committment

complection, complexion

concensus, consensus

conterversy, controversy

definite, definate

dependent, dependant

describe, discribe

description, discreption

descrepancy, discrepancy

dilema, dilemma

disappoint, dissapoint

dissapate, dissipate

embarrass, embarass

ettiquete, etiquette

exceed, excede

existence, existance

exorbitant, exhorbitant

fourty, forty

grammar, grammer

guage, gauge

harrass, harass

humorous, humorus

hypocrasy, hypocrisy

imatate, imitate

inadvertent, inadvertant

independant, independent

indispensible, indispensable

inate, innate

insistent, insistant

maintenance, maintanence

mecanics, mechanics

mileage, milage

miniscule, minuscule ✓

<u>necessary</u>, necessery
<u>ninety</u>, ninty
ocassionally, <u>occasionally</u>
<u>occurred</u>, occured
<u>occurrence</u>, occurence
<u>parallel</u>, paralell
<u>perform</u>, preform
<u>permanent</u>, permenant
perserverance, <u>perseverance</u>
<u>personnel</u>, personel
porportion, <u>proportion</u>
<u>precede</u>, preceed
<u>privilege</u>, privelege
<u>probably</u>, probaly
procede, <u>proceed</u>
proceedure, <u>procedure</u>
<u>quandary</u>, quandery

<u>recede</u>, receed
<u>receive</u>, recieve
<u>recommend</u>, reccomend
<u>repetition</u>, repitition
<u>seize</u>, sieze
<u>separate</u>, seperate
<u>sieve</u>, seive
<u>similar</u>, similiar
<u>stopped</u>, stoped
<u>succeed</u>, succede
supercede, <u>supersede</u> ✓
<u>superintendent</u>, superintendant
<u>technique</u>, techneque
undoubtably, <u>undoubtedly</u>
<u>vacuum</u>, vaccuum
<u>whether</u>, wheather

ACKNOWLEDGMENTS

First of all, I'd like to thank our clients for their ongoing confidence in our training programs: writing, oral presentation, interpersonal skills (listening, meetings, conflict resolution, negotiations), customer service, and personal productivity. Our clients have provided samples, discussed their feedback on strategies, and shared their successes and results with us. Seeing the big-picture impact makes the business all the more rewarding for us personally as well as for us as a training organization.

But more than thanks to our clients "in general," I want to thank those specific individuals who have sponsored us into their organizations. I appreciate all their efforts in "spreading the word" about what these communication concepts could do for their organizations. My thanks to each of you individually.

Also, I'd like to thank Doris S. Michaels, who agented this book for me. She's a delight to work with.

Special thanks also to Mitch Ivers, my editor at Pocket Books and an author in his own right, who has shepherded this project through the publishing house with such personal enthusiasm and influence.

Finally, I'd like to thank those in our office who have worked tirelessly and without complaint to help put this manuscript into final form: Scott Stein, Anita Slusher, Polly Fuhrman. And thanks to all the rest of you for "picking up the slack" in the interim. You're a great team.

OTHER RESOURCES
BY DIANNA BOOHER
AVAILABLE FROM
BOOHER CONSULTANTS

Workshops

To-The-Point E-Mail
Effective Writing
Technical Writing
Developing Winning Proposals
Good Grief, Good Grammar
eService Communications
Customer Service Communications
Presentations That Work (oral presentations)
Communicate with Confidence (interpersonal skills)
Listening Until You Really Hear
Resolving Conflict Without Punching Someone Out
Leading and Participating in Productive Meetings
Negotiating So That Everyone Feels like a Winner
Increasing Your Personal Productivity
Managing Information Overload

Speeches

Communication: From Boardroom to Bedroom
From the Information Age to the Communication Age: The 10 Cs
The Gender Communication Gap: "Did You Hear What I Think I Said?"
Communicating CARE to Customers

Write This Way to Success
Platform Tips for the Presenter: Thinking on Your Feet
Get a Life Without Sacrificing Your Career
You Are Your Future: Putting Together the Puzzle of Personal Excellence
The Plan and the Purpose—Despite the Pain and the Pace
The Worth of a Woman's Words
Ten Smart Moves for Women

FOR MORE INFORMATION

Dianna Booher and her staff travel internationally, presenting training workshops on communication and delivering motivational keynote speeches on life balance and personal productivity topics. For more information about booking Dianna or her staff, please contact:

Booher Consultants, Inc.
4001 Gateway Dr.
Colleyville, TX 76034–5917
Phone: 800-342-6621

mailroom@booherconsultants.com
www.booherconsultants.com

INDEX